Wealth Without Waste

Wealth Without Waste

Frugal Where It Counts, Generous Where It Matters

Ravi Khatekar

Mindful Pages

Published in 2026

ISBN: 9789376558452 (PB)
ISBN: 9789376553761 (eBook)

Published by

Mindful Pages
Imprint of Alpha Editions LLC
312 W. 2nd St #1834
Casper, WY 82601, USA

This book was developed using advanced writing tools to support the drafting and ideation process. All content has been thoughtfully curated, refined, and reviewed to ensure quality and relevance.

Content

Introduction

On 9 January 2007, at the Moscone Center in San Francisco, Steve Jobs walked onstage and pulled a rectangle of glass and aluminium out of his pocket. The room's applause rose in a hard, clean wave; the air had that faintly sweet smell of warmed electronics and carpet glue that clings to conference halls. It was theatre, but it was also a hinge in everyday life. Within a decade, a device like that would not merely sit in a hand. It would sit between a person and almost everything they might buy, watch, summon, subscribe to, or outsource. The promise was obvious: less friction, more freedom. The cost was quieter. The cost was a drip.

Comfort can still feel brittle. It shows up in households that, on paper, are winning. A good income arrives reliably. The mortgage is paid. The fridge is full. The car starts. Holidays happen. Services appear at the door with the soft ping of a notification. The coffee machine has its own personality. And yet, towards the end of the month, there is that small tightening in the chest: not panic, not poverty, but a sense that money is moving faster than attention can track. Something is being spent—perhaps not badly, but blindly.

In the UK, the Office for National Statistics reported in 2024 that households were spending more on services than a decade earlier, part of a longer shift in consumer life away from physical goods and towards recurring access. That trend does not require anyone to be reckless. It requires only busyness and decent cashflow. A household can be perfectly competent and still end up with a financial life that behaves like an untended garden: vigorous growth, plenty of colour, and a slow strangling of the paths people actually want to walk.

The modern affluent life is not ruined by one dramatic extravagance. It is shaped by the accumulation of small agreements, each one reasonable in isolation. A streaming bundle here, a premium storage plan there, a cleaner who makes Tuesday afternoons bearable, the delivery fees that buy back minutes, the upgraded seat that makes travel less punishing, the childcare add-ons that smooth a week. None of this resembles a moral failure. It resembles the default settings of a civilisation designed to monetise ease. When money is exchanged for reduced hassle, the transaction feels harmless; the price is not the pounds leaving the account so much as the quiet erosion of optionality.

Optionality is the true luxury, and it is strangely easy to lose at high incomes because the loss does not look like deprivation. It looks like a calendar that cannot breathe. It looks like a bank balance that refills and empties with unnerving symmetry. It looks like generosity postponed because the household has become a finely tuned machine that needs constant fuel. The deeper paradox is that the very comforts purchased to create time and space can, if left to sprawl, produce the opposite: a life that costs so much to operate that it becomes cautious, defensive, and oddly narrow.

The mechanism has a name in behavioural economics: lifestyle creep. The phrase is accurate and far too polite. "Creep" suggests a gentle drift, but what often happens is more like a set of invisible contract signings. A pay rise arrives; it lands in the account; the household feels relief for perhaps a week. Then the phone gets upgraded because the old one is "basically dead". The restaurant bill rises because work has been grinding and everyone deserves a night off. The children's activities expand because childhood is short and opportunities feel morally urgent. A new baseline forms. The next pay rise is absorbed before it even arrives, because the life has already expanded to meet it.

Comparison accelerates the process, and it rarely announces itself as jealousy. It arrives disguised as normality. In affluent circles, the reference group's "ordinary" is expensive: the type of school, the number of holidays, the assumption of renovations, the definition of a "reliable" car, the expectation that each adult keeps up with their own professional wardrobe and the social life that oils career progression. Social proof is a powerful force because it operates beneath conscious thought. People copy what looks stable. They copy what looks sensible. In a world where many costs are hidden behind monthly direct debits and contactless taps, copying another household's lifestyle can mean inheriting their financial architecture without ever seeing the blueprint.

A second force is less discussed: invisible commitments. These are not indulgences at all; they are obligations and conveniences that arrive as solutions. The cleaner is a solution to exhaustion. The food deliveries are a solution to late meetings. The tutoring is a solution to school anxiety. The upgraded data plan is a solution to remote work. These are rational responses to real constraints. The problem is not that they exist. The problem is that, once installed, they behave like permanent fixtures, and they multiply. A household can become a museum of solved problems, each exhibit paid for monthly, each one once justified, now rarely revisited. The drip is the point.

There is an older story about money that does not fit this reality. It is the story of the traditional budget: a grid of categories, each assigned a number, each tracked faithfully. For some people, that is calm. For busy high earners, it often becomes a second job, or worse, a moral tribunal. The issue is not that numbers are useless; it is that line-by-line tracking asks for a level of daily attention that competes with work, children, health, ageing parents, and the simple desire to have a life. When the system demands perfection, it tends to produce either guilt or rebellion. Both are expensive.

A more honest lens starts elsewhere: with alignment. Money is not only a tool for purchasing goods; it is a way of translating values into visible behaviour. That translation is frequently distorted by speed. The faster money moves, the more it expresses defaults rather than decisions. A household that cares deeply about friendships may find itself too tired to host because the weekly outgoings have tightened the schedule. A household that says it values freedom may find itself trapped in recurring costs that require constant high performance at work. A household that wants to be generous may find itself waiting for some mythical month when everything is "sorted"—a month that never arrives because the machine has been built to consume all surplus.

The idea of waste needs reframing. Waste is not merely buying cheap things that break. Waste can be buying excellent things that do not earn their place. Waste can be paying for convenience that saves time in theory while encouraging patterns that create more time pressure in practice. Waste can be spending that dulls attention, so people stop noticing what they are really trading: hours of life for habits that barely register. A £25 subscription that no one uses is obvious waste; a £2,500 annual pattern that becomes invisible is more dangerous. The harm is not financial ruin. The harm is a life that becomes oddly unresponsive to its own stated priorities.

There is a temptation, especially among capable people, to treat this as a discipline problem. If only there were more willpower, more restraint, more "being sensible". That framing is both inaccurate and unkind. A high-functioning household can be extraordinarily disciplined in work and caregiving and still have spending that is scattered, simply because the environment is designed to scatter it. Modern commerce is frictionless by design. Cards are stored. Trials roll into renewals. One-click purchasing exists. Notifications arrive precisely when fatigue is highest. The rational response is not heroic self-control; it is better design—an environment where the default supports the life people actually want.

Design begins with seeing. Consider a Thursday evening in May 2018, in London, when Parliament passed the Data Protection Act to implement the EU's GDPR regime in the UK. Most households noticed it, if at all, as a flurry of emails about updated privacy policies. The more significant change was subtler: it reminded organisations to treat data as an asset and to build systems around its capture. The same logic has been applied relentlessly to payment behaviour. Companies have become adept at converting momentary interest into monthly revenue, and at making cancellation slightly harder than signing up. This is not a conspiracy; it is commercial competence. The implication is that a household's attention is a scarce resource with competitors, and those competitors are well funded.

Still, not every sense of tightness is self-inflicted. There are regions, industries, and seasons where costs rise sharply or income becomes uncertain. There are caregiving responsibilities that make "optimising" feel insulting. There are structural pressures—housing markets, school places, healthcare gaps—that can swallow money with no hint of indulgence. Any serious approach to spending has to hold this truth without flinching: some constraints are real, and no amount of cleverness transforms them into ease. And yet even within real constraints, there is usually a margin where alignment can be improved, not through deprivation, but through clarity.

Clarity is not the same as austerity. A household can cut spending and feel poorer if the cuts land on what genuinely brings meaning, while low-value spending remains untouched. Conversely, a household can spend more in a few places and feel richer, if that spending reduces friction where it matters and increases joy where it counts. The difference lies in a value hierarchy, whether conscious or accidental. Without an explicit hierarchy, the market supplies one: convenience, novelty, and status rise to the top because they are loudly advertised and easily purchased. Relationships, health, and contribution are quieter; they do not arrive in a box.

One practical way to see the hierarchy is through the idea of "enough". Enough is not a number that ends desire forever. It is a threshold that prevents endless upgrading from masquerading as progress. A household might have enough in technology when devices are reliable and functional, and the marginal improvement is mostly bragging rights. It might have enough in dining out when it still feels like a treat rather than a default solution to fatigue. Enough in travel might mean fewer trips but more presence, less frantic collection of experiences. The metric is not moral virtue. The metric is whether the spending creates a life that feels steadier and more open.

Openness matters because generosity is not best left to leftovers. When giving is postponed until "later", it often becomes a performance of guilt: a burst of donation after a crisis, a rushed cheque at the end of the tax year, a sudden decision driven more by emotion than by coherence. Planned generosity behaves differently. It becomes part of the household's identity, a regular commitment that shapes choices upstream. A family that sets aside money for giving each month—quietly, without drama—ends up making different decisions about subscriptions, upgrades, and lifestyle ratchets, not because they are saintly, but because they have introduced a design constraint. The constraint does something willpower rarely does: it keeps the question of "enough" alive.

One can see this in the aftermath of real events. After the Grenfell Tower fire in June 2017 in North Kensington, London, there was an immediate outpouring of public donations, goods, and volunteer time. It was generous, heartfelt, and in places chaotic. Some donations were exactly what was needed; others were unusable, a mismatch between impulse and information. The incident became, among many other things, a case study in how giving works best when it is deliberate, coordinated, and resourced in ways that respond to need rather than to the giver's desire to feel helpful. The lesson is not cynicism about generosity. The lesson is respect for it. Serious giving deserves structure.

Structure is often misunderstood as rigidity. In reality, the most useful financial systems for busy earners tend to be light, forgiving, and automatic. When money has clearly assigned roles—essentials, irregular costs, pleasure, giving—it becomes harder for low-value spending to masquerade as harmless. When recurring costs are mapped visually, patterns emerge: a cluster of charges after payday, a slow bleed in the second half of the month, a "harmless" set of conveniences that adds up to a second mortgage payment. When the system is designed to run with minimal attention, it survives stressful seasons. It does not rely on perfect behaviour. It relies on thoughtful defaults.

Thoughtful defaults also change how purchases are judged. Cost-per-use is not a trick for justifying expensive things; it is a way of exposing both false economies and false luxuries. A coat that is worn daily for five winters and repaired once is not merely a coat; it is a stable choice that reduces mental noise. A cheap item purchased repeatedly because it breaks is not frugality; it is an ongoing tax on time and patience. Meanwhile, a high-end gadget bought for an imagined lifestyle and used twice is not enjoyment; it is a story purchased at retail price. The numbers matter, but so does the honesty in the estimate.

Honesty becomes even more important with big commitments. One-off windfalls—bonuses, inheritances, unexpectedly strong years—have a habit of becoming permanent expenses in disguise. A new car on finance is not simply a car; it is a monthly obligation that narrows future choices. A school fee is not merely an educational decision; it is a long-term cashflow structure that can crowd out flexibility and, sometimes, kindness. The moment that feels like celebration can quietly become a ratchet: a new baseline that is hard to reverse without emotional pain. The human brain is excellent at adapting upward. That talent is not always helpful.

The question, then, is not whether a household is spending too much. For affluent people, that is often the wrong diagnosis. The question is whether spending is doing its job. Does it buy back time that is actually used for what matters, or does it simply create more obligations? Does it support relationships, or does it outsource intimacy into transactional convenience? Does it create freedom, or does it demand constant high earnings to maintain? Does it make generosity easy and consistent, or does it make giving feel risky? These are not moral questions. They are engineering questions about a life.

Most months end the same. The pay arrives, the bills leave, the subscriptions sip quietly, the conveniences fill the gaps, and the remaining money is absorbed by the sheer friction of living well. Then, occasionally, there is a jolt: a conversation that goes badly because one person thinks the household is "fine" and the other feels secretly anxious; a bonus that disappears without changing anything; a moment of wanting to help someone and realising that help would feel financially dangerous. Those jolts are diagnostic. They reveal where the system has drifted from the household's declared values.

That drift is not corrected by shame. Shame makes people hide, and hidden money decisions become brittle. Correction comes from precision: the ability to see what matters, to measure what is actually happening, and to design a flow that reflects both ambition and humanity. Precision does not mean obsessing over pennies. It means refusing to let the largest part of adult life—how resources are traded for time—run on autopilot designed by strangers with excellent marketing departments.

Somewhere in the background, the drip continues. It is the sound of a modern life paying for itself, month after month, often without anyone deciding anew. The better question is which drips deserve to remain because they water what matters, and which are simply the price of not looking. When the numbers are kind and the calendar is full, neglect can look like success. It takes maturity to notice the difference.

The forward tension is simple and uncomfortable: when the next opportunity arrives—a bonus, a move, a tempting upgrade, a request for help, a new recurring service that promises to make life easier—which constraint will take precedence? Comfort, status, and ease all make persuasive cases. Freedom and generosity are quieter advocates, and they require a household to have done its thinking in advance. The diagnostic question is not whether the purchase can be afforded in the moment, but whether it increases the household's capacity to say yes to what it claims to value, without borrowing peace from the future.

Chapter 1
Redefining Wealth And Waste

In 1899, in Chicago, Thorstein Veblen published *The Theory of the Leisure Class* and gave polite society a small, sharp mirror. He was not writing about people who could not pay their bills. He was writing about people who could, and who still managed to feel pressed—pressed to display, pressed to keep up, pressed to translate prosperity into visible proof of prosperity. Veblen's phrase, "conspicuous consumption", has since become a shorthand, a smirk, a way to point at someone else's shiny watch. Its more unsettling implication is that spending is rarely just spending. It is signalling, soothing, belonging, compensating, chasing an image of safety. Once that is true, the question of "enough" stops being numerical and becomes psychological.

The modern version of Veblen's observation does not live only in jewellery or cars. It lives in the small, constant transactions that feel like nothing. A household upgrades its phones because the contract renewal arrives with a cheerful discount and a mild threat of inconvenience. It adds another streaming service because one new show becomes the shared language of friends at work. It pays for delivery because the week is a relay race between school gates and late meetings. It pays for a cleaner because Sunday is the only day that still belongs to the family. The money leaves in soft, regular drops. No single drop makes a sound. Then, one evening, someone opens the banking app and feels the same tightness they swore they would never feel again: that odd sense of being well-off and, simultaneously, cornered.

Affluence can be a kind of glass box. It looks spacious from the outside. From within, it can feel narrow. That is the paradox worth naming early, because it rescues the reader from the most useless interpretation: that the discomfort must mean incompetence. Many high-income households are not failing. They are operating a complex system with too many moving parts and too little reflection built in. The constraints are real, even when the income is high, because the household's cost of being itself has quietly risen to match its earnings.

The first engine of this constraint is lifestyle creep, which is less a creep than a series of small, irreversible decisions made under time pressure. A household begins by paying for relief, then discovers that relief becomes the new baseline. The car that once felt like a luxury becomes simply "reliable". The holiday that once felt like a splurge becomes the only way to recover from work. The dining out that once marked celebration becomes the default way to feed everyone on a Wednesday. The earlier self, who would have found all this astonishing, vanishes into the routine. The raises arrive and are already spoken for, because the household has become a machine that needs more fuel merely to feel normal.

Comparison is the second engine, and it rarely feels like comparison. It feels like ambient reality. People do not line up their spreadsheets next to friends and choose envy. They absorb norms. They notice what peers do and internalise it as sensible, as safe, as responsible. Parents watch other parents choose certain schools, activities, tutors, camps, and quietly recalculate what counts as "giving a child a fair shot". Professionals observe how colleagues dress, where they eat, which events they attend, and infer what seriousness looks like. None of this requires vanity; it requires social intelligence. But social intelligence, left unchecked, can convert someone else's priorities into one's own expenditure.

The third engine is the least visible: invisible commitments. These are the subscriptions, the retainers, the annual renewals, the silent direct debits, the insurance upgrades, the "small" monthly costs that are attached to bigger choices. They are also the commitments that start as rational solutions to real problems. Childcare arrangements, therapy, tutoring, commuting costs, support for relatives, professional memberships, specialist software, storage, health services that fill gaps. This category includes things one would never mock. That is precisely why it becomes dangerous when left unattended. Invisible commitments do not feel like consumption; they feel like life. They are the structural costs of coping. Once installed, they behave like fixtures in a house: no one thinks about them until a leak becomes obvious, and by then the water has already travelled.

The pressure affluent people feel is often a pressure of maintenance. They have built a life that requires continual inputs to keep it pleasant, smooth, and socially legible. That maintenance cost can be oddly high because it is not only financial. It is cognitive. It takes attention to manage multiple accounts, renewals, apps, logins, memberships, household services, and the constant parade of decisions disguised as conveniences. When attention is spent here, it is not spent elsewhere. Something gives. Usually, what gives is the very thing money was meant to protect: presence, calm, the capacity to be generous without fear.

A common response to this unease is to reach for traditional budgeting: the stern spreadsheet, the categories, the monthly targets. It is the financial equivalent of a crash diet, and it fails for many of the same reasons. It asks for daily vigilance in a life already crowded with demands. It turns money into a scoreboard. It punishes complexity. It tells a high-income household to behave like a low-income household without acknowledging that the problem is not simply "spending too much", but "spending without a clear hierarchy". Line-by-line tracking can be a noble hobby. For time-poor adults, it can become an instrument of self-reproach.

The deeper flaw is that traditional budgeting often treats values as an afterthought. It assumes that the goal is optimisation in the abstract—less spending, more saving—without asking what saving is for, what spending is for, or why certain categories matter more than others. It offers generic percentages, as if every household's best life could be reduced to the same pie chart. That approach tends to produce two unhelpful outcomes. One is the brittle month: a period of forced restraint followed by a backlash purchase because the system feels punitive. The other is the guilty month: the household hits its "targets" but feels poorer, because it has cut the things that nourish it while leaving the invisible commitments untouched.

What affluent, busy households need is not more moralising. They need a better instrument. A classic budget is like a microscope used for navigation: it magnifies detail but does not tell you where you are going. What matters is the flow of money through the household and what that flow says about the household's priorities. The objective is not to account for every pound. The objective is to make sure pounds, hours, and attention are not being traded for a life nobody actually wants.

That is where the phrase "wealth without waste" earns its keep, because it refuses the lazy equation that expensive equals wasteful and cheap equals virtuous. Some of the most wasteful spending is cheap and frequent, because it buys nothing durable—no time, no meaning, no ease that lasts longer than an afternoon. Some of the most valuable spending looks expensive, because it buys stability: a service that prevents burnout, an item that lasts and reduces hassle, an experience that strengthens relationships rather than merely filling a feed with photos. Waste is not a moral category; it is a functional one. Waste is spending that undermines freedom, either by creating obligations or by draining attention, or by locking a household into a lifestyle that demands constant high performance to sustain.

Freedom is often spoken about as if it were a finish line: earn enough, save enough, and eventually it appears. In lived life, freedom is usually a margin, a breathing space that exists or does not exist month by month. It is the ability to absorb a surprise without panic. It is the ability to say no at work without feeling financially endangered. It is the ability to take time when someone you love needs you. It is the ability to make a decision that is slightly less profitable and far more humane. People do not lose this freedom by buying one reckless thing. They lose it by accepting a dozen recurring costs that nibble away the margin until the margin becomes a myth.

And then there is generosity, which is too often treated as the reward for perfect financial behaviour. The story goes like this: build the ideal system, clear the debt, maximise the savings, and then, when everything is secure, become generous. The problem is that "everything secure" is a mirage. Life changes. Costs appear. Needs escalate. A household can always invent a reason to postpone giving. Generosity, left for later, becomes fragile. It depends on mood. It becomes seasonal. It turns into an act of guilt management rather than a stable expression of values.

A different framing is both more demanding and more liberating: generosity as a design constraint. When a household builds giving into its financial life as something ordinary and expected, it forces sharper choices elsewhere. The household cannot simply allow subscriptions and upgrades to multiply indefinitely; it must decide what earns its place. In return, generosity does something subtly profound. It anchors the sense of enough. It interrupts the endless logic of accumulation. It reminds people, in a culture that equates worth with consumption, that money is also a tool for connection and repair. It is hard to remain perpetually unsatisfied while giving consistently, because giving makes abundance visible in a way that buying rarely does.

This is not sentimental. It is practical. When a household has breathing room, it can give without the hidden fear that generosity will destabilise the core. When a household gives deliberately, it tends to protect breathing room, because it becomes harder to justify spending that is merely habitual. The relationship is circular, like a well-designed system that reinforces itself. The alternative is also circular: a life built to consume surplus will perpetually feel like it needs more surplus. The drip is always there, and the only question is what it is watering.

Modern life makes these questions urgent. The subscription model has moved beyond entertainment into software, fitness, food, learning, storage, transport, even domestic services. Convenience has become a marketplace, and fatigue is its most reliable customer. Digital payment systems make spending painless, which is precisely why spending can become thoughtless. The acceleration is not merely technological; it is cultural. People are told, implicitly and constantly, that a good life is one where friction has been eliminated. Yet friction is not always the enemy. Some friction protects values. A little friction prevents impulse purchases. A little friction forces reflection. A little friction can be the difference between spending that is aligned and spending that is automatic.

There is also a philosophical question hiding beneath the practical one: what is wealth for? For some, it is comfort and security, full stop. For others, it is autonomy, the ability to shape time. For others, it is contribution, the chance to make something better than they found it. Most people hold several answers at once, and that is not hypocrisy; it is humanity. The trouble begins when the household's spending behaves as if only one answer matters—usually the one that is easiest to purchase quickly. Comfort and ease are important. They simply cannot be the only gods in the pantheon, because they are insatiable. There is always a smoother service, a more seamless upgrade, a more exclusive experience. A life organised around removing discomfort will end up, paradoxically, amplifying it, because it trains attention to notice every inconvenience as an emergency.

A credible counter-example deserves respect here. Some people are genuinely fulfilled by high-maintenance living: they love the abundance, the services, the premium versions, the constant variety. They are not secretly hollow. They are simply different. For them, the "waste" critique may feel like moral policing dressed as prudence. That objection matters, because it guards against a smug minimalism that mistakes personal taste for ethical superiority. The reconciliation is straightforward. Waste is not a judgement about taste. It is a judgement about fit. If high-spend living genuinely supports freedom, relationships, and chosen contribution, and if it does not create anxiety or brittleness, then it is not wasteful in the sense that matters here. The test is not austerity. The test is whether life feels expandable or contractive, open-handed or defensive, intentional or reactive.

The chapter that follows takes aim at the most corrosive financial emotion among the comfortable: the sense that one is doing well and still somehow failing. That emotion thrives in secrecy and in fog. Once it is named, it can be treated like a design problem. Design problems have solutions that do not require self-punishment. They require clarity about what matters, and systems that protect it.

The work begins by looking directly at the paradox of constrained affluence and refusing to sentimentalise it. It then treats the traditional budget with appropriate scepticism—not because discipline is bad, but because a rigid instrument can produce the wrong kind of discipline: vigilance without wisdom. From there, the chapter turns towards the central lens of this book: spending judged by contribution, not by price tag. The final movement links that lens to a pair of forces that most people treat as opposites—freedom and generosity—and shows why they often rise and fall together.

A household does not need to become spartan to become free. It needs to become precise. It needs to know which costs are ballast and which are holes in the hull. It needs to decide, with adult calm, which drips are worth keeping because they water the garden it truly wants, and which are simply the sound of a life running on default settings. The page turns when that decision becomes possible.

Why affluence feels constrained

On 15 September 2008, in New York City, Lehman Brothers filed for bankruptcy. The headlines carried the drama, but the more enduring effect was domestic and quiet: highly paid people—traders, lawyers, consultants, executives—went home and discovered that a large income does not automatically translate into a large margin. Months earlier, many of them had looked secure. Their lives were well-appointed, their calendars full, their spending comfortably smooth. Then one shock exposed the structure underneath: fixed commitments were heavy, optionality was light, and the household's cost of "normal" had climbed so high that even a short disruption felt like threat. Money moves, quietly, every day.

The peculiarity is that the feeling persists even when nothing collapses. Plenty of high-income households report a steady, low-grade pressure in perfectly ordinary years: not the acute fear of missing rent, but the discomfort of watching the month narrow despite apparent success. The salary is high. The breathing room is not. That mismatch is not proof of moral weakness. It is a clue about design: the household's financial system may be absorbing income in ways that are invisible until the space is gone.

Begin with something concrete: the moment a pay rise lands. A professional receives an email, a contract, a new number. There is a brief lift—measurable even in behaviour. They book a celebratory meal, upgrade something overdue, relax for a week. Then the world obligingly provides "needs" that were previously tolerable discomforts. A faster internet plan because remote meetings keep glitching. A better phone because the battery is unreliable and reliability now matters. A cleaner because weekends are being eaten by laundry and resentful silence. A more expensive supermarket routine because cooking from scratch feels like another project. The household does not *waste* the raise in one flamboyant act. It commits it, drip by drip, to a smoother version of the same life. Psychologists have a name for part of this: hedonic adaptation, the tendency for gains to become the new baseline of normal (Brickman & Campbell, 1971). The implication is disarming. The raise can vanish without indulgence, simply because comfort rapidly stops feeling like a luxury and starts feeling like a requirement.

The same pattern applies to time. Affluent people often buy convenience to reclaim hours, yet many feel more rushed than before. The show is visible: a takeaway bag on the counter at 9 p.m., a courier text arriving during a meeting, a taxi ordered in a hurry, a subscription renewed because cancelling would take six clicks and a phone call. Name the concept: frictionless consumption. Explain it plainly. When spending becomes effortless, it is more likely to express fatigue than intention. The implication is not that convenience is bad; it is that convenience, repeated, can become a habit that quietly converts income into upkeep rather than freedom.

Comparison intensifies the pressure because it shifts the definition of "enough" without a formal meeting. The social scientist James Duesenberry argued in 1949 that people judge consumption partly relative to others, not purely by absolute income (Duesenberry, 1949). That is an old idea, but it keeps finding new costumes. In practice, it looks like parents recalibrating what schooling is "responsible" by observing their peers. It looks like professionals adjusting how often they eat out because everyone in the group does. It looks like upgrading a car not because the old one is failing, but because it is no longer socially invisible. The behaviour is measurable: recurring costs ratchet upwards after exposure to new norms, and they rarely ratchet down. The implication is a soft kind of coercion. A household can be financially disciplined and still have its standards set by the people it lunches with.

Thorstein Veblen saw this dynamic long before the subscription economy, writing in 1899 about status-driven consumption as a social language (Veblen, 1899). The modern twist is that the language has become more granular. It is no longer only the visible purchases—watches, cars, holidays—that matter. It is the continuous signals: the activities children do, the gym one belongs to, the neighbourhood one lives in, the services one casually mentions. Even when nobody is trying to show off, belonging has a price. The implication is not cynicism about society. It is realism: humans are cooperative animals, and cooperative animals pay attention to the group's standards. Money leaks through the seams of belonging.

Then there are invisible commitments—the costs that do not arrive as a conscious choice but as the monthly consequence of earlier choices. To see them, picture a bank statement as a coastline. Big rocks are obvious: mortgage, childcare, council tax. The tricky part is the tide of small withdrawals: storage, software, streaming, insurance add-ons, subscription boxes, upgraded plans, donations that began with good intentions, memberships joined in hopeful phases of life. Each is defensible alone. Together, they can form a second mortgage in everything but name. Name the concept: commitment creep. Explain it with specificity. It is not "overspending"; it is the accumulation of contracts—formal and informal—that claim future income before the future arrives. The implication is that the household can feel squeezed not because it spends extravagantly, but because it has promised too much of tomorrow to yesterday's decisions.

This is where traditional budgeting advice often misfires for high-income, time-poor people. The classic approach treats the problem as excess consumption and prescribes more tracking. The show is familiar: an app, a spreadsheet, a month of diligent categorising, then a slow abandonment. The friction is not laziness. The friction is opportunity cost. Time spent micro-logging purchases is time not spent sleeping, working, exercising, being with family, thinking. Behavioural economists have studied how humans use mental shortcuts—heuristics—because attention is finite (Kahneman, 2011). A system that requires continuous fine-grained attention competes with everything else, and it usually loses. The implication is important: when a tool fails repeatedly for competent people, it is often the wrong tool, not a character flaw.

Even when the tracking is done, traditional budgets often create a moral atmosphere: success feels like virtue, deviation feels like failure. That atmosphere tends to produce two predictable behaviours. One is secret spending—small purchases hidden to avoid conflict or guilt. The other is binge spending after restraint—an expensive weekend framed as "making up for being good". Psychologists and economists have explored how self-control is not a limitless resource; it fluctuates with stress and fatigue (Baumeister et al., 1998, though later debates about the size and consistency of ego-depletion effects are part of the scholarly record). The implication is not that people are doomed. It is that rigid budgets can encourage the very volatility they were meant to prevent.

A more accurate description of the affluent squeeze is that it is often structural. Consider the behavioural pattern of "set and forget". A household sets up direct debits. It signs up for services. It arranges childcare. It renews insurance. It chooses a lifestyle that requires constant smooth functioning. Then it forgets—not in the sense of ignorance, but in the sense of not revisiting. The show is obvious to anyone who has ever tried to cancel a service: it takes longer to escape a commitment than it did to enter it. The concept is inertia, a force that behavioural economics treats as powerful precisely because it is ordinary (Thaler & Sunstein, 2008). The implication is stark: a household can be financially capable and still drift into a high-cost default because cancelling, renegotiating, or redesigning requires attention, and attention is already spent.

A contemporary example makes the point without moral drama. On 3 February 2022, the UK's energy regulator Ofgem announced a major rise in the energy price cap, reflecting wholesale price pressures that would soon affect household bills across the country (Ofgem, 2022). The shock landed unevenly, but it had a revealing feature: it hit many affluent households not because they were irresponsible, but because their fixed commitments had already absorbed most flexibility. When fixed outgoings are high, any external increase—energy, childcare, commuting—feels like a personal failure even when it is plainly not. The visible behaviour is the same across income levels: people delay decisions, they grow tense, they reduce discretionary spending in ways that feel punitive, they become risk-averse at work. The implication is psychological as well as financial. A small reduction in margin can reduce generosity, creativity, and calm, even when the absolute income remains enviable.

There is a second example, older but instructive, because it shows how quickly "normal" can reprice itself. When Apple released the iPhone in June 2007 in the United States and later expanded internationally, it was not merely selling a device; it was selling an interface for everyday spending—apps, services, upgrades, digital add-ons—many of which would later shift into recurring subscriptions. The show is the behavioural change: more frequent micro-transactions, more stored payment details, less deliberate purchasing. Name the concept: transaction frequency. Explain it. When the number of purchase decisions increases, each decision receives less attention. The implication is that affluence becomes easier to dissipate because it is being asked to fund not a few large decisions but hundreds of small ones. The drip becomes a system.

Affluence also carries a subtler constraint: responsibility. Higher incomes often come with more people depending on them—children, partners, employees, relatives, sometimes entire communities or organisations. The household may be the backup plan for others. That creates an internal pressure that can look like a desire for luxury but is often a desire for safety. The behaviour is visible: higher insurance coverage, more conservative choices, duplicate systems "just in case", paid help to prevent domestic collapse. Name the concept: risk management spending. Explain it honestly. When people feel responsible for others, they pay to reduce failure points. The implication is that what looks like indulgence from outside may be, from inside, an attempt to keep the whole structure from wobbling.

This is where the common moral story about affluent spending becomes not only unhelpful but inaccurate. Many high earners are not shopping for status; they are shopping for stability. They are buying predictability in a life that feels unpredictable. They are buying reclaimed time in a calendar that feels hostile. They are buying relief from domestic friction to protect relationships. Those motives deserve respect. The question is not whether the motives are legitimate. The question is whether the purchases actually deliver what they promise, or whether they merely create a more expensive version of the same stress.

A limitation should be stated clearly, because it prevents the argument becoming smug. Some people feel unconstrained at high incomes because they deliberately keep fixed costs low. They may live below their means, choose a modest home relative to income, avoid recurring commitments, or hold strong cultural norms against visible consumption. Research on high-wealth households has often noted that many accumulate wealth precisely by resisting lifestyle inflation, keeping spending stable while income rises (Stanley & Danko, 1996). That counter-example matters. It shows that constraint is not inevitable. The reconciliation, though, is equally important: resisting lifestyle inflation usually requires either time, strong social insulation, or both. It is easier when peers share similar norms, when housing choices are not forced by schooling, when professional signalling is less intense, and when the household has the bandwidth to design its system rather than merely cope. In other words, the counter-example proves possibility, not simplicity.

There is also a distinction between being constrained and being *aware* of constraint. Some households do not feel squeezed because they do not look closely. They run on confidence and credit, trusting that future income will cover present commitments. That approach can work for long stretches. It is also brittle. The behaviour is visible: high balances carried, recurring costs signed without scrutiny, reliance on future bonuses to "catch up". Name the concept: deferred reckoning. Explain it without melodrama. When spending decisions borrow from anticipated income, the household is trading future flexibility for present ease. The implication is a vulnerability that often only becomes visible when something changes—health, job, interest rates, family needs. The feeling of constraint can be a kind of intelligence: a warning light rather than a failure.

To treat this as a design problem, one must first see the architecture. Affluence becomes constrained when a household's recurring commitments—financial and psychological—expand to consume the margin that would otherwise provide freedom. The market encourages this because recurring revenue is prized. Social groups encourage it because norms spread. Individuals encourage it because relief is seductive. None of these forces require anyone to be foolish. They require only a life lived at speed.

The motif worth keeping in mind is the drip. A single drip is nothing. A thousand drips is a flood, and the flood is not dramatic; it is ambient. If a household feels uneasy despite strong income, the most honest diagnostic is not "what is wrong with them?" but "where is the margin going?" Not in the abstract, but in observable form: how many fixed monthly withdrawals exist, how often spending happens without deliberate choice, how many subscriptions would go unnoticed for two months, how much income is pre-committed before the month begins. Those are not moral metrics. They are structural ones.

The final tension is that affluence offers a genuine gift—choice—while simultaneously creating conditions that can erode choice. Each commitment reduces decision space. Each upgrade raises the baseline. Each comparison shifts the target. Each convenience can become a dependency. The open question, the one that should not be answered too quickly, is whether the next increase in income will widen the margin or thicken the commitments. When the next raise or bonus arrives, will it become freedom, or will it become another drip?

Limits of traditional budgets

In April 2014, in London, the Behavioural Insights Team published a short report called *EAST*, arguing that the most reliable way to change behaviour is to make it Easy, Attractive, Social and Timely. It was written for policy, not personal finance, yet it described domestic money with uncomfortable accuracy. People do not fail because they are unaware of what they "should" do. They fail because the system around them makes the right behaviour difficult to sustain. When financial advice assumes endless attention, it ignores the first constraint of modern affluence: not pounds, but bandwidth.

A high-income household rarely lacks information. It often lacks calm. The traditional budget—columns, categories, targets, discipline—promises control through detail. It is seductive: a moral geometry of life. Then the household tries it, usually in a burst of resolve after a tense conversation or a surprising bill, and discovers the hidden price. Every purchase becomes an administrative act. Every deviation feels like a confession. A budget can be tyrannical.

The classic model comes from a world where the primary financial challenge was scarcity and where the pace of spending was slower. Many households had fewer payment channels, fewer recurring services, fewer micro-decisions disguised as convenience. Even when money was tight, the cognitive environment was often simpler. The modern affluent household lives in the opposite condition: relative abundance combined with decision saturation. It may contain two demanding careers, children, ageing parents, and a logistics schedule that would make a small airline nervous. Asking such a household to track every coffee, parking fee, app subscription, work lunch, school trip, and late-night delivery is not a lesson in responsibility; it is a request for a second unpaid job.

The problem shows up in a very specific scene. Someone sits at a kitchen table at 11:30 p.m. with a laptop open, pulling transactions into a spreadsheet or an app. They categorise, adjust, split payments, debate whether a purchase belongs under "household", "kids", or "miscellaneous". The work is strangely intimate. It requires memory, judgement, and honesty when energy is lowest. Name the concept: cognitive load. Psychologists have long described how mental effort is finite and how complex tasks become harder when working memory is taxed (Kahneman, 2011). The implication is practical: a system that demands fine-grained attention at the end of a long day will be abandoned not because the person is weak, but because the person is human.

Even before abandonment, the detail can mislead. Traditional budgets reward the appearance of precision: a clean set of categories, tidy limits, a sense of mastery. Yet the household's real financial life is shaped less by whether £18.50 was "groceries" or "entertainment" and more by a few structural decisions—housing costs, childcare arrangements, commuting patterns, recurring subscriptions, family support, and the quiet habit of upgrading. The show is visible in the monthly statement: dozens of small transactions and a handful of huge ones. Name the concept: signal versus noise. Explain it plainly. The categories produce noise because the household's freedom is determined by the big commitments that compress margin, not by the perfect classification of minor spending. The implication is that traditional budgeting can create the illusion of control while leaving the architecture untouched.

The tyranny has another face: guilt. A rigid budget does not simply record reality; it judges it. A household "fails" the budget when real life intrudes—when a child gets ill and meals are ordered, when work explodes and taxis replace trains, when a relative needs support, when the boiler breaks, when a long-delayed holiday is finally booked. The system frames these moments as lapses. The show is behavioural: people hide purchases, avoid opening the app, postpone money conversations, and then overspend in a burst of defiance because the budget feels like a scolding parent. Name the concept: moral accounting. Explain it. When a tool turns spending into virtue and deviation into shame, it does not improve decisions; it damages honesty. The implication is corrosive: guilt becomes another leak, draining attention and making the household less likely to face the real drivers of cost.

Generic budgeting advice adds a further mismatch: it assumes that values can be captured by percentages. The famous rules—whether "50/30/20" or any other division—offer a pleasing simplicity, but simplicity is not the same as accuracy. A household with expensive childcare and modest tastes will look "out of balance" on paper. A household that spends heavily on travel because it keeps extended family connected may be told it is indulging. Another household may spend aggressively on home renovations because it hosts constantly and finds that hospitality is its deepest joy; the budget sees only a category overrun. The show is a number—an arbitrary line crossed. Name the concept: value blindness. Explain it. Percentages ignore the fact that households allocate money to serve different versions of a good life. The implication is that a generic budget can punish the very spending that gives life meaning, while leaving low-value defaults undisturbed because they fit neatly into a category.

There is a second kind of blindness, more subtle and more modern: the traditional budget struggles with the subscription economy. A household can sign up to a service in two minutes and then forget it for two years. The budget may show it as a small line item, too small to provoke action, yet cumulatively these items can form a substantial part of fixed outgoings. The show is measurable: count the number of recurring transactions under £20; then count how many are genuinely noticed month to month. Name the concept: attention drift. Explain it. Recurring micro-costs are designed to be forgettable, and a line-by-line budget tends to normalise them by absorbing them into a category instead of challenging whether they should exist at all. The implication is that the budget becomes a bookkeeper for drift rather than a defence against it.

The cultural story of budgeting also carries an implicit ideal: that the financially responsible person is perpetually vigilant. That ideal is incompatible with the reality of high-performing, time-poor lives. Vigilance has costs. It can turn money management into a constant low-level hum of self-surveillance, the financial equivalent of checking work email on holiday. The show is psychological rather than numerical: a person feels anxious even when they are "on track", because the system has trained them to monitor. Name the concept: scarcity mindset by design. Behavioural researchers have explored how perceived scarcity—of time, money, or attention—narrows focus and increases error, even when resources are adequate (Mullainathan & Shafir, 2013). The implication is paradoxical: a rigid budget can make a comfortable household feel poorer, not because it is poorer, but because the tool keeps attention locked on constraint.

A named example helps anchor this. In September 2008, in San Francisco, Mint.com launched as an online budgeting and aggregation tool, promising to automate the categorisation and bring clarity to spending; it became widely used and was later acquired by Intuit in 2009. Automation solved some friction, but it did not solve the deeper problem: categorisation is not the same as decision-making. The show is familiar to anyone who has watched a dashboard: charts update, categories shift, colourful insights appear, and the household's fundamental commitments remain unchanged because the tool is excellent at describing what happened and less effective at shaping what should happen next. Name the concept: retrospective control. Explain it. Traditional budgeting tools focus on the past—transactions, categories, historical averages—while the affluent squeeze is largely about future commitments and the ability to protect margin. The implication is that clarity can coexist with helplessness if the system is not designed around what matters most.

None of this means budgets never work. A credible counter-example deserves its full dignity. In 1904, in Tokyo, Hani Motoko—Japan's first female journalist—popularised *kakeibo*, a household ledger method encouraging reflection on spending and saving. It has endured for more than a century because it matches a particular temperament and culture: patient, deliberate, comfortable with ritual, and oriented towards mindful sufficiency. For some people, especially those who find satisfaction in recording and reflecting, a detailed budget is not tyranny; it is calm. The show is behavioural: they keep the ledger consistently, feel in control, and make better choices because the act of writing changes the act of buying. Name the concept: self-monitoring as reinforcement. Explain it. Recording can strengthen awareness and curb impulse because the purchase is no longer private; it must pass through a moment of acknowledgement. The implication is a valuable limitation: the critique of traditional budgets is not universal. It is contextual.

The reconciliation is where the argument becomes useful. Methods succeed when they fit three things: the household's time, the household's emotional style, and the household's real problem. For a household with limited income, tight tracking may be necessary because small differences matter. For a household with ample income but limited bandwidth, the problem is rarely the lack of a detailed ledger. It is the presence of too many commitments and too little alignment. Precision matters, but it must be directed at the right layer. A microscope is marvellous. It is not a compass.

This is why rigid budgets can fail even when people "try harder". The failure is not a lack of discipline; it is a mismatch between instrument and objective. The objective for busy, comfortable households is not to suppress all discretionary spending. It is to protect freedom, reduce regret, and build predictable space for generosity and meaning. That objective requires a different posture: less policing of minor transactions, more design of cashflow. Cashflow is a living rhythm—income arriving, obligations leaving, choices being made in between. The show is temporal: what happens immediately after payday, what happens mid-month, what happens when a large bill hits, what happens when a windfall arrives. Name the concept: rhythm over rules. Explain it. A purpose-led cashflow plan pays attention to timing and commitments, because timing determines whether the household experiences calm or scramble. The implication is that the household can regain breathing room without turning life into accounting.

A purpose-led approach also respects emotional bandwidth. A budget that demands constant micro-decisions makes money management the emotional centre of the household. That is rarely desirable. The more humane alternative treats money decisions as occasional, high-quality choices rather than constant low-grade monitoring. The show is visible: fewer conversations about whether a particular purchase "broke the budget", more conversations about whether recurring costs still earn their place; fewer late-night categorisation sessions, more periodic reviews of commitments and margins. Name the concept: decision quality. Explain it. When attention is scarce, the best strategy is often to reduce the number of decisions and increase the quality of the remaining ones. The implication is that the household's system should protect attention, not consume it.

This shift matters because the emotional damage of a punitive budget is not limited to the person doing the tracking. It spreads. Partners interpret the budget as control or criticism. Children absorb an atmosphere where money is either taboo or tense. The household begins to associate financial clarity with conflict. The show is relational: a conversation starts with numbers and ends with old resentments. Name the concept: financial communication spillover. Explain it. Tools shape tone. A rigid budget tends to create winners and losers—who stayed "within limits", who did not—while a purpose-led cashflow plan is more likely to frame choices as shared trade-offs. The implication is not merely nicer conversations; it is better outcomes, because cooperation is itself a financial asset.

The quiet motif here is the instrument. Budgets are often treated as if they were morality, when they are merely tools. Use the wrong instrument and the music sounds harsh, even if the musician is skilled. Use the right one and the same household can feel calmer without becoming stingy. The practical challenge is to choose an instrument that fits the actual constraints of modern affluence: plentiful transactions, abundant temptation, limited attention, and a life that cannot be paused for monthly accounting.

The unresolved tension is worth leaving intact because it is the hinge the rest of the chapter turns on. If detail does not reliably create direction, what does? When the next month begins and the payments start dripping out—subscriptions, services, renewals, conveniences—will the household continue to measure itself by whether it obeyed a set of categories, or by whether its cashflow protected the margin that makes freedom and generosity possible? The test is simple, and it is not comfortable: when time is short and spending is easy, which instrument will the household trust?

Wealth without waste defined

In June 1889, in New York, Andrew Carnegie published an essay in *The North American Review* that would later be nicknamed the "Gospel of Wealth". He was already one of the richest industrialists alive, and he chose, in that moment, to argue that surplus wealth was not merely a private trophy but a public responsibility. The piece landed like a thrown stone in a still pond: it did not end inequality or settle the ethics of capitalism, but it changed the social vocabulary around money. Wealth was no longer only something to possess; it became something to *direct.* That distinction matters because it separates accumulation from purpose, and comfort from meaning.

Carnegie's world was loud with furnaces and rail, ours with notifications and monthly renewals, yet the underlying question is the same: what is money *for* once the basics are handled? The modern affluent household often answers without speaking. It answers by default—by maintaining an expensive normal, by smoothing friction, by purchasing relief, by drifting into obligations that look sensible in isolation. The result is frequently a life that is comfortable and strangely tight, as if prosperity has been poured into a container with a hairline crack.

Not all costs are waste.

That sentence is simple, but it is the hinge on which the whole idea turns. In many households, "waste" is imagined as moral failure: frivolity, vanity, careless indulgence. That picture is inadequate. It misidentifies the enemy. Waste, in the sense that erodes a good life, is not primarily about buying "luxury" objects; it is about misalignment—money, time, and attention flowing away from what a person claims to value, and towards what happens to be easiest, loudest, or most socially validated in the moment. The central lens here is therefore not price but contribution.

Consider a familiar scene. A professional couple arrives home late. The kitchen is untidy. The children need packing for tomorrow. There is a work email that cannot be ignored. A delivery app solves dinner in twelve seconds. The household pays, the food arrives, and peace returns—briefly. Show: the transaction is not only about calories. It is about reducing domestic friction and preventing exhaustion from spilling into irritation. Name: relief spending. Explain: relief spending often buys something real, yet it can also become a default response to stress, repeating so frequently that it stops purchasing relief and starts purchasing habit. Implication: the household may be spending to protect relationships, while simultaneously building a cost structure that makes relationships more fragile by increasing pressure elsewhere. The same spend can be both understandable and quietly corrosive, depending on frequency, context, and what it displaces.

This is why "wealth without waste" cannot be defined as frugality in the old sense. It is not a vow of minimalism. It is not a personality trait. It is a way of judging trade-offs. A household may buy something expensive and be practising wealth without waste if that purchase reliably increases freedom, steadiness, or connection. Another household may buy something cheap and be practising waste if that purchase increases hassle, regret, or the need for repeated replacements. The difference is not the receipt total. The difference is what the spending *does* in the household's lived life.

The idea sounds abstract until it is attached to visible behaviours. Take time. Time is not a sentimental concept; it is an inventory. It can be counted: evenings, weekends, school runs, hours of sleep, hours of conversation that are not interrupted by a screen. A household that spends money to recover time and then uses that time to work more hours has not truly purchased freedom. It has purchased the ability to keep the machine running. Show: a cleaner is hired, the house is immaculate, and the "saved" Saturday morning becomes a block of emails. Name: substitution effect in time use. Explain: buying time often creates a temptation to fill it with more tasks rather than with what the household actually values. Implication: the spending may be justified on the surface but misaligned in effect, because it strengthens the treadmill rather than stepping off it.

Researchers have studied a related phenomenon with unusual clarity. In a 2017 paper in *Proceedings of the National Academy of Sciences*, Ashley Whillans and colleagues reported that people who spend money to save time—such as paying for services that reduce unpleasant chores—tend to report greater life satisfaction, even after accounting for income (Whillans et al., 2017). That finding does not turn convenience into a commandment. It does, however, offer a more intelligent question than "Is this indulgent?" The sharper question is: does the spending *reliably* convert money into time that is then used for what matters, or does it merely rearrange pressure?

Attention is the third leg of the definition, and it is the most neglected. Attention is the gatekeeper of choice. When attention is fractured, money behaves like water: it takes the easiest route downhill. The modern economy competes aggressively for attention because attention predicts spending. Subscription models, autoplay, saved cards, one-click checkouts, and timed discounts are not neutral conveniences; they are designs that reduce the moments in which a person might pause and decide. Show: a household continues paying for three streaming services, two cloud storage plans, and a fitness app nobody opens. Name: attention tax. Explain: the more recurring commitments exist, the more attention is required to audit them, and the more likely people are to avoid auditing because avoidance is emotionally pleasant. Implication: waste grows not through extravagance but through neglect, and neglect is often the product of fatigue rather than irresponsibility.

A definition of wealth without waste must therefore include a criterion that sounds almost moral but is actually mechanical: *does this spending increase or decrease a household's margin of choice?* Margin of choice can be observed. It shows up in whether a person can say no to an extra work commitment without anxiety. It shows up in whether a surprise expense triggers argument. It shows up in whether generosity feels easy or risky. It shows up in whether a household can take a slower path—cook, walk, repair, host—without feeling punished by time. When spending compresses that margin, it is waste in the most consequential sense, even if it looks respectable.

This framing also resolves an apparent contradiction: the same purchase can look "wasteful" to outsiders and be the opposite. A family might spend a large sum on an annual trip to see grandparents, because geography has scattered the family and relationships decay without presence. Another family might spend far less, but on a constant flow of forgettable upgrades that produce no enduring joy. The first spend may be costly yet aligned; the second may be modest yet wasteful. The tool here is not judgement but discernment.

A named example makes the point from the opposite direction: restraint that is costly. In September 2016, in Amsterdam, the Repair Café Foundation—begun in 2009 by Martine Postma—continued its now-global model of community repair events where volunteers help people fix household items rather than discard them. The appeal is not primarily thrift; it is the restoration of agency. Show: people bring a toaster, a lamp, a jacket; they sit, wait, talk, and watch something broken return to use. Name: durability culture. Explain: durability culture treats objects as maintainable rather than disposable, and it often requires more time and attention up front—diagnosing, repairing, sourcing parts. Implication: what looks like "saving money" is also a way of saving attention over the long run, because fewer replacements means fewer shopping decisions, fewer disappointments, fewer trips to the bin. The waste being resisted is not only financial; it is the constant churn of choice.

That churn matters because waste has a psychological signature. Waste feels like regret. It feels like a home filling with "useful" things no one uses. It feels like recurring charges that provoke irritation whenever they are noticed. It feels like buying something to soothe a hard day and then noticing, later, that the hard day is still there. A household practicing wealth without waste is not necessarily spending less; it is experiencing less regret, because spending is more often congruent with declared priorities.

This is where generosity belongs inside the definition rather than appended to it. Generosity is often treated as a separate virtue—something admirable but optional. In practice, generosity functions as a calibration mechanism. It forces a household to ask, repeatedly, whether it has enough. It interrupts the fantasy that satisfaction arrives after the next upgrade. It also changes what "waste" looks like. A subscription that might feel harmless becomes more visible when a household knows that the same monthly amount could support a cause, a relative, a neighbour, a community effort. The comparison is not meant to induce guilt. It is meant to clarify opportunity cost, which is simply the fact that resources used one way cannot be used another.

Here the Carnegie example returns, not as a moral sermon but as an engineering insight. Carnegie's argument was contentious then and remains contentious now, yet it captured a structural truth: money that is not given a purpose will be given one by the surrounding culture. In a consumer society, that purpose is usually consumption. If generosity is included as a deliberate channel for surplus, it competes with consumption in a quiet, stabilising way. It creates a second gravitational pull. The household stops asking only, "What will make life easier?" and begins asking, "What is this ease for?"

A second named, checkable example shows how this can become concrete without grandiosity. In June 2010, in New York, Bill Gates and Warren Buffett announced the Giving Pledge, encouraging billionaires to commit publicly to giving away the majority of their wealth. The pledge has been praised, criticised, and debated, but the structural move is clear: it turns generosity into a constraint on accumulation and consumption, not merely an afterthought. Show: a wealthy person publicly commits to give, and that commitment shapes decisions that follow. Name: pre-commitment. Explain: pre-commitment is a behavioural tool, studied across psychology and economics, in which future choices are shaped by a decision made in advance. Implication: when generosity becomes pre-committed, it reduces the space for lifestyle creep to claim every surplus pound, because surplus already has an assignment beyond the self.

At this point, an honest limitation is necessary, because a contribution-based lens can be misused. People are imaginative storytellers. They can justify almost anything by declaring it "aligned". A costly purchase can be wrapped in the language of efficiency, wellbeing, family bonding, professional necessity. Show: a household upgrades repeatedly—phone, car, kitchen—each time with a plausible rationale, each time insisting it is "worth it". Name: rationalisation. Explain: rationalisation is the mind's habit of constructing acceptable reasons after a desire has already formed; it is a documented feature of human cognition, not a vice unique to spenders. Implication: defining wealth without waste requires more than eloquent self-description; it requires observable evidence that the spending produces the claimed benefits—more margin, less regret, more time used well, more consistent generosity, or a stable increase in what the household actually values.

This is where the quiet motif becomes useful: the plumb line. A plumb line is a simple tool builders use to check what is truly vertical. It does not argue. It does not flatter. It reveals tilt. In the same way, wealth without waste is less a philosophy than a plumb line for decisions. Does the spending hang straight with the household's stated priorities, or does it pull towards the easy default? The test is not aesthetic. It is structural.

A good plumb line also reveals that values conflict. A household may value freedom and also value providing every opportunity to children. It may value generosity and also value comfort, safety, privacy. It may value time and also value excellence at work. Wealth without waste does not pretend these tensions disappear. It refuses the childish belief that a perfect system eliminates trade-offs.

Instead, it treats trade-offs as the real work. When spending is judged by contribution, the household is forced to ask not only "Is this nice?" but "What does this cost us *elsewhere*?" That "elsewhere" might be time, mental peace, relational warmth, or the ability to give without fear.

This definition also rescues "waste" from moralistic aesthetics. Waste is not owning nice things. Waste is owning nice things that create dependency, clutter, distraction, or a baseline so expensive that a household must continually run at high speed just to maintain it. Waste is not spending on joy. Waste is spending that produces a thin, restless joy that expires quickly and requires replenishment. Waste is not paying for help. Waste is paying for help that merely masks a deeper mismatch between commitments and capacity. In each case, the most reliable indicator is a behavioural one: does the household's life feel more spacious after the spend, or more tightly wound?

The plumb line appears again in a deceptively small place: the end of the month. The bank balance may be fine. The question is whether the household feels free. Can it absorb a friend's crisis without calculating what kindness will cost? Can it take a day off without panic? Can it say yes to a generous impulse without a silent recoil? These are not sentimental questions. They are diagnostics of margin, which is the substrate of both freedom and generosity.

The forward test, then, is not whether a person can defend a purchase as "reasonable", because almost anything can be defended once it is already bought. The forward test is whether, before the next commitment becomes another monthly drip, the household can hold the plumb line steady and ask a single, unnerving question: will this spend widen our margin of choice, or will it quietly narrow it while pretending to be comfort?

Freedom and generosity connection

On 27 November 2012, in New York City, the 92nd Street Y and the United Nations Foundation helped launch what became known as GivingTuesday, a public attempt to make generosity as culturally legible as shopping days. The timing was not accidental. It arrived after Black Friday and Cyber Monday, when spending is ritualised, advertised, and socially contagious. The new proposition was simple: give, too, and do it together. Whatever one thinks of branded generosity, the launch captured a truth that affluent households often feel but rarely name. Consumption has a calendar. Generosity often does not. When giving is left to whim, it behaves like a mood; when it is treated as part of life's operating system, it becomes something sturdier—something that can coexist with comfort instead of being perpetually postponed by it.

The paradox sits in the quietest corner of domestic finance. People pursue financial breathing room for the same reason divers carry oxygen: without it, everything becomes reactive. And yet generosity is frequently treated as the thing that can wait until breathing room is abundant and permanent, as if life ever offers permanent conditions. Here is the twist. The households that give deliberately often protect breathing room more successfully than those who treat giving as an optional extra. Not by magic. By design.

Margin makes generosity feel safe.

Begin with a scene that happens in thousands of minor variations. A couple hears that a colleague's partner has been diagnosed with something serious; a neighbour's boiler fails; a local school needs funds for a child whose family is struggling. The amounts involved are rarely enormous. The point is the moment: a desire to help meets the household's internal sense of risk. Show: the hand hovers over the "send" button; the mind runs a quick calculation; the body registers a flicker of unease. Name: perceived fragility. Explain: when a household has allowed fixed commitments to swell, even small acts of giving can feel like they threaten stability, because the margin is thin and the next bill is already looming. Implication: people who are objectively affluent can still experience generosity as danger, which is a painful distortion of what wealth is supposed to make possible.

The relationship runs in the other direction as well. Consider the household that gives regularly—modestly, predictably, without theatrics. Show: a recurring transfer leaves the account each month; it is noticed in the same way a mortgage payment is noticed: as part of reality. Name: pre-commitment. Explain: behavioural economics has long observed that humans are more consistent when future choices are constrained by decisions made in advance, because the decision is moved from the heat of the moment to a cooler context (Thaler & Sunstein, 2008). Implication: when generosity is pre-committed, it becomes less vulnerable to mood, fatigue, or the latest spending temptation; it also forces the household to build around it, rather than treat it as leftover.

That last point is where generosity starts to look like freedom's ally rather than its rival. Freedom is often imagined as the ability to buy anything. In lived terms, it is more often the ability to *decline*—to turn down demands, to avoid lifestyle ratchets, to choose time over money when it matters. Those choices require slack. Show: a professional can say no to a project that would destroy a family holiday; a family can absorb a sudden expense without panic; a person can take time to care for a parent without immediately calculating the financial haemorrhage. Name: breathing room. Explain: breathing room is not a spiritual abstraction; it is a measurable property of cashflow and commitments, visible in how much of income is already promised before the month begins. Implication: households that protect breathing room protect freedom, because freedom is not a philosophical stance but a structural condition.

Now the uncomfortable link: generosity both depends on breathing room and helps create it. The dependence is obvious. When the core costs of life are not right-sized, giving becomes sporadic and anxious, or becomes performative and resentful. The creation effect is subtler. Planned giving functions like a constraint that disciplines the rest of the system. A household that knows a portion of its resources is set aside for giving is less able to treat every surplus pound as fuel for upgrades. It must choose which comforts genuinely earn their place. The household becomes, almost accidentally, more deliberate.

A named example makes the mechanism visible. In April 2010, in New York, Bill Gates and Warren Buffett announced the Giving Pledge, encouraging billionaires to commit publicly to giving away the majority of their wealth. It has attracted praise and critique in roughly equal measure, and it does not solve the moral complexity of vast fortunes. But structurally, it demonstrates a principle: when giving is treated as a prior commitment, it reshapes everything that follows. Show: a public pledge narrows the space for later rationalisations. Name: identity constraint. Explain: public commitments change behaviour because they bind identity—"this is the kind of person I am"—and identity is a powerful driver of consistency. Implication: even at a far smaller scale, when giving becomes part of identity rather than a discretionary gesture, it changes what feels acceptable elsewhere in the budgetary landscape.

This is where the notion of "enough" gains teeth. Without a practice that repeatedly reintroduces the idea of sufficiency, the affluent household is exposed to a cultural algorithm that is relentless: more comfort, more speed, more convenience, more exclusivity. It is not malicious; it is simply profitable. Generosity interrupts the algorithm because it makes the opportunity cost of endless upgrades visible. A household can purchase another subscription or another small convenience, or it can keep faith with a chosen act of contribution. The question is no longer moralised; it becomes concrete. Two outcomes compete.

Psychology offers evidence that the competition matters emotionally. In 2008, Elizabeth Dunn, Lara Aknin, and Michael Norton published a study in *Science* reporting that people who spent money on others tended to report greater happiness than those who spent it on themselves, even after accounting for income (Dunn, Aknin & Norton, 2008). The finding has been replicated and extended in various contexts, though like all social science it depends on definitions and measurement choices. Still, it illuminates a behavioural truth that many people recognise in their own lives: purchases aimed at self-comfort often fade quickly, while giving can lodge in memory as meaning. The implication is not a command to give. It is a corrective to a common assumption—that personal consumption is the most reliable route to satisfaction once basic needs are met.

And yet generosity is not automatically virtuous or psychologically clean. A limitation is necessary here because without it the argument becomes sentimental, and sentimentality is another form of waste.

Giving can be used as status signalling. It can be impulsive in ways that are ineffective or even harmful. It can be a substitute for presence: money sent instead of time offered, guilt discharged rather than responsibility met. It can also be financially destabilising when done from a place of thin margin and social pressure. Show: a household agrees to a donation at a fundraising event because everyone is watching; later, they quietly feel angry or afraid. Name: coerced generosity. Explain: when giving is driven by external pressure or status anxiety, it can produce resentment and increase the sense of fragility. Implication: generosity that is not deliberate can undermine the very freedom it is supposed to express.

The reconciliation returns to design. Deliberate generosity is different from reactive generosity in the same way a planned meal is different from scavenging when starving. One is a choice made with information and calm. The other is a response to immediate cues. When giving is deliberate, it can be consistent without being destabilising; when it is reactive, it tends to be either sporadic or emotionally expensive. This distinction matters especially for affluent households because they are often surrounded by cues: charity events, school fundraising, workplace appeals, social media campaigns. Without a pre-decided posture, the household is tugged by every story and every invitation, and the result is not noble; it is chaotic.

A second named, checkable example shows generosity functioning as a cultural system rather than a private impulse. On 16 March 1988, Comic Relief held its first Red Nose Day in the United Kingdom, turning fundraising into a national ritual that mixed humour, spectacle, and social participation. The style is not to everyone's taste. The structure is instructive. Show: a recurring public event creates a predictable moment for giving; people expect it, plan around it, and participate together. Name: temporal anchoring. Explain: humans behave more consistently when actions are tied to recurring cues—dates, seasons, public rituals—because the cue reduces the cognitive effort required to initiate the behaviour. Implication: generosity becomes less fragile when it has a rhythm, and rhythm is a cousin of breathing room; both reduce reactivity.

The connection between breathing room and generosity also works through risk perception. A household with thin margin experiences life as a series of threats: the next bill, the next surprise, the next expensive problem. In that state, hoarding becomes rational. Show: people cling to a buffer, delay giving, postpone help, and justify it as prudence. Name: defensive finance. Explain: when the household's system is brittle, it encourages self-protection even in the face of genuine compassion. Implication: a household can become psychologically narrower as it becomes financially busier, and this narrowing is not stinginess; it is fear.

Increase breathing room and something loosens. Not just cashflow, but posture. A household with slack can respond to life with less calculation. That responsiveness is a form of freedom that feels, to many people, more valuable than luxurious objects. It allows a person to be the kind of friend, sibling, neighbour, or colleague they want to be. It allows giving to be a steady practice rather than an occasional crisis response. The key is that breathing room is not created solely by earning more. It is created by right-sizing the core and resisting the quiet drift of commitments.

Generosity, once embedded, then protects that right-sizing. It introduces an alternative use for surplus that is not immediately consumable by lifestyle creep. It also changes the internal narrative of money. Instead of money existing only to purchase comfort and reduce friction, it becomes a medium of connection. That shift is psychologically potent because it reorients attention away from scarcity. When people give deliberately, they repeatedly rehearse the fact that they have enough to share. That rehearsal is not naïve optimism. It is a behavioural antidote to the cultural script that insists nothing is ever enough.

A motif can hold the argument together: the air gap. In engineering, an air gap is a simple separation that prevents failure from propagating. In household life, breathing room is an air gap between income and obligation, and generosity can function as an air gap between surplus and consumption. Without these gaps, everything touches everything; stress transmits instantly; a single surprise becomes a cascade. With them, the system absorbs shocks. People remain kind. People remain flexible. The money stops behaving like a frantic current and starts behaving like a flow with channels.

There is an ethical dimension here that should not be exaggerated and should not be dodged. It is possible to be financially free and ungenerous. It is possible to give and still feel trapped. The connection is not deterministic. It is probabilistic, shaped by habits, social environments, and the architecture of commitments. The point is that when generosity is treated as structurally central rather than morally decorative, it tends to produce a household that is less tempted by empty upgrades and more oriented towards what lasts: relationships, contribution, calm. That is not sainthood. It is a practical route to contentment in a culture that sells restlessness.

The forward test is therefore not whether generosity is admirable. Most people already agree that it is. The test is whether the household's financial design makes generosity easy and safe, or awkward and frightening; whether breathing room is being protected as a core asset, or quietly traded away for conveniences that do not actually expand life. The next time a new recurring comfort presents itself—another service, another upgrade, another "small" monthly drip—the unresolved question will be whether the household keeps the air gap intact, or lets it close, and discovers later that freedom and generosity were never enemies at all, merely rivals for the same fragile margin.

Chapter 2
Designing Intentional Cashflow

In 1494, in Venice, a Franciscan friar named Luca Pacioli published a dense, practical book with a title that sounds like a shelf collapsing: *Summa de arithmetica, geometria, proportioni et proportionalità*. Tucked inside was a method merchants already used and Pacioli described with unusually clear patience—double-entry bookkeeping. The point was not paperwork for its own sake. It was orientation. A trader could look at ink on a page and understand, not merely what had happened, but what was happening: which ventures were profitable, which were draining, which promises had been made to the future without being noticed at the time. Outside, the city's canals moved with the tide; inside, the ledger made another kind of tide visible.

That is the odd, modern irony. Most affluent households have more powerful "ledgers" than Pacioli could have imagined—apps, bank feeds, cards that record every transaction to the second—yet they often have less orientation. Money arrives and leaves with exquisite automation, and the experience is frequently a blur: a salary lands, a dozen debits siphon off, a week of taps and swipes passes, a large payment hits, and the month ends with the same faint question: where did it go, exactly, and why does it feel tighter than it should? The machinery of finance has become frictionless; the understanding has not.

Cashflow is not a budget. It is a rhythm. It is not a moral scoreboard. It is the household's circulation system, and like any circulation system, it can be healthy or strained, generous or constricted, resilient or brittle. People often talk about "income" as if it were the whole story, but income is only the inflow. The lived experience of money is shaped by timing—when bills hit, when subscriptions renew, when school costs cluster, when travel is booked, when convenience spending spikes under stress. Two households can earn the same amount and feel utterly different, not because one is virtuous and the other irresponsible, but because the timing and structure of their commitments produce different internal weather.

The first move towards intention is almost absurdly simple: stop treating money as a single monthly number and start treating it as a flow. The month is not a smooth line; it is a landscape with cliffs and valleys. A household that is paid monthly and charged weekly experiences a different terrain from one that is paid fortnightly and charged annually for half its services. A household with school fees clustered in certain terms experiences a different terrain from one with steady costs. A household that books holidays in a single burst feels a different terrain from one that pays gradually. When people feel "bad with money" despite competence elsewhere, it is often because they are trying to navigate terrain with a single number in mind. Terrain does not yield to wishful thinking.

The modern household's terrain has become more jagged for a particular reason: commitments have become easier to create and harder to see. Streaming services, software subscriptions, delivery memberships, cloud storage, gym contracts, warranty extensions, the premium versions of ordinary things—these are not dramatic purchases. They are little pipes installed quietly under the floorboards. Once installed, they pull money month after month with barely any noise. The household can be attentive and still fail to register the cumulative effect because the human brain is better at noticing large, discrete events than small, recurring ones. A direct debit of £9.99 is designed to slide beneath the mind's alarm threshold. Multiply it enough times and the household's margin is gone, with nothing to show for it except the eerie feeling of being prosperous and pinned.

Design begins, therefore, with a map. Not a forensic accounting exercise. A map that is honest enough to be useful and simple enough to be bearable. The most consequential insight many households have is not that they spend "too much", but that their money bunches. It arrives in one moment, leaves in another, and the space in between is filled by spending that feels trivial at the time and significant in retrospect. When people see the bunching, they stop arguing with themselves about discipline and start asking a more intelligent question about structure: if the bills hit in a cluster, why is the household still acting as if it has a steady weekly allowance? If irregular costs keep arriving as "surprises", why are they being treated as surprises rather than as part of reality?

The emotional tone of this matters. Mapping without fixing is psychologically difficult for conscientious people, because it forces them to sit with ambiguity. It asks for observation rather than immediate action. Yet observation is precisely what breaks the spell of the drip. A household that can look at its flow without flinching gains a form of power that does not require austerity. Clarity is not control, but it is the precondition of control. It also has an unexpected side effect: it reduces shame. When people see how much of their spending is structured and timed rather than "chosen" in each moment, they tend to treat themselves less like sinners and more like engineers.

Once the flow is visible, the old language of "needs versus wants" can be rescued from childishness. The binary framing has always been too blunt for adult life, and it becomes comical when applied to affluent households. A need is not only "food" and a want is not only "champagne". People have stability needs: costs that protect health, relationships, and the ability to work without collapse. People also have meaningful wants: spending that is not required for survival but is central to a life that feels rich. The mistake is to call everything discretionary frivolous and then wonder why discipline fails. When a household treats all joy as optional, it eventually rebels. When it treats all convenience as necessary, it eventually becomes expensive.

The nuance shows itself in contested categories—housing, schooling, travel—where identity and values are entangled with money. A larger home may be status theatre for one household and the practical foundation of multigenerational care for another. Private schooling may be a social norm in one community and an emergency response to unmet needs in another. Travel may be a consumer trophy for one person and the only way to keep a family intact across continents for another. The categories do not carry meaning on their own. Meaning arises from what the spending *enables* and what it *costs*. The map of cashflow creates space for this more adult kind of assessment: not "Is this a need?" but "What stability does this buy, what joy does this buy, and what does it displace?"

At this point, many people reach instinctively for strict budgets, because strictness feels like seriousness. But strictness is often a form of denial: a refusal to accept that life contains variability and that a household's values cannot be expressed through a fixed monthly grid without becoming brittle. A better metaphor is not the cage but the guardrail. Guardrails do not dictate the exact path taken. They prevent the worst accidents. They acknowledge that humans drift, that weeks get busy, that judgement fluctuates, that temptation is engineered. A guardrail system respects adult reality: decisions will not always be perfect, so the environment should make it harder for small drifts to become structural damage.

The most important effect of guardrails is that they protect priorities without demanding constant attention. They shift effort away from daily policing and towards periodic calibration. That is an enormous relief for time-conscious professionals because the hidden cost of traditional budgeting is not only the time spent tracking; it is the time spent thinking about tracking. Mental overhead accumulates. A household that is always "watching spending" often ends up watching life, too, through a thin lens of constraint, even when money is abundant. Guardrails offer a different posture. They allow spending to happen without anxiety while still containing low-value drift. They make it possible to be comfortable without being careless.

Cashflow design also asks for respect towards seasons. Some months are heavy with birthdays, travel, school demands, work deadlines. Some seasons require more convenience, more outsourcing, more smoothing. Pretending otherwise is a recipe for guilt. The aim is not to eliminate variability but to stop variability from becoming chaos. That is why rhythm matters. A household that can anchor quick reviews to existing routines—already-established moments of planning—does not need heroism. It needs a minimum effective dose of attention, applied consistently. Consistency is not the same as obsession. A few small, well-timed check-ins can outperform hours of tracking done sporadically in a panic.

There is a philosophical dignity in this approach. It treats money management as part of living well rather than as a perpetual penance. It assumes that intelligent people are capable of making good trade-offs if the decision environment is designed to support them. It also refuses a strange modern superstition: that automation will solve everything. Automation is wonderful at moving money. It is terrible at deciding what money should mean. If the household never pauses to assign meaning, automation simply accelerates defaults. A designed cashflow plan is a way of recovering authorship. It does not fight modern finance with purity. It uses structure, timing, and a clearer hierarchy to make the flow serve the life.

A quiet motif threads through all of this: the tide chart. Sailors do not curse the sea for rising and falling. They consult the chart. They plan departures and arrivals with humility towards the water's rhythm. Household cashflow deserves the same attitude. Income arrives on particular days. Bills land on particular days. Certain costs surge at predictable times. When people treat the month as flat, they feel ambushed by predictable tides. When they treat it as a rhythm, they regain calm—not by controlling the ocean, but by navigating it.

The deeper payoff is not merely a neater financial picture. It is a different experience of choice. A household that understands its flow can distinguish between genuine scarcity and temporary tightness. It can tell the difference between a month that feels constrained because bills have clustered and a life that is constrained because commitments have grown too heavy. It can see where money vanishes unnoticed and where it bunches in ways that create stress. It can stop arguing about whether a particular purchase was "allowed" and start talking about what the household is optimising for: freedom, relationships, generosity, presence.

The page turns when a household moves from reactive money to intentional cashflow—when it stops treating the bank balance as a mood and starts treating it as a designed system with rhythms, guardrails, and clear trade-offs. The unresolved question that hangs over every subsequent choice is simple and sharp: when the next busy week arrives and the tide rises, will the household's money move according to its values, or according to whatever is easiest in the moment?

Mapping current money flows

On 13 January 2018, in London, the UK's Open Banking regime went live for the largest banks under the direction of the Competition and Markets Authority, requiring new ways of sharing account data with customer permission through secure interfaces. The technical change was concrete. People could, with a few taps, pull multiple accounts into a single view, watch transactions appear almost in real time, and see their financial lives rendered as tidy feeds of incoming and outgoing numbers. The cultural promise was equally clear: if the data is visible, the decisions will improve.

And yet visibility is not the same as understanding. A feed of transactions is like a box of scattered map tiles—accurate fragments without orientation. A household can stare at perfect data and still feel vaguely ambushed by the month, because what matters is not merely *what* was spent but *when*, and how those timings interact with the household's commitments, habits, and seasons. The problem is rarely ignorance. The problem is shape.

A map makes money legible.

That is the task here: to see the shape of cashflow as it actually behaves, before any attempt to correct it. Modern households live inside streams of money that move quickly and quietly, and the mind is not built to hold those streams in working memory. The brain excels at spotting large, dramatic events. It is far less reliable at tracking dozens of small, recurring withdrawals and interpreting their combined effect. The month becomes a feeling rather than a system, and feelings are a poor instrument for navigation. A map, by contrast, is humble. It does not moralise. It simply reveals where the ground rises and where the water gathers.

Begin with the way money arrives. Many professionals experience income as a single monthly pulse, a deposit that lands like a tide coming in overnight. Show: the balance rises sharply; relief and possibility follow; a few days later the balance drops as direct debits and standing orders siphon off their share. Name: income rhythm. Explain: income rhythm is the timing pattern of inflows, and it shapes everything that follows because a household's sense of abundance or constraint is strongly influenced by when it sees money, not only how much arrives. Implication: a household paid monthly may feel rich and then suddenly tight, even if the overall month is stable, because the rhythm creates a psychological rollercoaster.

The next thing the map reveals is that bills do not behave like income. Many major obligations—mortgage or rent, council tax, childcare, utilities, insurance—strike on their own schedules, often clustered early in the month. Show: a household may watch a third or half of the month's income leave within a few days of payday, then experience the remaining weeks as a slow squeeze. Name: bill clustering. Explain: bill clustering occurs when multiple fixed commitments hit in a narrow time window, creating an artificial sense of scarcity that can drive reactive behaviour, such as cutting joy spending harshly mid-month or relying on convenience spending in the final week because energy is low and the "tight" feeling is high. Implication: the household can misdiagnose the problem as overspending when the deeper issue is timing: the flow is lumpy, and lumpiness triggers poor decisions.

Card and app spending then fills in the middle like weather. Some spending is predictable—food shops, transport, lunches. Much is contingent: it spikes with stress, travel, deadlines, social invitations, children's needs, fatigue. Show: a week of late meetings produces more taxis and deliveries; a quiet week produces fewer transactions; a busy month produces an extra layer of "small" purchases that feel necessary in the moment. Name: contingent spending. Explain: contingent spending is behaviourally driven; it responds to time pressure, emotional load, and convenience cues more than to long-term plans. Implication: without seeing how contingent spending correlates with particular weeks and pressures, a household tends to blame itself in general terms—"we're careless"—rather than noticing the specific conditions that trigger drift.

A cashflow map, therefore, is less like a budget and more like a tide chart. It shows when the water rises and falls, where it pools, and where it drains away unseen. The practical value is that it reclassifies surprise. If a household can see that certain costs always arrive in predictable clusters—school terms, annual renewals, seasonal travel—those costs become part of the terrain rather than emotional ambushes. The mind relaxes, not because the costs disappear, but because they are no longer interpreted as personal failure.

This shift is not merely psychological; it changes the household's behaviour in observable ways. When people feel ambushed, they either clamp down too hard or avoid looking. When they feel oriented, they can make fewer, better decisions. Behavioural economists have described the power of "salience"—the degree to which something stands out and therefore influences decisions (Kahneman, 2011). A cashflow map increases the salience of timing and commitments, which are the drivers that most often determine whether a month feels calm or cramped. The implication is that mapping is not busywork; it is a way of directing attention to the variables that actually matter.

A second historical snapshot illuminates why timing is so easy to miss. On 27 June 1967, in Enfield Town, North London, Barclays installed what is widely cited as the world's first cash machine, a precursor of the modern ATM. The machine did not only dispense cash; it changed the experience of money. Cash became accessible outside bank hours, reducing friction and making spending feel more continuous. Over subsequent decades, cards and digital payments extended that continuity until money became almost invisible, a background utility rather than a tangible medium. Show: purchases no longer required a deliberate trip to a bank or the physical parting with notes; they required a tap. Name: friction reduction. Explain: as friction falls, the mind's perception of cost often falls with it, because fewer sensory cues accompany the transaction. Implication: the household may spend more frequently in smaller increments without feeling the cumulative drain, and the month can feel mysterious even when the data is technically available.

This is why mapping must include *frequency* as well as totals. A household might assume that the problem is a handful of big purchases, when the map shows a constant drizzle of small ones: coffees, app add-ons, delivery fees, impulse upgrades, convenience purchases justified as "only a tenner". Show: the bank feed contains a high count of transactions below a psychologically painless threshold, each one defensible. Name: micro-leakage. Explain: micro-leakage is not about extravagance; it is about the ease with which small costs escape scrutiny when they occur frequently and are paid invisibly. Implication: a household can feel constrained not because it has one expensive habit, but because it has ten small ones that collectively behave like a fixed bill.

A map also reveals something that often surprises high earners: the importance of "in-between money". This is the portion of income left after fixed commitments—mortgage, taxes, childcare, insurance, core bills—have taken their share. Show: two households with identical gross incomes can have radically different in-between money if one has higher fixed costs or more recurring commitments. Name: discretionary margin. Explain: discretionary margin is where freedom actually lives; it is the part of the month where choices can be made without destabilising the base. Implication: debates about individual purchases are often proxy battles. What matters is whether the household has built a base that leaves room for anything else at all.

The map becomes even more revealing when it includes irregular costs, which are "irregular" only in the sense that they do not occur monthly. Annual insurance renewals, birthdays, holidays, home maintenance, professional fees, school trips, car repairs—these are not random meteor strikes. They are part of living. Show: a household treats these expenses as surprises, pays them from the month's margin, and then experiences the month as tight and volatile. Name: predictable irregularity. Explain: many expenses feel unpredictable only because they are not integrated into the household's mental model of cashflow; they occur on longer cycles, so they are easy to ignore until they arrive. Implication: the household's month-to-month stress can be driven less by extravagance and more by the repeated collision between a monthly mindset and yearly realities.

A limitation matters here, because mapping can become its own trap. Some people respond to financial unease by gathering endless data: multiple apps, dashboards, categories, alerts. Show: the household gains visibility but also gains noise; it checks balances compulsively, treats every fluctuation as meaningful, and becomes anxious despite having strong cashflow. Name: surveillance drift. Explain: when the act of monitoring becomes an emotional coping strategy, it can increase anxiety rather than reduce it, because the household is constantly exposed to numbers without a framework for interpretation. Implication: mapping is only useful when it produces orientation rather than obsession; the point is to understand the tide, not to stare at the water all day.

The reconciliation is that a map should be intentionally imperfect. It should prioritise the variables that shape experience: the timing of inflows, the timing and clustering of fixed commitments, the broad bands of discretionary spending, and the recurring drips that are easy to miss. Precision at the wrong layer is a form of avoidance. When people get lost in categorising every coffee, they are often escaping the more important questions about commitments, timing, and the life those commitments are funding.

Two named, checkable examples from recent consumer finance show why this matters. When Mint.com launched in September 2008 in San Francisco, it made transaction data easier to see, but many users reported that awareness did not automatically translate into changed behaviour; the tool excelled at retrospective clarity. When the UK's Open Banking regime went live in January 2018 in London, it improved account aggregation and data sharing, but households still faced the same human problem: the data was granular, the month was lumpy, and decisions were being made under fatigue. Show: better data arrives; the household still feels squeezed. Name: data-action gap. Explain: the distance between seeing and changing is not bridged by information alone; it is bridged by a model of what matters, and by a structure that translates observation into fewer, higher-quality decisions. Implication: mapping is the necessary first step because it supplies the model with reality, but it is not sufficient on its own.

Mapping also has a relational dimension that is often missed. In many households, one person holds the money map in their head and the other experiences only the atmosphere: tension near the end of the month, vague anxiety around certain purchases, irritation when bills hit. Show: arguments begin with "we can't afford this" and end with "you never tell me what's going on". Name:

informational asymmetry. Explain: when only one person can see the flow, money becomes a source of power and insecurity, even without anyone intending it. Implication: a shared map reduces conflict because it turns money from a moral debate into a shared picture of reality—where the tide is, where the ground is high, where the leaks are.

The deeper significance of mapping is that it restores agency without demanding austerity. It replaces the foggy question "why does this feel tight?" with more precise questions: where does money bunch, where does it vanish, and which timings create avoidable stress? It gives names to patterns that would otherwise be interpreted as personal inadequacy. It also changes what a "good month" means. A good month is not one in which nothing unexpected happens. A good month is one in which the flow can absorb reality without panic, and in which the household's spending expresses priorities rather than fatigue.

The tide chart returns here because it captures a final truth: the month has forces larger than any individual transaction. Salary cycles, billing cycles, school calendars, insurance renewals, seasonal spending, and social rhythms create predictable movement. The household's task is not to fight that movement with guilt, but to understand it well enough to navigate. Without a map, people improvise—and improvisation is expensive.

The forward tension is simple, and it is diagnostic. When the household looks at its own flow—its inflow pulses, its clustered obligations, its drizzle of micro-spending, its predictable irregularities—does the pattern suggest a life with margin, or a life that consumes margin as fast as it appears? The next chapter's work depends on a sober answer to a question that no dashboard can answer on its own: is the household steering the tide, or merely being carried by it?

Separating needs and wants

In 1943, in New York City, Abraham Maslow published "A Theory of Human Motivation" in *Psychological Review*, offering a hierarchy that has since leaked into everything from management training to late-night self-help conversations. Its concrete outcome was not a new law or a new institution, but a new way of sorting human desire: some needs press on the body, some on the psyche, some on the longing to matter. The hierarchy became popular because it felt true in the hand, like a good tool. People could pick up their own lives and begin to separate what was essential from what was merely attractive. It was a powerful idea.

The trouble begins when a powerful idea becomes a blunt one. In personal finance, "needs versus wants" is often treated as an easy binary: rent is a need, holidays are wants, end of discussion. For people living near the edge, the binary can be serviceable because the stakes are survival and the margin is thin. For affluent households, the same binary becomes both inaccurate and quietly cruel. It turns legitimate stability into "indulgence" and makes meaning sound like a guilty hobby. The labels slip.

Words shape behaviour.

That is why this distinction matters. A household that mislabels its spending tends to mismanage its emotions about spending, and those emotions—shame, defensiveness, secretiveness—are not side issues. They alter decisions. They alter relationships. They alter whether the household can look honestly at its own cashflow without flinching. The goal here is not to grant permission for anything, nor to scold; it is to make the categories fit adult life.

Begin with the simplest layer: survival needs. Show them as behaviours rather than ideals. A person requires shelter that is physically safe, food that sustains, warmth, basic healthcare access, transport that makes earning possible, and a minimum level of stability in the home. Name the concept: survival needs. Explain it plainly. These are needs that, when unmet, produce immediate harm—illness, exposure, hunger, disintegration of work capacity. Implication: when survival needs are threatened, many other decisions become noise, because the nervous system will prioritise immediate security above long-term plans.

Affluent households often assume they are far beyond this layer, and sometimes they are. Yet survival needs can reappear in disguise. Consider the professional who earns well but lives in a housing arrangement that is technically "fine" and practically unstable: a long commute that steals sleep, a damp flat that triggers recurring illness, a neighbourhood where walking home at night feels unsafe. The household may call a move to a better area a "want", because the spreadsheet says rent would rise and the current situation is not catastrophic. Show: the person arrives at work exhausted, pays for more convenience food, spends more on taxis, feels chronically on edge. Name: hidden survival stress. Explain: when basic conditions are compromised, people often compensate through spending that looks discretionary—deliveries, caffeine, "treats"—because they are trying to self-regulate. Implication: calling the original problem a "want" can keep the household stuck in a costly pattern of compensation.

Now move to the layer that the binary model tends to flatten: stability needs. These are not survival in the narrow sense. They are the costs that prevent a household from becoming brittle. They create resilience. They reduce the chance that one shock becomes a cascade. Show stability as something measurable: the proportion of take-home pay committed to fixed obligations; the number of days a household can cover essentials if income pauses; the frequency with which unexpected bills trigger conflict. Name: stability needs. Explain: stability needs buy predictability, not luxury. They include insurances, maintenance, childcare arrangements that allow work to function, tools and services that protect health and time in ways that are not glamorous but are real. Implication: when stability needs are underfunded, the household may appear "frugal" yet live in constant reactivity, which is a costly way to be alive.

This is where many affluent households get tangled, because stability needs can look expensive. Paying for childcare that reliably covers work commitments can be a stability need even if it dwarfs other categories. Maintaining a car that is safe and dependable can be a stability need even if the vehicle is nicer than a minimalist would choose. Paying for occasional help at home can be a stability need if it prevents chronic conflict or burnout. The household's error is not that it wants stability. The error is that it fails to name stability as its own category, so it vacillates between resentment ("we spend too much") and denial ("we deserve it"), instead of evaluating whether the spending genuinely reduces fragility.

A named example clarifies how categories depend on context. In March 1940, in the United Kingdom, the Ministry of Food began systematic rationing during the Second World War. The policy's visible behaviour was severe constraint: ration books, queues, strict allocation of staples. The concept is obvious: society redefined needs under pressure. What counted as essential was narrowed, enforced, and shared. The implication for a modern household is not that it should live like wartime Britain. It is that "need" is never purely a personal preference; it is shaped by circumstances. When constraints change, categories change. Pretending that needs and wants are fixed and universal is historically naïve.

A third layer completes the adult picture: meaningful wants. The phrase sounds like an apology, which is part of the problem. Many finance discussions treat "want" as synonymous with frivolous. Yet much of what makes life worth living sits in the category of wants: friendships, beauty, play, curiosity, travel, hospitality, generosity, craft, learning. Show meaningful wants as visible patterns: the dinners that keep friendships alive; the annual trip that maintains extended family bonds; the hobby that makes a person less brittle; the home environment that supports calm. Name: meaningful wants. Explain: these are discretionary in the sense that a body can survive without them, but central in the sense that a person's life becomes thin without them. Implication: when a household suppresses meaningful wants under the banner of "being sensible", it often creates a pressure cooker—resentment builds, then erupts as impulsive spending that is less meaningful and more expensive.

The classic binary fails precisely because it cannot distinguish meaningful wants from low-value drift. A household can spend heavily on something that looks like a want and is, in function, a stability investment—say, travel to see grandparents because the family is scattered. Another household can spend modestly but constantly on things that are neither stability nor meaning—endless small upgrades, forgettable convenience, subscriptions used twice.

Both households will have "wants" in the ledger. Only one has wants that earn their place.

Housing is the first arena where the labels fight back. For one family, a larger home in a particular postcode is a status symbol; for another, it is the only workable solution to caring for an elderly parent while keeping two careers intact. Show the trade-off in observable terms: commuting time, childcare logistics, sleep hours, frequency of family meals, stress levels. Name: functional housing. Explain: housing is not merely a roof; it is a platform that shapes time, relationships, and health. Implication: calling a move "a want" because the household will not freeze without it can obscure the reality that the current arrangement is extracting costs elsewhere—often in time and mental peace, which then gets repurchased at retail price through convenience spending.

Schooling is the second arena. Private education can be status theatre. It can also be a response to specific needs: a child's learning differences, safety concerns, a local system that does not fit. Two households can make similar choices for opposite reasons. Show: a family pays for tutoring, therapy, or specific educational environments; another pays because "everyone does". Name: motive clarity. Explain: the same expenditure can be a stability need for one household and a comparison-driven want for another, and the difference lies in the observable reason: what problem is being solved, what outcome is being sought, what alternative options exist. Implication: without motive clarity, households tend to argue about cost rather than function, and cost arguments rarely settle anything because they ignore the underlying fear—fear of failing a child, fear of social judgement, fear of regret.

Travel is the third arena, and it reveals how easily the word "want" becomes a moral trap. For some, travel is a trophy—collecting destinations, posting proof, returning unchanged. For others, it is relational infrastructure: maintaining friendships across distance, preserving family rituals, building shared memories that outlast the month. Show the difference as behaviour: the number of trips versus the depth of presence; the degree of exhaustion on return; whether the travel reduces or increases domestic stress. Name: relational travel. Explain: travel can be a meaningful want when it strengthens bonds and refreshes capacity, and it can be waste when it functions mainly as status signalling or escape from an unlivable routine. Implication: the question is not "is travel a need?" but "what does this travel *do* to the household's stability and meaning?"

A limitation is essential, because even the three-layer model can become another set of rigid labels. Some expenses refuse tidy classification. Disability-related accommodations can look like "extras" to outsiders and be essential to functioning. Cultural obligations—supporting extended family, funding rites of passage, participating in community—may be experienced as stability and meaning intertwined, not separable. Health-related spending can be both deeply necessary and deeply variable. Show: a household faces a cost that is not optional in practice, even if it would be labelled "discretionary" by generic rules. Name: category spillover. Explain: real life contains expenditures that sit across layers, and forcing them into a single box can produce distorted decisions or unnecessary shame. Implication: the categories should be treated as lenses, not verdicts; their job is to improve understanding, not to police identity.

Reconcile the limitation by returning to the quiet motif: the labels. The point is not to perfect the label-maker; it is to stop sticking the wrong labels on the wrong things. When a household calls stability a "want", it tends to underfund resilience and then pay more later in emergency mode. When it calls low-value drift a "need", it tends to normalise habits that quietly erode margin. When it calls meaningful wants "frivolous", it tends to create a brittle life that compensates through impulsive spending. The labels matter because they determine which costs are defended, which are questioned, and which are silently resented.

A second named example shows how quickly labels can change when society changes. In March 2020, in the United Kingdom, the government announced a national lockdown in response to COVID-19. Many middle-class households suddenly experienced a reclassification of needs: reliable internet became a working necessity, not a convenience; a quiet corner became a scarce resource; home delivery shifted from indulgence to risk management; childcare became an existential constraint rather than a line item. The point is not to relitigate the pandemic. The point is to observe, with precision, that "need" is partly a function of context and responsibility. The implication is practical and enduring: households should expect their categories to shift with life stages and external conditions, and should treat that shifting as normal rather than as failure.

This nuanced separation also changes how "discipline" is understood. Discipline is not primarily the ability to say no to wants. It is the ability to say yes to the right wants and no to the wrong defaults. Show discipline as a pattern: a household repeatedly protects stability and meaning while trimming drift, not through constant monitoring but through clear priorities. Name: selective constraint. Explain: selective constraint is what adults do when resources are finite: they constrain low-value spending so that meaningful spending can exist without guilt and without fragility. Implication: a household that learns to distinguish survival, stability, and meaningful wants can become both more generous and more comfortable, because it stops fighting itself with childish binaries.

The labels return one last time as a forward test. When the next contested expense appears—a move, a school decision, a holiday, a new recurring service—the question will not be whether it is a "need" or a "want" in some universal sense. The question will be whether it functions, in this household, as survival, as stability, or as meaning, and whether the label being applied is honest or merely convenient. The unresolved tension is the one that reveals everything: is the household using categories to see reality more clearly, or using categories to justify whatever it has already decided?

Creating spending guardrails

On 1 July 1956, in the United States, President Dwight D. Eisenhower signed the Federal-Aid Highway Act, funding what became the Interstate Highway System. The concrete outcome was asphalt, bridges, and speed at a continental scale. Yet the system's most quietly civilising feature was not the tarmac. It was the guardrail: a simple metal constraint that assumed a human truth—that drivers drift, that weather changes, that attention lapses—and that built safety into the environment rather than demanding perfect behaviour from every individual, every mile.

Good money systems need the same humility. A household can be intelligent, conscientious, and well paid and still drift into lower-value spending when tired, busy, or socially pulled. That drift is not a defect; it is a feature of being alive. Traditional budgets often respond to drift with punishment: tighter categories, stricter limits, more tracking. Guardrails respond with design: broad boundaries that prevent the worst collisions while allowing life to move.

Guardrails beat willpower.

That is the premise worth taking seriously. A strict budget imagines a flawless driver who never swerves. A guardrail imagines a competent driver who sometimes does. The point is not to excuse careless choices; it is to prevent ordinary human inconsistency from producing structural damage—lost margin, rising commitments, generosity postponed because the month feels brittle. Guardrails aim at safety and freedom, not perfection.

The first step is to acknowledge what guardrails are not. They are not detailed categories for every purchase. They are not a moral scoreboard. They do not require daily logging. They are ranges—deliberately imprecise—placed around the areas where drift is most likely to happen and most likely to matter. Show: a household notices that restaurant spending and convenience deliveries balloon during deadlines, and that subscription creep accumulates quietly. Name: drift zones. Explain: drift zones are spending areas that expand under stress and social cues; they are not inherently bad, but they are the easiest places for money to leak without delivering proportionate value. Implication: if a household contains drift zones, it can protect the rest of the system by setting boundaries around them, rather than trying to police every transaction.

A guardrail approach starts where the cashflow map left off: with timing. The month is not a neutral container. Bills cluster, income arrives in pulses, and discretionary spending tends to follow emotional rhythms rather than calendar logic. Show: a household is paid on the last working day of the month; mortgage and childcare leave on the first; the first week feels flush, the third week feels tight. Name: temporal mismatch. Explain: when spending boundaries ignore pay cycles, people spend according to perceived abundance early in the month and then clamp down later, which produces volatility and resentment. Implication: guardrails that align with pay cycles reduce volatility by creating steadier decision conditions; they replace "we're fine" and "we're doomed" with a more stable baseline.

This alignment is not mere convenience. It improves decision quality. Behavioural research has repeatedly shown that context—fatigue, timing, choice overload—affects judgement (Kahneman, 2011). A household does not make its worst spending decisions when calm and rested. It makes them when time is short and the mind is already full. Guardrails take that seriously. They reduce the number of moments in which a tired person must make a fine-grained choice, because the system has already decided what "normal range" looks like for that category in that season.

The psychological difference between a strict cap and a range is not cosmetic. A strict cap turns a small overrun into failure. A range treats variability as expected. Show: a household sets a hard monthly limit on eating out and "breaks" it by £30, then feels guilty and declares the system broken. Name: brittle targets. Explain: brittle targets create all-or-nothing thinking; they treat the month as a test rather than a living system. Implication: when people feel they have failed, they are more likely to abandon the tool entirely, which returns the household to the drift it was trying to contain.

Ranges also reduce argument. They move money conversations away from individual purchases and towards patterns. That is not a soft point. In households, conflict is costly; it drains attention and makes transparency harder. Show: one partner questions a £12 lunch; the other hears criticism; the real issue—recurring costs eroding margin—goes unaddressed because the debate collapses into personality. Name: transaction fixation. Explain: focusing on single purchases is emotionally provocative and analytically weak, because the household's financial experience is shaped by aggregates and commitments, not by one lunch. Implication: guardrails that focus on broad patterns allow households to discuss spending without turning it into a referendum on character.

A named, checkable example from behavioural policy illustrates why simple signals outperform complex monitoring for most people. In April 2014, the UK's Behavioural Insights Team, based in London, published *EAST*, arguing that behaviour change tends to succeed when it is made Easy, Attractive, Social, and Timely. The lesson transfers neatly. Show: a system that requires daily categorisation competes with life; a system that uses a few simple signals can run under stress. Name: minimal viable monitoring. Explain: when attention is scarce, the best monitoring is sparse but meaningful—focused on indicators that correlate with outcomes people care about, such as discretionary margin or the growth of recurring commitments. Implication: guardrails are effective partly because they make monitoring possible without turning it into a hobby.

Guardrails also clarify what deserves precision. High-income households often waste energy policing low-impact categories while ignoring high-impact ones. The classic example is arguing about coffees while carrying a fleet of subscriptions, insurance add-ons, and premium plans that nobody has evaluated in years. Show: the household reduces small pleasures and still feels tight because fixed commitments remain heavy. Name: misplaced precision. Explain: precision applied to small, emotionally charged items can function as a distraction from bigger structural choices that require calm and negotiation. Implication: guardrails redirect attention to where it has leverage in the non-silly sense: the decisions that shape recurring outgoings and therefore shape freedom.

Two named, checkable developments in consumer finance show how environments can be designed to assist rather than to police. When the UK's Open Banking regime went live in January 2018 under the Competition and Markets Authority, it enabled account aggregation and spending insights with reduced manual effort. When Mint.com launched in September 2008 in San Francisco, it popularised automated categorisation. Both improved visibility, but visibility alone did not guarantee better behaviour; what mattered was whether the tools supported timely decisions rather than retrospective regret. Show: people see charts after the month ends and feel chastened; they do not change the conditions under which spending occurs. Name: hindsight friction. Explain: many budgeting systems deliver feedback too late, when the money is already spent, turning insight into self-criticism rather than into choice. Implication: guardrails work best when paired with early signals—simple cues that a category is drifting before the month has hardened into history.

Signals are the quiet workhorses of guardrails. A signal is not a detailed report. It is a prompt that attention should be applied briefly, before drift becomes structural. In household terms, signals are behavioural and temporal: an unusual cluster of delivery charges in a week; a rising count of recurring payments; the second "small" subscription added in a month; the moment discretionary margin begins to thin earlier than usual. Signals are not moral alarms. They are information. Their power lies in timeliness.

The motif of the guardrail deserves a second appearance here because it makes a deeper point about dignity. Guardrails do not insult the driver. They respect physics. Spending guardrails do not insult the household. They respect psychology. They assume fatigue, distraction, social pressure, and occasional impulse. They build around those realities. A household that adopts guardrails is not declaring itself weak; it is declaring itself honest.

A credible limitation should be stated, because guardrails can be misused. Some people set ranges so wide that the guardrails become decorative, offering the comforting sensation of a system without any real constraint. Others set ranges so narrow that the system becomes a disguised strict budget and resurrects the same guilt dynamics. Show: one household declares "fun money" with no boundary and watches it swell; another sets a range so tight that any social event creates anxiety. Name: false guardrails. Explain: a guardrail must be placed where it can actually prevent harm without preventing life; too wide and it does nothing, too narrow and it becomes a wall. Implication: the effectiveness of guardrails depends on calibration to real patterns, which is why mapping comes first; the environment must be shaped according to what the household actually does, not what it wishes it did.

Reconcile this by returning to the point of guardrails: protect big priorities by containing low-value drift. The "big priorities" are visible in outcomes: stable margin, reduced recurring commitments, less end-of-month brittleness, more capacity for planned generosity, fewer arguments rooted in money fog. A guardrail that does not protect these outcomes is not a guardrail. It is theatre.

This is also where the distinction between flexibility and looseness matters. Flexibility respects variability; looseness ignores consequences. A flexible system anticipates that some months contain travel, family needs, work intensity, or rare opportunities. It allows movement inside ranges without panic. It also treats recurring commitments with appropriate seriousness, because recurring commitments are not flexible; they are promises. The guardrail mindset therefore pairs softness in day-to-day variability with firmness about what becomes fixed. That is a sophisticated posture: relaxed where it can be relaxed, strict where it must be strict.

The real sophistication, though, is that guardrails make trade-offs explicit without being punitive. If a household spends at the top of its range in one area, it knows that other areas must stay closer to the bottom if margin and generosity are to remain intact. That knowledge does not require an app's scolding notification. It requires a shared picture of the flow and a few agreed boundaries. The result is a system that can run during hectic seasons because it does not demand constant attention; it demands occasional honesty.

The guardrail metaphor returns one last time in the only way that matters: at speed. Households spend fastest when they are tired and busy, when a child is melting down, when a project deadline looms, when social invitations pile up, when the week has already been too much. At speed, perfect decisions are a fantasy. Guardrails are realistic.

The forward test is therefore simple and slightly uncomfortable. When the next month begins and money starts moving—salary landing, bills clustering, small drips accumulating—will the household rely on memory and willpower, or will it trust a few well-placed guardrails and timely signals to keep the system on the road?

Cashflow rhythms for busyness

On 7 October 1913, at Ford's Highland Park plant in Michigan, the moving assembly line began to reshape industrial life. The outcome was measurable: according to the historian David A. Hounshell's account of American mass production, the time to assemble a Model T chassis fell dramatically once work was organised into a paced flow rather than a series of heroic, stop-start efforts (Hounshell, 1984). That shift was not only mechanical. It was psychological. Instead of relying on constant supervision and individual vigilance, the system embedded rhythm into the environment. Work moved forward because the line moved forward.

The affluent household is not a factory, and nobody should want it to be. Yet the basic lesson transfers with surprising elegance. When money management is treated as a periodic burst of willpower—an evening of spreadsheets, a weekend of sorting receipts—it competes with fatigue and usually loses. When it is treated as a rhythm—small, regular pulses of attention anchored to existing routines—it survives busy seasons because it is no longer asking the household to perform heroics. It is asking the household to keep time.

Busyness is not a character flaw.

It is a condition. For high-functioning people, busyness often arrives as a by-product of responsibility: demanding work, caregiving, children's schedules, ageing parents, community ties, the relentless logistics of modern life. In such circumstances, the scarcest resource is not information and often not even money. It is attention. Attention has limits, and the limits are not negotiable. Psychologist Daniel Kahneman described attention as a finite capacity in which mental effort is allocated and depleted across tasks (Kahneman, 2011). The implication is plain: any cashflow system that requires frequent, high-effort engagement will be abandoned precisely when it is needed most—during pressure.

The most common failure mode is easy to recognise. Show: a household intends to "get on top of money", downloads an app, categorises diligently for two weeks, then misses a week because work explodes or a child becomes ill, then avoids reopening the app because the backlog feels like guilt. Name: the backlog trap. Explain: when a system penalises missed time with extra work, it creates an emotional debt; people avoid the system to avoid the feeling. Implication: the household returns to autopilot, but now with a fresh layer of self-reproach, which makes the next attempt even harder.

The alternative begins with a different assumption: financial clarity does not require constant monitoring; it requires timely monitoring. Show: a household does not need to know the category of every £7.40 purchase to protect its margin; it needs to notice when recurring commitments grow, when discretionary spending drifts early in the month, and when a cluster of bills will compress the next fortnight. Name: the minimum effective dose. Explain: in medicine the phrase refers to the smallest intervention that produces a meaningful effect; in household systems it points to the smallest amount of attention that preserves orientation and prevents drift. Implication: the household can build a system that works during chaos because it asks for minutes, not hours, and because it focuses those minutes where they change outcomes.

There is an evidence-backed reason rhythms matter. Habits form when a behaviour becomes linked to a stable cue and repeated enough times that it requires less conscious effort. Researchers Wendy Wood and Dennis Neal have argued that much daily behaviour is habitual rather than deliberative, driven by context cues more than by conscious goals (Wood & Neal, 2007). The cashflow question, then, is not "how does a household stay motivated?" but "what cues can carry the behaviour when motivation is low?" The implication is liberating: a household can rely less on mood and more on design.

A rhythm also reduces the psychological burden of the task. Show: a person who tries to do a full monthly finance review in one sitting often experiences dread, because the task feels large and morally loaded. Name: task aversion. Explain: people avoid tasks that feel ambiguous, time-consuming, or emotionally punishing; avoidance is not irrational, it is a protective behaviour. Implication: breaking money attention into smaller, regular pulses makes the task less emotionally heavy and therefore more sustainable, without requiring anyone to become unusually disciplined.

The practical question becomes: where do rhythms attach in a busy life? The clue is that most busy people already have rhythms. They plan their week. They check calendars. They handle a small block of admin. They glance at email. They refill prescriptions. They do school bags. The point is not to create a new ritual that competes with everything else; it is to piggyback on an existing one. Psychologist Peter Gollwitzer's work on implementation intentions showed that "if–then" plans—linking an action to a cue—can increase follow-through because the cue triggers behaviour with less deliberation (Gollwitzer, 1999). The implication is not that life becomes robotic; it is that tiny structures can protect important behaviours from being crowded out.

Consider a weekly planning moment. Show: a household looks at the next seven days and sees travel, social plans, a child's activity, a deadline, and one evening that will be late. Name: anticipatory cashflow awareness. Explain: spending is often driven by the week ahead; a late week invites convenience spending, a travel week invites higher transport costs, a social week invites dining out. Implication: a brief, routine glance at cashflow in the same moment as calendar planning can reduce the number of surprise pressures, because the household is no longer reacting blind to predictable conditions.

Now consider the monthly moment when many bills cluster. Show: direct debits leave, subscriptions renew, insurance or childcare payments hit, and the account balance shifts sharply. Name: the bill window. Explain: because many obligations are timed early in the month, the early-month window is when a household's discretionary margin becomes real rather than imagined. Implication: a quick, consistent check at this moment has disproportionately high value; it reveals whether the month is spacious or tight *before* spending habits settle into motion.

The key is to keep the monitoring lightweight and specific. A rhythm that requires interpretation of dozens of categories will not survive. A rhythm that asks a household to notice a few structural indicators might. The indicators are visible behaviours rather than abstract virtues: the count of recurring payments; the size of fixed commitments relative to income; whether discretionary spending is tracking within the guardrails; whether any unusual costs are approaching. These are not moral metrics. They are navigational.

This is where guardrails and rhythms meet. Guardrails create boundaries; rhythms create maintenance. Without maintenance, guardrails drift into irrelevance. Without guardrails, rhythms become anxious monitoring. Together, they form a system that can run on limited attention: a small pulse checks whether the household is still between the rails. The motif here is the metronome. A metronome does not play the music. It keeps time so the music does not collapse into chaos. The household's brief reviews are the metronome: they keep the financial rhythm steady enough that life can be lived without constant recalculation.

A named, checkable example from behavioural policy captures the design principle cleanly. In April 2014, the UK's Behavioural Insights Team in London published *EAST*, emphasising that behaviour change works better when made Easy and Timely, among other features. The crucial element here is timeliness: interventions placed at the moment of decision outperform interventions delivered long after the fact. The implication for cashflow is sharp. A monthly post-mortem may produce insight and shame; a small, timely check before the busy week begins can change the week's behaviour without drama.

The most robust systems also acknowledge another human feature: self-control fluctuates. Some days a person is calm and future-oriented; some days they are depleted and short-term. The early "ego depletion" literature suggested that self-control can function like a limited resource, although later research has debated the size and consistency of this effect (Baumeister et al., 1998; subsequent replication debates are part of the record). The point does not depend on any single study. Ordinary observation is enough: people make poorer decisions when exhausted. The implication is that money systems must be built to work *when judgement is worst*, not only when it is best.

This is why the minimum effective dose matters. A household does not need to become more virtuous to become more intentional; it needs to reduce the number of high-stakes decisions that occur when everyone is tired. A rhythm does this by shifting attention upstream. Show: rather than debating a late-night delivery order in the moment, a household has already noticed that the coming week contains three late nights and has planned for that reality. Name: upstream design. Explain: upstream design places structure before the stress arrives, which reduces reliance on willpower in the stressed moment. Implication: the household spends with less regret not because it becomes ascetic, but because it has fewer moments of reactive spending.

A limitation should be stated clearly, because rhythms can become performative. Some people respond to anxiety by checking finances compulsively, refreshing balances, scanning feeds, treating every fluctuation as meaningful. Show: a household looks ten times a day, feels briefly soothed, then feels more anxious because the number keeps changing and the mind keeps attaching stories to it. Name: monitoring as coping. Explain: when monitoring is used to manage emotion rather than to inform decisions, it can become a loop that increases preoccupation without improving outcomes. Implication: the goal of rhythms is orientation, not surveillance; they should reduce the time money occupies the mind, not expand it.

The reconciliation lies in intent and scope. A useful rhythm is bounded: it happens at particular moments, for a small duration, with a specific question in mind. The metronome appears again: it clicks, briefly, and then falls silent so the music can play. This is not an argument for ignorance. It is an argument for proportion. Money deserves attention. It does not deserve domination.

A second named, checkable example illuminates why small, scheduled check-ins often beat sporadic overhauls. When the UK's Open Banking regime became operational in January 2018 under the Competition and Markets Authority, it enabled more continuous visibility of transactions. Continuous visibility can tempt continuous checking. Yet the real advantage of better data is that it allows a household to schedule lighter reviews without losing accuracy—because the information is accessible when needed. The implication is that modern tools are best used to support rhythms, not to create a permanent financial dashboard addiction.

There is also a social dimension. In many households, one person becomes the "finance brain" by default. That person absorbs the cognitive load, carries the worry, and occasionally explodes. A rhythm can redistribute that load by making the check-in a shared routine rather than a solitary burden. Show: two people glance at the same map and notice the same cluster of bills and the same upcoming expenses. Name: shared visibility. Explain: shared visibility reduces suspicion and reduces the tendency to treat money conversations as accusations; it turns them into joint navigation. Implication: the household gains not only better cashflow management but a calmer relational climate, which is itself a form of wealth.

Ultimately, cashflow rhythms are an application of a simple, adult principle: systems should respect reality. Reality includes unpredictability, fatigue, changing seasons, and the fact that people have better things to do than micro-track every purchase. A rhythm honours that by asking for small, regular acts of attention that keep the household between the rails. The payoff is not merely a smoother month. It is the return of mental space—less time spent wondering whether the household is "fine", more time spent living.

The unresolved test arrives whenever life accelerates, which is often. When a hectic season begins—deadlines, travel, school demands, family needs—does the household's money management become another collapsing project, or does the metronome keep time well enough that the system continues to run, quietly, in the background?

Chapter 3
Building Your Value Hierarchy

In 1971, in Palo Alto, Stanford psychologist Walter Mischel began a series of experiments that would later be remembered as the "marshmallow test". A child was offered a simple bargain: eat one treat now, or wait and receive two. The image has been repeated so often it has become a cultural shorthand for self-control. Yet the most interesting detail is not the marshmallow. It is the room. The child is not deciding in a vacuum. The child is deciding inside an environment thick with cues—temptation, trust, boredom, imagination—and inside a private story about whether waiting will be rewarded. Later critiques and replications complicated the original narrative, pointing to the roles of socioeconomic context and trust in the promised future, but the deeper lesson remains intact: choices are not only about willpower; they are about what a person believes is worth waiting for, and whether their world makes that belief feel safe.

Affluent adults make marshmallow decisions constantly. They do it with property and schooling, with holidays and home improvements, with "just this one upgrade" and "we deserve a treat". They do it with the silent question beneath every purchase: is this the good life, or merely the expensive life? The difficulty is that adult treats are disguised. They arrive as services, subscriptions, status norms, convenience defaults. They are marketed as sensible. They are socially validated. They rarely announce themselves as temptation. So the household waits for what, exactly? More comfort? More security? More options? Or a specific form of life that is felt, relational, and particular?

A life needs a hierarchy.

Without one, money becomes a democracy where every desire gets an equal vote, and the loudest desires—convenience, novelty, status—tend to win. The result is not necessarily bankruptcy. The result is drift: a household that can afford many things but experiences its money as strangely unhelpful, because spending is scattered across low-value defaults rather than concentrated on what actually makes life feel rich. The preceding chapter dealt with the mechanics of cashflow and the virtue of guardrails. This chapter steps upstream of mechanics. It asks what the system is meant to serve.

The phrase "values" is often abused. It is used as a decorative word in corporate missions and holiday speeches, and many thoughtful people have learned to distrust it. Here, values are not slogans. They are *preferences with consequences*. They show up in how a household spends evenings, how it responds to requests for help, how it treats time, which relationships it protects, and what it is willing to trade away to preserve what it loves. Values are not what people say in the abstract. They are what they repeatedly choose when reality presses.

The pressure is unusually intense now because the market has become extraordinarily good at selling pseudo-values. It can sell "self-care" in the form of a product. It can sell "family time" in the form of a holiday package. It can sell "freedom" in the form of a premium service that removes friction. It can sell "belonging" in the form of a postcode, a school, a set of brands that signal competence. These offers are not always cynical. They are simply efficient: they turn human longing into purchasable units. Without a clear hierarchy, a household ends up paying retail for meaning and receiving only the packaging.

A value hierarchy is not a list of virtues. It is a ranking of what matters most when trade-offs are unavoidable. Every household has one already, whether it is explicit or accidental. The accidental version is constructed by habit and social environment. The explicit version is constructed by reflection and honest conversation. The difference is profound. When the hierarchy is accidental, spending feels reactive; the household experiences money as something that happens to it. When the hierarchy is explicit, spending becomes selective; the household uses money like a tool rather than like a mood.

The first task, then, is not to "set goals" in the generic sense. Goals are often vague and easily gamed. "Security" can mean anything from a larger emergency fund to a prestigious school to a bigger house. "Travel" can mean a once-a-year pilgrimage to see family or a constant churn of escapism. The work is to define what genuinely lights people up—experiences that restore them, relationships that deepen them, contributions that make them feel at home in the world—and to distinguish these from surface-level wants that are mostly about status, habit, or momentary relief. This is harder than it sounds because status wants often masquerade as stability, and habit wants often masquerade as "just how we live". Naming does not eliminate desire. It makes desire legible.

Once what matters is clearer, a second challenge appears: the absence of enough. Many affluent households live with a subtle, chronic sense that they are not quite there yet. The upgrade horizon keeps moving. The "right time" to enjoy never arrives. There is always a reason to postpone: a future school cost, a potential redundancy, the next promotion, a housing market that never behaves, parents who may need care. These are not imaginary concerns. They are real uncertainties. Yet when uncertainty becomes a permanent veto on enjoyment and generosity, the household ends up living as if it is always on probation. The irony is that probation is expensive. It often produces compensatory spending—small treats and conveniences—to soothe the feeling of deprivation in the present.

The idea of "enough thresholds" is the antidote to vague restraint. A threshold is a boundary that is humane because it is specific. It recognises that sufficiency is not the same as scarcity. "Enough" in housing might mean a home that supports rest and relationships, even if it lacks a certain kind of prestige. "Enough" in clothing might mean a small rotation that works well, even if it does not keep pace with trends. "Enough" in technology might mean devices that function reliably, even if they are not the newest. "Enough" in dining out might mean a frequency that still feels like pleasure rather than like default. Thresholds do not remove desire. They prevent desire from becoming the only compass.

This is where the chapter begins to look less like philosophy and more like craft. Once values and thresholds exist, reallocation becomes possible. The most effective changes in affluent households are rarely achieved through blunt cutting. They are achieved through trading. A household does not have to live with less overall. It has to live with less in the places that do not matter much and more in the places that matter deeply. The distinction is not obvious until it is made. Many people discover, with mild embarrassment, that they have been paying heavily for forgettable conveniences while starving the few experiences that actually nourish them—hosting friends, taking a meaningful trip, supporting a cause, creating time for a relationship to breathe. The trade is not deprivation. It is liberation from low-value noise.

The modern relevance is obvious. Subscription models, convenience markets, and status signalling have become so ambient that they can easily occupy the prime real estate of a household's spending without ever being chosen deliberately. Meanwhile, what people say they want—time, closeness, contribution—often requires fewer purchases but more intention. The market can sell a holiday, but it cannot sell presence. It can sell a cleaner, but it cannot sell a household that uses the saved time to be kinder rather than busier. It can sell a premium lifestyle, but it cannot sell a shared sense of enough. That is the household's work.

The work becomes even more delicate when values differ within the same home. Many money conflicts are not truly about money. They are about competing visions of safety and happiness. One partner may treat saving as love; the other may treat experiences as love. One may feel calm with a large buffer; the other may feel alive with generous spending on hospitality. One may be scarred by a childhood of scarcity; the other by a childhood of emotional distance. When these histories collide, the spreadsheet becomes a battlefield. The solution is not to find the mathematically correct answer. It is to build a shared hierarchy broad enough to hold both people without erasing either of them.

This is why value alignment is not a sentimental aside. It is an efficiency strategy in the truest sense: it reduces repeated conflict and wasted emotional energy. When households do not agree on what money is for, they end up renegotiating every purchase as if it were a referendum on the relationship. That is exhausting. When a household has a shared hierarchy—plus a respectful space for individual priorities—many day-to-day choices become easier. Not easy in the sense of painless, but easy in the sense of clear. The arguments change tone. They become experiments rather than ultimatums, trade-offs rather than accusations. A household can disagree without treating disagreement as betrayal.

A subtle motif threads through this chapter: the compass. Cashflow systems and guardrails keep the vehicle steady. The value hierarchy sets direction. Without direction, steadiness is merely efficient drifting. With direction, even modest resources can create a life that feels abundant because they are concentrated on what matters. The compass is not a moral judge; it is an instrument. It does not tell anyone what to love. It helps them notice what they already love, and whether their spending is pointing the same way.

The emotional payoff of this work is not purity. It is relief—the relief of no longer having to justify every choice with a story about deserving or discipline. When values are clear, "nice to have" and "worth it" stop being vague slogans and become discernible categories. The household can stop performing affluence and start living it, in the only sense that counts: having enough freedom to choose well, enough alignment to feel calm, and enough surplus to be open-handed without fear.

The page turns with a question that is simultaneously practical and existential. When the next tempting upgrade, lifestyle ratchet, or socially validated expense arrives, will the household reach for it because it is available and normal, or will it consult the compass and ask what that choice would displace—time, margin, generosity, relationship, a quieter kind of joy that cannot be bought at the last minute?

Defining what matters most

In 1726, in Philadelphia, Benjamin Franklin began what he called his "project of moral perfection", drawing a small grid in his notebook to track thirteen virtues week by week. The outcome was not sainthood—Franklin admitted, in his *Autobiography*, that he never achieved the spotless ledger he imagined—but something more durable: a method for noticing the gap between what a person claims to value and what their days actually express. The scene is almost comically domestic: ink, paper, a mind attempting to discipline itself by measurement, the scratch of a pen and the quiet hope that a life can be steered rather than merely lived.

The method looks quaint beside modern dashboards and banking apps, yet the underlying problem has hardly changed. People can name admirable values in the abstract and still spend their time and money as if guided by a different set of priorities. They can say "family" and then build a week that never permits unhurried conversation. They can say "freedom" and then accumulate commitments that require constant high earnings to maintain. They can say "generosity" and then treat giving as something reserved for a future month that never arrives. Values hide inside daily habits.

That hiddenness is the central obstacle for affluent households. Scarcity forces priorities into the open because choices are brutally constrained. Comfort does the opposite. Comfort makes almost everything possible, at least in the short term, which means almost everything can be rationalised. The result is a peculiar fog: the household has resources, yet cannot easily distinguish between what it *wants* and what it is merely accustomed to wanting. Defining what matters most is the act of clearing that fog—not by producing a slogan, but by turning values into something that can guide actual trade-offs.

Begin with the kind of scene that produces the most expensive confusion: a decision that is technically affordable and emotionally ambiguous. A household considers a larger home. The numbers work, just. The new place would be more impressive, more comfortable, more aligned with what peers seem to be doing. It would also increase fixed costs, reduce flexibility, and tighten the margin that makes spontaneous kindness and genuine rest possible. Show: the conversation toggles between justification and doubt, between the language of "deserving" and the language of "sensible". Name: value ambiguity. Explain: when values are not explicit, the mind fills the gap with proxies—status, convenience, fear of missing out, fear of regret—because proxies are easy to feel and hard to argue against. Implication: the household risks locking itself into a higher-cost life without ever deciding whether the higher cost is paying for what it truly cares about, or merely paying for a socially legible version of success.

The heart of the matter is that values are not interchangeable. "Security" is not a single thing. For one person it means a large buffer and low fixed commitments; for another it means a prestigious school that signals future opportunity; for a third it means living near family so childcare and care for ageing relatives is possible without collapse. "Travel" is not a single thing. For one household it is a form of belonging—going back to grandparents, maintaining an extended family across borders. For another it is the accumulation of destinations, a way of proving a life is interesting. The same word can conceal opposite priorities, which is why generic goals often fail as guides. They comfort the mind without directing it.

Economists have a term that sounds clinical and is, in practice, deeply human: revealed preferences. In 1938, the economist Paul Samuelson published "A Note on the Pure Theory of Consumer's Behaviour" in *Economica*, laying groundwork for the idea that what people choose reveals what they value, regardless of what they claim to value. This is not an accusation. It is an observation about how choice operates. Show: the calendar is always full of work, always thin on friendships; the bank statement is rich in convenience fees, poor in planned generosity; the household repeatedly upgrades devices but delays time with family. Name: revealed values. Explain: values become real not in declarations but in repeated allocation of scarce resources—time, attention, money, emotional energy. Implication: a household that wants to know what it truly values can learn by examining patterns rather than intentions, because patterns do not flatter.

This is where the affluent reader often feels a sting, and it is important to handle it with respect. Many people are not failing to live their values because they are shallow. They are failing because modern life is structured to make low-value spending and high-value distraction easy. Convenience purchases arrive as small reliefs; status purchases arrive as socially validated "responsible" choices; both are smooth, quick, and rewarded. Meanwhile, the things most people claim to value—presence, deep relationships, contribution—are rarely smooth. They require time, attention, and sometimes discomfort. The market can sell the appearance of a value faster than it can support the practice of one. The compass needle is constantly tugged.

A named piece of evidence sharpens this point without reducing it to a cliché. In 2010, in *Proceedings of the National Academy of Sciences*, Daniel Kahneman and Angus Deaton analysed large survey data and reported a nuanced relationship between income and wellbeing: higher income was associated with higher life evaluation, while emotional wellbeing showed diminishing returns beyond a certain point in the United States at that time (Kahneman & Deaton, 2010). The exact thresholds in popular retellings have been debated and updated, and they vary by context, but the central implication is robust enough to be useful here. Once basic pressures are eased, the quality of life becomes less about sheer income and more about what income is *for*: how it is used to shape time, stress, relationships, and meaning. Affluence widens choice; it does not automatically supply direction.

Direction requires more than preference. It requires hierarchy. A hierarchy does not mean a life becomes narrow. It means the household decides what it is willing to trade for what. Consider the difference between a surface-level want and a deep one. A surface-level want tends to be externally triggered: a colleague's new car, a social media advertisement, a neighbour's renovation, a limited-time offer, a sudden desire to feel "caught up". It produces a short spike of excitement followed by a return to baseline. A deep want tends to be internally anchored: it persists over time, survives changing fashions, and produces a lasting increase in ease or connection. Show: a person buys a costly gadget and uses it twice; another spends the same amount hosting friends regularly and finds the house becomes a warmer place to live. Name: durable satisfaction. Explain: durable satisfaction often correlates with repeated use, relational reinforcement, and identity coherence—spending that supports the person one is becoming, rather than the person one is trying to appear to be. Implication: without a value hierarchy, a household can spend heavily and still feel undernourished, because its spending is feeding momentary cues rather than durable satisfactions.

The household's value hierarchy also has a temporal dimension. Many affluent people hold their values hostage to a future self. They tell themselves they will prioritise family when work calms down, prioritise health when the next project ends, prioritise generosity when the mortgage is smaller, prioritise friendships when the children are older. Sometimes those seasons come. Often they do not. The years are not a tidy ladder; they are a field of weather. Show: the household postpones what it claims matters and then compensates with spending that soothes the discomfort of postponement—treats, upgrades, convenience, distraction. Name: deferred living. Explain: when a household delays its values, it tends to purchase short-term relief to tolerate the delay, and that relief can become a habit that makes the delay longer by consuming time and margin. Implication: the hierarchy remains theoretical, and money continues to serve the immediate rather than the important.

A second named, checkable example makes the role of environment impossible to ignore. In March 2020, the UK entered national lockdown in response to COVID-19, and many households experienced an abrupt reordering of priorities. Commuting and certain forms of consumption collapsed overnight; time at home expanded; relationships were tested; health anxieties changed what felt essential. Some people discovered they missed restaurants less than they missed friends. Others discovered they missed privacy more than they missed holidays. The point is not to romanticise a difficult period. It is to observe a clear mechanism: when the environment changes, the hierarchy becomes visible. Show: spending patterns shift because routines shift; what people had been buying to cope is no longer available, and the underlying needs appear. Name: forced clarity. Explain: the crisis removed certain defaults and compelled households to confront what they actually required to feel stable and alive. Implication: in normal times, intentional reflection can achieve some of the same clarity without requiring disruption, because it can separate true priorities from purchased coping mechanisms.

Still, there is a limitation worth stating plainly: values are not always stable, and they are not always neatly articulable. People change. Children arrive. Parents become ill. Careers evolve. Communities shift. A household can define what matters most and still discover, a year later, that the definition needs revision. Moreover, some values conflict. A person can value autonomy and also value deep belonging, which sometimes requires obligation. A household can value generosity and also value leaving a financial inheritance. A person can value excellence at work and also value unhurried family life, and there is no magical reconciliation that produces maximum of both. Name: value plurality. Explain: humans hold multiple goods, and the goods occasionally collide. Implication: a value hierarchy is not a final proclamation; it is a living instrument that helps a household navigate collisions without pretending they do not exist.

The reconciliation is where the hierarchy earns its keep. A living hierarchy does not promise harmony; it promises honesty. It allows trade-offs to be made consciously rather than by drift. It turns vague arguments—"we spend too much", "we never do anything fun", "we should be saving more"—into sharper questions that can actually be answered. What is being protected here: security, status, time, relationships, contribution, peace? What is being sacrificed, and is that sacrifice acceptable? What is merely habitual, and what is genuinely life-giving? The compass needle does not remove storms, but it helps a household choose a heading during them.

This is also why values must be expressed in concrete terms, not in noble abstractions. "Family" might mean two protected evenings a week without screens. "Friendship" might mean hosting once a month rather than constantly meeting in restaurants. "Freedom" might mean keeping fixed commitments below a chosen proportion of income. "Generosity" might mean a regular practice rather than occasional guilt-driven bursts. These are not prescriptions; they are translations. A value that cannot be translated into an observable behaviour is too vague to guide spending when temptation arrives.

Translation exposes status wants with unusual clarity. Status is not always silly. It can be professionally useful. It can be culturally meaningful. It can even be a form of signalling safety in uncertain environments. The problem is not status itself. The problem is unconscious status spending that masquerades as stability or taste. Show: the household pays for a prestige upgrade and then feels a brief lift followed by the same anxiety. Name: borrowed identity.

Explain: when purchases are used to borrow a sense of competence or belonging, the effect is often short-lived because identity cannot be permanently rented; it must be built through lived experience and relationships. Implication: households that confuse status with value can remember the purchase but not the life it created, because it created mostly an image.

The most revealing question is also the simplest: what experiences leave the household feeling more itself? Not more impressive, not more comfortable in the moment, but more aligned—more coherent, more warm, more capable of generosity without fear. When people answer that question honestly, patterns emerge. They often involve time and people more than objects. They involve fewer recurring purchases and more deliberate ones. They involve less noise.

The north star metaphor is overused in business and still useful here, precisely because navigation requires a fixed reference point. A household's value hierarchy is that reference: not a fantasy destination, but a way of maintaining direction while tides and weather change. The work is not to produce the perfect list. The work is to keep the compass needle from being hijacked by the nearest shiny thing, the loudest norm, the quickest relief.

The forward test arrives the next time the household faces a plausible, affordable upgrade that comes with a good story attached. The question will not be whether the story sounds reasonable. It will be whether the choice moves the compass needle towards the life the household says it values—or whether it merely follows the strongest current and calls it intention.

Creating enough thresholds

In 1955, in Pittsburgh, Herbert A. Simon published "A Behavioral Model of Rational Choice", arguing that real human beings do not optimise endlessly; they satisfice. The concrete outcome was a new, disarmingly humane idea in economic and decision theory: when choices are complex and time is finite, people set an aspiration level and accept an option that is "good enough" (Simon, 1955). Simon was not writing a lifestyle manual. He was describing cognition under constraint. Yet the implication lands directly in the middle of affluent life, where the number of available upgrades is effectively infinite and the cost of endless choosing is paid in attention.

Enough is the household waterline.

A waterline is not a moral boundary. It is a functional one. Below it, the boat becomes unstable. Above it, the boat can move. The same is true of "enough" thresholds in a household: they establish the point at which extra spending stops improving life in proportion to its cost and starts raising the baseline in ways that quietly shrink freedom. Without a waterline, the household can keep adding weight—bigger house, better car, more subscriptions, more upgrades—until it is technically afloat and practically brittle.

Affluent households struggle with "enough" because modern consumption rarely presents itself as excess. It presents itself as reasonable refinement. The upgrade offers are incremental: slightly faster, slightly nicer, slightly more convenient, slightly more exclusive. Each step feels small. The cumulative effect is structural. Show: a household begins with a simple phone plan, then adds more storage, then adds device insurance, then adds a new device because the old one is "fine but annoying", then adds accessories and subscriptions that fit the new device. Name: baseline inflation. Explain: baseline inflation occurs when what once felt like a luxury becomes a requirement, and the household's sense of normal shifts upward without any conscious decision to live at a higher cost. Implication: "enough" becomes elusive not because the household is greedy, but because the reference point keeps moving.

Psychology has described part of this movement for decades. In 1971, Philip Brickman and Donald Campbell discussed what later became known as the hedonic treadmill: people adapt to improvements, returning towards a baseline level of satisfaction after changes in circumstance (Brickman & Campbell, 1971). This is not a claim that joy is impossible or that people are doomed to numbness. It is a claim about adaptation. Show: a new kitchen renovation is thrilling for a month; then it becomes the kitchen. A premium car feels like triumph; then it becomes the car. Name:

adaptation. Explain: adaptation is the mind's efficiency mechanism, turning the new into the normal so attention can be spent elsewhere. Implication: if a household relies on upgrades to generate lasting satisfaction, it will need a steady stream of upgrades to keep the feeling alive, and that stream is expensive in both money and attention.

This is where the idea of thresholds becomes liberating rather than restrictive. A threshold is a decision boundary that reduces the number of times a household must renegotiate "is this worth it?" It converts a vague aspiration—"we should be more sensible"—into a concrete posture—"this is enough for us here." The posture is not austere. It is specific. Show: rather than debating every dinner out, the household recognises that dining out beyond a certain frequency stops feeling special and starts functioning as fatigue management. Name: diminishing returns. Explain: diminishing returns means that each additional unit of spending buys less additional benefit than the one before; it is a basic economic idea that becomes painfully personal in lifestyle spending. Implication: when a household sets an "enough" threshold near the point where returns diminish, it protects enjoyment instead of suppressing it, because it keeps the thing from becoming numbingly normal.

The adult distinction to make is between sufficiency and scarcity. Scarcity is an involuntary constraint that produces anxiety, hoarding, and compensatory behaviour. Sufficiency is a chosen boundary that produces calm, because the household trusts that its needs and meaningful wants are met within it. Trust is not an abstraction here; it is visible. It shows up in behaviour: fewer impulse upgrades, fewer anxious comparisons, fewer late-night "treat" purchases that are really emotional repair. When sufficiency is real, the household can postpone certain purchases without feeling deprived, because the baseline is already humane.

A named historical example captures how easily "not enough" can be manufactured by a single upgrade. In 1769, in Paris, Denis Diderot wrote an essay often translated as "Regrets for My Old Dressing Gown", describing how a new robe made the rest of his belongings feel shabby, pulling him into a costly chain of replacements. The piece is witty and uncomfortable because it names a familiar mechanism: one improvement can reclassify everything around it as inadequate. Show: the robe arrives; the desk looks poor; the chair looks wrong; the room explains its own insufficiency. Name: the Diderot effect. Explain: the Diderot effect describes how new purchases can trigger a cascade of related purchases to restore a sense of coherence, often without increasing real wellbeing. Implication: without thresholds, a household can be dragged into coherence spending—buying not for function or joy, but to stop things feeling mismatched.

Thresholds matter most in categories that combine identity and repetition: housing, clothing, tech, and eating out. Housing is the most consequential because it sets fixed commitments and therefore sets the household's margin. A "good-enough" housing threshold is not a number that applies to everyone; it is a function. Show: a home that supports sleep, allows ordinary family life to happen without constant friction, and does not demand every adult's maximum earning capacity just to keep the lights on. Name: functional sufficiency. Explain: functional sufficiency means the home is sized and located to support the household's priorities—time, relationships, stability—rather than to satisfy a status narrative. Implication: when housing moves above the household's waterline, everything downstream becomes more fragile: generosity feels risky, work becomes harder to refuse, and small surprises feel bigger.

Clothing illustrates a different mechanism: the boundary between taste and churn. A wardrobe can be a tool or a treadmill. Show: a person buys frequent "just in case" items, accumulates clutter, and still feels they have nothing to wear because the purchases were not coherent. Name: incoherent accumulation. Explain: incoherent accumulation is what happens when buying is driven by occasional desire, sales, or social pressure rather than by a clear sense of what actually gets worn. Implication: a threshold based on function—enough outfits for work, enough for weekends, enough for events—can reduce regret and increase satisfaction, because the household spends less time shopping and more time living inside a wardrobe that fits.

Technology is where "enough" is most aggressively contested, because the market is built around upgrades and the social environment treats newness as competence. Show: a device works, but is a year old; battery life is slightly worse; the camera is slightly less sharp; the thought arises that replacing it would be "practical". Name: novelty as utility. Explain: when novelty is framed as necessity, people overpay for marginal improvements and underestimate the cost of the ecosystem—accessories, insurance, subscriptions, the attention spent setting up, comparing, deciding. Implication: a tech threshold that emphasises reliability and sufficiency protects attention as much as money; it limits the number of times a household must revisit the question of "should we upgrade?"

Dining out is the category where sufficiency is often easiest to feel and hardest to defend, because it sits at the intersection of fatigue, social life, and pleasure. The difference between "meaningful" and "default" becomes visible in the calendar. Show: a household eats out frequently and barely remembers the meals; it pays for convenience and calls it enjoyment. Name: forgettable spending. Explain: forgettable spending is not sinful; it is simply low return. It tends to happen when people are busy and depleted, and it becomes expensive precisely because it is frequent. Implication: an "enough" threshold can protect the meals that truly matter—celebrations, friend dinners, date nights—by preventing the category from becoming an unexamined coping mechanism.

A sample household makes the idea concrete without turning it into a morality play. Imagine a couple with two children, both adults working demanding jobs, living comfortably and feeling oddly tight. Their cashflow map shows the usual clusters: mortgage, childcare, subscriptions, then a drizzle of convenience spending when weeks go long. Their value hierarchy points to two things that reliably make life feel rich: time with extended family and hosting friends at home. Their "enough" thresholds begin to take the shape of a waterline. In travel, enough means one longer family trip each year to see relatives properly, rather than multiple shorter breaks that feel like collecting experiences and returning exhausted. In technology, enough means the household replaces devices when reliability genuinely declines, rather than when a contract offers a tempting upgrade. In dining out, enough means fewer midweek takeaways that vanish into fatigue, and more planned meals that create actual memories. The result is not deprivation. It is coherence.

Coherence is what thresholds buy. They reduce the number of micro-negotiations inside the household and the number of times a person must argue with themselves. They also reduce status anxiety because the household is no longer trying to win at everything. It has chosen where it wants to be excellent and where it is content to be merely sufficient. That choice is quietly radical in an affluent culture that encourages constant upgrading. It is also deeply practical, because a household cannot optimise every domain without paying a heavy price in time, money, and peace.

There is a further benefit: thresholds protect generosity. When "enough" is undefined, surplus is unstable. It is eaten by the next upgrade, the next lifestyle ratchet, the next quiet commitment. When thresholds exist, surplus becomes more predictable, and predictable surplus is what makes planned giving possible without fear. The household's waterline becomes a design constraint: keep the core below it, and generosity can be steady rather than occasional.

A credible limitation must be admitted, because the concept can be misapplied. For some households, "enough" language has been weaponised—used to shame people who are still genuinely anxious about stability, or who carry responsibilities that make a larger buffer rational. Context matters. The same threshold that feels liberating to one person can feel unsafe to another, especially if they have experienced sudden income loss, precarious family situations, or environments where support is unreliable. Kahneman and Deaton's 2010 analysis, often misquoted as a simplistic "money buys happiness until X", is a reminder that subjective wellbeing depends on context and stressors as much as on raw income (Kahneman & Deaton, 2010). The reconciliation is straightforward: thresholds are not a universal austerity rule. They are a personalised tool for reducing regret and protecting margin *once* the household's baseline is genuinely humane.

A second limitation is that thresholds can become rigid identity theatre: a household clings to an "enough" boundary long after life has changed, treating it as virtue rather than as an instrument.

Children grow. Careers shift. Health changes. Parents need help. A threshold set in one season may be wrong in another. The answer is not to abandon thresholds but to treat them like a waterline that must be checked when the boat's load changes. A growing family carries different weight. A new responsibility changes stability needs. The tool must remain alive.

What makes thresholds powerful is that they convert vague restraint into clear trade-offs. They turn "we should spend less" into "we have chosen what enough looks like here so we can spend more where it matters." They shift the emotional tone from punishment to authorship. They also expose the real question behind most upgrading: is the purchase solving a genuine problem, or is it attempting to buy a feeling—of safety, of belonging, of being the kind of person who has it together?

The unresolved test returns whenever the market offers a plausible improvement. A new phone, a larger home, another subscription, a more premium version of an ordinary thing. The household will be able to afford it. The question is whether it can afford the *baseline* it creates. Will the purchase raise the waterline and quietly reduce margin, or will the household hold its threshold and keep the surplus available for what it has already decided matters most?

Trading low value for high

In 1776, in London, Adam Smith published *The Wealth of Nations* and gave a language to something merchants already understood in their bones: resources are finite, and choices have costs. Smith's most enduring contribution was not a sanctification of greed, as caricatures sometimes suggest, but an insistence on trade-offs—what economists later formalised as opportunity cost. If labour, time, and capital are spent one way, they are not available another way. The concrete outcome was a shift in how societies talked about prosperity: not as a pile of coins, but as a pattern of allocation.

Spending is allocation. Always.

For affluent households, that sentence is the antidote to a particular kind of self-deception: the belief that because there is enough money for many things, there is no meaningful sacrifice involved in any single purchase. There is sacrifice. It simply hides. It hides in the margin that could have been freedom. It hides in the attention that could have been presence. It hides in the generosity that could have been consistent. When money feels tight despite comfort, the problem is often not that people have too little; it is that too much is being allocated to low-return spending that does not noticeably improve life.

Low value does not mean cheap. It means forgettable.

That is the first conceptual shift. In many households, the most expensive spending is not the dramatic splurge. It is the steady drizzle of "reasonable" conveniences and default upgrades that are barely remembered. Show: the household pays for food delivery on a Wednesday because everyone is tired; it pays for another streaming service because one show is popular; it upgrades a phone plan because the offer arrives at the right moment; it keeps multiple subscriptions "just in case". Name: low-return consumption. Explain: low-return consumption is spending that provides a small, transient benefit but carries an outsized cumulative cost because it is frequent, recurring, or habitually repeated. Implication: a household can spend heavily and still feel undernourished, because its money is feeding short-lived relief rather than lasting satisfaction.

The good news is that the remedy is not self-denial. It is reallocation. The household does not need to reduce life to grey austerity. It needs to take resources—money, time, attention—out of low-value channels and pour them into high-value ones. High value is not synonymous with luxury. It is spending that reliably increases what the household actually cares about: relationships, calm, freedom, contribution, craft, health, beauty, learning. High-value spending often has a particular texture. It produces memories. It reduces recurring stress. It creates time that is used well. It produces a steadier sense of enough.

Begin with a scene many households recognise: the evening takeaway. Two adults arrive home late. The children are hungry. The kitchen is messy. Cooking feels like punishment. A delivery app provides relief. Show: the purchase solves a real problem in that moment—food arrives, tension drops, everyone eats. Name: acute relief spending. Explain: acute relief spending can be wise and humane when it prevents a household collapsing into conflict or exhaustion; it becomes low value when it becomes the default response to routine fatigue. Implication: the question is not "should takeaways ever happen?" The question is whether the household is buying relief repeatedly instead of altering the conditions that create the need for relief, and whether the money spent on repeated relief could be redirected towards something more sustaining.

A sample family illustrates the shift without turning it into a morality tale. Imagine a household with two working adults and two children, living comfortably and feeling persistently squeezed. Their bank feed shows frequent takeaways, small delivery fees, duplicate entertainment subscriptions, and occasional upgrades justified as "we need to make life easier". Their value hierarchy says something different: the adults miss friends; the children thrive when the house is lively; the family feels most itself when hosting—unhurried dinners, laughter, a sense that life is not only work and logistics. The household does not need to spend less overall. It needs to trade.

The trade is concrete. Instead of four midweek takeaways that blur together, the household chooses fewer, more deliberate convenience meals and allocates the freed money and attention to a hosted dinner once or twice a month. Show: the grocery shop shifts from default convenience to a planned menu; a friend arrives; children play; adults talk; the evening becomes memorable. Name: conversion of spending into meaning. Explain: the same resources—money for food, time for preparation, attention for planning—produce a different outcome because the household is now purchasing not merely calories but connection. Implication: the household's sense of richness increases even if the total food spend is similar, because the spending is now aligned with a declared priority and yields durable satisfaction rather than transient relief.

The mechanism here is measurable. The household can compare frequency and recall. How many transactions in a category produce a memory worth keeping? How often does the spending create time that is actually used for relationships rather than for more work? How often does the spending reduce stress in a way that lasts longer than the evening? These are not mystical questions. They are metrics of contribution. A low-value category typically has high frequency and low recall. A high-value category tends to have lower frequency and higher recall, or a repeated pattern that produces consistent wellbeing, such as a service that prevents chronic stress. Reallocation is the act of shifting the balance between those profiles.

Behavioural science suggests why this works psychologically. A 2008 paper in *Science* by Elizabeth Dunn, Lara Aknin, and Michael Norton reported that people who spent money on others tended to report greater happiness than those who spent it on themselves, controlling for income (Dunn, Aknin & Norton, 2008). The relevance here is not a moral command to give. It is a clue about the texture of high-value spending: spending that involves connection—whether generosity, hospitality, shared experiences—often yields more durable satisfaction than spending aimed solely at the self. The implication is that reallocating from solitary convenience to relational experiences can increase felt wealth without increasing total expenditure.

The same principle applies to duplication, which is one of the stealthiest low-value drains in affluent life. Duplication is rarely chosen deliberately. It accumulates through inertia. Show: multiple streaming subscriptions, overlapping cloud storage plans, two gym memberships used intermittently, duplicated insurance cover, recurring app payments that solve similar problems. Name: redundant commitments. Explain: redundant commitments persist because cancelling requires attention, and because each commitment seems small when viewed alone. Implication: redundancy consumes not only money but mental space; it increases the number of things that can go unnoticed and the number of small withdrawals that erode margin.

Default upgrades are another classic low-value sink. They often arrive at the precise moment when people are least able to evaluate them: contract renewals, device upgrades, service plan "improvements". The offer is framed as prudent—pay a little more for better service—and the household accepts because it wants to reduce hassle. Show: a household upgrades a phone plan, then a broadband package, then a subscription tier, each time feeling it is choosing ease; the month becomes tighter without any single purchase feeling significant. Name: baseline creep. Explain: baseline creep occurs when small recurring upgrades accumulate into a higher fixed cost of living, reducing freedom because fixed costs are the hardest to reverse. Implication: reallocating away from default upgrades creates disproportionate benefits because it restores margin—the household's capacity to choose.

A named, checkable example of the psychology of cascading consumption helps clarify why trades often feel harder than they are. Denis Diderot's 1769 essay about his new dressing gown describes how one improved item made everything else feel shabby, prompting a chain of replacements. The Diderot effect has become a shorthand for consumption cascades: the purchase that forces further purchases to preserve coherence. Show: a household renovates one room, then feels compelled to update the next; buys a new car and suddenly the older car feels "embarrassing"; upgrades one device and then buys accessories and subscriptions to match. Name: coherence spending. Explain: coherence spending is driven by the desire for the environment to match a new standard; it is less about functional improvement and more about relieving the discomfort of mismatch. Implication: reallocation requires resisting coherence spending because it is a thief of surplus; it turns one deliberate improvement into a chain reaction that crowds out higher-value priorities.

The most effective reallocation is not random trimming; it is targeted substitution. Substitution is a concept economists use in describing how people shift consumption when relative prices or preferences change. In household terms it looks like replacing a frequent, low-recall spend with an occasional, high-recall spend that serves a declared value. Replace multiple forgettable restaurant meals with fewer, memorable hosted dinners. Replace impulse upgrades with planned, durable purchases that reduce hassle over years. Replace duplicate subscriptions with one or two services actually used. Replace constant small treats with one experience that feels genuinely restorative. The point is not to become puritanical. It is to stop buying the same thin satisfaction repeatedly.

A limitation matters here, because the phrase "low value" can sound judgmental or naïve about busyness. Some conveniences are not low value; they are stability infrastructure. A cleaner can prevent a household from collapsing into conflict. Childcare support can prevent careers from derailing. Occasional delivery can keep a week from breaking. The mistake is not convenience. The mistake is convenience without intentionality, convenience that becomes automatic even when the original pressure has changed, or convenience that consumes the very time it was meant to protect because it encourages a schedule that remains overloaded. The reconciliation is functional evaluation: does the spending reliably reduce fragility and free time that is used for what matters, or does it simply smooth an overcommitted life while raising the cost of maintaining that overcommitment?

There is also a human limitation: people resist reallocation because it threatens identity. Some low-value spending is not about utility at all; it is about being a certain kind of person—successful, modern, generous, relaxed, tasteful. Cutting it can feel like downgrading the self. This is why reallocation works best when it is framed not as loss but as exchange: trading an identity that is performed through consumption for an identity expressed through lived experience and contribution. Show: a household stops subscribing to every prestige service and starts investing in a few experiences that align with its hierarchy; it feels more itself, not less. Name: identity realignment. Explain: identity becomes less fragile when it is built on actions and relationships rather than on possessions and default upgrades. Implication: reallocation can produce emotional relief as well as financial margin, because it reduces the need to keep up appearances that do not actually nourish.

Modern relevance sharpens the argument. The subscription economy and frictionless payments make low-value spending effortless and high-value spending harder. A takeaway requires two minutes; hosting requires planning. A new subscription requires one click; cancelling requires attention. A premium upgrade requires acceptance; choosing "enough" requires a moment of resistance. This asymmetry is not personal weakness. It is design. Reallocation is, therefore, an act of counter-design: the household deliberately reshapes defaults so that resources flow towards chosen goods rather than towards whatever is easiest to buy when tired.

The motif that holds this together is the lens. Reallocation is not about becoming stricter. It is about changing what is seen as a "good spend". A lens that focuses on contribution makes the trade visible. It reveals that the household has been paying for what is forgettable while underfunding what is memorable. It reveals that the month feels tight not because the household lacks money, but because its money has been fragmented into low-return drips.

The unresolved test arrives at the moment when the household is tired and a low-value default presents itself as relief. The app is open. The upgrade offer is there. The subscription trial is tempting. The question is not whether the household can afford it. The question is whether it wants to allocate another portion of life's finite resources to something it will scarcely remember—or whether it will trade that drip for something that will still feel like wealth a year from now.

Aligning partners on values

In 1992, in Seattle, John Gottman and Lowell K. Levenson published research from the University of Washington that claimed something both bold and oddly domestic: by observing how couples interacted, it was possible to predict with striking accuracy which marriages would later dissolve. The concrete outcome was not a romance myth but a set of measurable patterns—physiological arousal, conversational dynamics, the kinds of bids for connection that were accepted or ignored—treated with the cold clarity of a lab (Gottman & Levenson, 1992). The work has been debated, refined, popularised, sometimes oversold, yet its underlying message remains bracingly useful for money: conflict is rarely about the surface topic. It is about what the surface topic symbolises.

Money is never just money.

In a household, spending and saving are proxy languages. A purchase can mean "I'm exhausted" or "I'm proud" or "I want to belong" or "I'm frightened of the future". Refusing a purchase can mean "we're being responsible" or "you're being controlled" or "my childhood is speaking" or "I don't trust the plan". When partners clash over money, they often imagine they are debating numbers. They are usually negotiating values, risk, identity, and whose definition of a good life gets to be the default.

Affluent households add a peculiar twist: because many things are affordable, disagreements are less likely to be about raw capability and more likely to be about meaning. Two adults can look at the same bank balance and feel opposite things. One sees a buffer and relaxes. The other sees a fragile castle built on continued high income and tightens. One sees travel as connection. The other sees travel as leakage. One sees a nicer home as stability. The other sees it as a trap. Without a shared value hierarchy, these disagreements repeat with minor variations, like the same argument in different costumes.

The first step towards alignment is to treat the household like a joint venture with two compasses rather than like a unit with one correct direction. Show the typical failure mode. A partner proposes an expense—a renovation, a holiday, a school decision, a recurring service—and presents it as obvious. The other partner hears not "proposal" but "decision already made". Resistance appears. Voices sharpen. Someone retreats into silence. Name the concept: unilateral framing. Explain: when one person frames a choice as self-evident, the other experiences disagreement as being cast as unreasonable or miserly, which activates defensiveness rather than curiosity. Implication: money becomes a battleground not because the household cannot solve the problem, but because the process triggers a status struggle—who gets to define what is sensible.

This is where values work becomes practical rather than poetic. Values are not "what we believe" in the abstract; they are "what we prioritise when trade-offs bite". In a household, the trade-offs bite constantly. A larger mortgage reduces optionality. A generous giving practice reduces the space for lifestyle creep. A premium convenience habit reduces discretionary margin. A choice in one domain silently commits the household in another. The value hierarchy is the method for deciding which commitments are allowed to become structural.

Partners often start this work in the wrong place. They begin with the spreadsheet. The spreadsheet matters, but it cannot resolve a values collision. When one person values security as low fixed costs and the other values security as "we must live in the best school catchment", the spreadsheet becomes a weapon rather than a tool. Show: a budget line is used like a verdict—"look, we can't"—or like a trump card—"look, we can"—while the real issue remains unspoken. Name: numeric displacement. Explain: numeric displacement is when numbers are used to avoid the discomfort of naming motives and fears. Implication: the household becomes fluent in costs and illiterate in meaning, which guarantees repeated conflict because the underlying question keeps returning.

A better approach is to surface each person's value hierarchy as a story, not a list. The story is composed of observable preferences: what each person protects under pressure, what each person regrets cutting, what each person tends to spend on when tired, what each person counts as "waste" and what they count as "worth it". A partner who resists dining out may not be stingy; they may be protecting freedom, remembering a parent who lost a job suddenly. A partner who pushes for experiences may not be reckless; they may be protecting aliveness, remembering a childhood where money was stable but love was thin. These are not excuses. They are explanations. Explanations lower heat.

Behavioural economics explains why these collisions can feel so intense. In 1979, Daniel Kahneman and Amos Tversky published "Prospect Theory" in *Econometrica*, describing loss aversion: most people experience losses more sharply than equivalent gains (Kahneman & Tversky, 1979). In household money arguments, "loss" is not only financial. A person can experience the loss of status, the loss of safety, the loss of autonomy, the loss of a dream, as vividly as the loss of pounds. Show: one partner hears "let's cut back" and feels a loss of dignity; the other hears "let's spend more" and feels a loss of safety. Name: asymmetric pain. Explain: because losses loom larger, partners can react strongly even to modest proposed changes, especially when the change threatens a value they hold as core. Implication: what looks like overreaction is often the nervous system defending a priority; ignoring that priority tends to escalate conflict rather than resolve it.

Alignment, then, is not achieved by persuading one person to adopt the other's priorities wholesale. That is not alignment; it is surrender, and it often breeds resentment. Alignment is achieved when the household can name a shared core and consciously reserve space for difference. The shared core might include stability, family time, generosity, a certain standard of comfort, and protection against the most feared risks. The reserved space might include individual priorities: one person's hobby, another's travel with friends, one person's preference for better clothing, another's preference for premium food. The point is not symmetrical spending. The point is mutual legitimacy.

The language used in these conversations matters because it shapes whether partners feel invited into problem-solving or pushed into defence. A household that frames trade-offs as moral judgements—"you're wasteful", "you're tight", "you don't care about the future", "you don't care about living"—turns money into character assassination. A household that frames trade-offs as experiments changes the tone. It sounds like, "Could we test this for three months and see what it changes?" or "What would we be saying no to if we say yes to this?" or "I'm not against the thing; I'm worried about what it does to our margin." Those phrases are not therapy. They are engineering language: they move from blame to design, from permanent identity claims to temporary hypotheses.

The motif worth threading here is the shared map. Earlier work in this book treats cashflow as a terrain and guardrails as safety features. In a relationship, a shared map is not only about money flows; it is about meaning flows. When both partners can see the same terrain—where money bunches, where commitments cluster, where drift occurs—arguments become less mystical. When both partners can also see the same north star—what the household claims to prioritise—trade-offs stop being personal attacks and start being navigational choices. A shared map does not eliminate disagreement. It prevents getting lost.

A named, checkable example of misalignment turning into costly drift appears in many households around housing. One partner pushes for a larger home in a prestigious area, partly for social belonging and perceived security; the other partner worries about fixed commitments and freedom. If the decision is made by fatigue or by unilateral framing—"this is what families like ours do"—the household often experiences a predictable aftermath: higher mortgage costs, higher maintenance, and a subtle increase in work pressure because stepping back feels riskier. The disagreement resurfaces later as resentment about time, not about the house. Show: arguments shift from "should we move?" to "why are you always working?" Name: downstream conflict. Explain: downstream conflict is when an unresolved values trade-off produces later arguments in a different domain because the original decision altered the household's structure. Implication: aligning values early is not an emotional luxury; it is a way of preventing structural decisions from creating predictable relational strain.

A second example appears around generosity, where values and identity are especially sensitive. One partner may see giving as a core expression of who they want to be; the other may see it as risk, especially if their internal model of safety requires a larger buffer. When this conflict is avoided, giving tends to become sporadic and emotionally charged—generous bursts followed by quiet panic or irritation. Show: a donation is made impulsively after a compelling story; later, the household feels tight and someone blames the giving. Name: reactive generosity. Explain: reactive generosity satisfies the immediate moral impulse but can threaten perceived safety, which triggers backlash. Implication: without alignment, generosity becomes a source of conflict rather than a shared practice that reinforces meaning.

The counter-example is important, because alignment talk can become sanctimonious if it implies every household must merge values into one unified philosophy. Some couples thrive with substantial autonomy and minimal shared decision-making. They keep finances largely separate. They agree only on a few essentials and leave most choices individual. That approach can reduce conflict, especially when partners have markedly different spending styles and both value independence. Name the limitation: pluralistic systems. Explain: pluralistic systems recognise that shared life does not require shared preferences in every domain; sometimes the most respectful solution is structural separation rather than constant negotiation. Implication: forcing full alignment can create more conflict than it resolves, because it turns everyday choices into endless negotiation.

The reconciliation is that "alignment" does not mean uniformity. It means coherence where coherence matters. Every household has a few decisions that are inherently shared because they create fixed commitments: housing, childcare structures, major recurring costs, and the broad shape of giving and saving. These are the domains where misalignment becomes downstream conflict because the commitments bind both people. Outside those domains, autonomy can be healthy. A household can agree on guardrails and thresholds for shared resources while ring-fencing personal priorities that do not threaten the system. That is not a compromise with second-best outcomes. It is a design that honours both shared life and individual personhood.

This perspective also reduces a common trap: treating one partner as the "responsible" one and the other as the "fun" one. Those roles are emotionally satisfying and structurally toxic. They create parent–child dynamics where one person polices and the other rebels. Show: one partner becomes the gatekeeper; the other hides spending; the household loses transparency and trust. Name: role polarisation. Explain: role polarisation occurs when partners outsource parts of adulthood to each other—one carries anxiety, the other carries desire—and then resent each other for the burdens they jointly created. Implication: aligning on values is partly an act of reclaiming shared adulthood, where both partners participate in both safety and joy.

Trust, in this context, is not a vague virtue. It is visible behaviour: sharing information without using it as ammunition, keeping promises about agreed boundaries, revisiting decisions when circumstances change, and resisting the temptation to "win" arguments by appealing to fear or shame. When trust is present, discussions can be brief and calm. When trust is absent, discussions become long and tense because every decision feels like a test of loyalty.

The shared map motif returns because it suggests a practical, non-dramatic way to approach difference. If both partners can name their top priorities—what they refuse to sacrifice lightly—and can also name what "enough" looks like in domains prone to drift, then the household stops trying to optimise everything. It chooses its arenas. It becomes lavish where it matters and restrained where it does not. That choice is easier to hold when it is held jointly, because a joint decision becomes part of the household's identity, not merely one person's preference.

The forward test is the next contested purchase, because the next contested purchase always arrives. It might be a move, a school choice, a holiday, a car, a renovation, a new recurring service that promises to make life easier. The household will have a chance, in that moment, to argue about the object—or to consult the shared map and ask the harder question: which value is each person protecting, what risk does each person fear, and can the decision be shaped as a time-bound experiment rather than a permanent victory for one compass over the other?

Chapter 4
Using Cost-Per-Use Math

In 1906, in Philadelphia, an engineer named Frederick Winslow Taylor published *The Principles of Scientific Management*, arguing—provocatively, and to many people offensively—that work could be measured, analysed, and improved through careful attention to time, motion, and output. The concrete outcome was not merely a book but a change in industrial imagination: managers began to treat inefficiency as something that could be detected and corrected rather than tolerated as fate. Taylor's methods were later criticised for reducing human labour to mechanical units, and those criticisms were not frivolous. Yet buried inside the controversy is a lesson that has aged well: measurement is powerful when it illuminates hidden waste, and dangerous when it pretends to be the whole story.

Households face a quieter version of the same dilemma. A single purchase can look cheap and behave expensive. Another can look expensive and behave cheap. The difference is not taste. It is time. A shirt worn twice and left at the back of a drawer costs more per use than a pricier one worn weekly for years. A bargain appliance that breaks early is not a bargain; it is a payment plan for annoyance. A premium purchase that sits unused is not an investment; it is decorative regret. Without a way to see through sticker price, affluent households are easy prey for false economies: buying cheap and often, or buying premium and idle, and calling both sensible.

Numbers can clarify. Not everything.

That balance is the spirit of this chapter. Cost-per-use is a deceptively simple calculation, but its real function is not arithmetic for its own sake. It is a corrective lens. It pulls attention away from the moment of purchase—the place where marketing is loudest and emotions are most persuadable—and towards the life of the thing: how often it will be used, how long it will last, and what it will demand in maintenance, accessories, energy, insurance, storage, and eventual disposal. In other words, cost-per-use is not a new kind of budgeting. It is a way of asking, with adult seriousness, what a purchase will *do* to a household over time.

The urgency is modern. Frictionless shopping, next-day delivery, subscription add-ons, and a culture of constant upgrades make it unusually easy to accumulate objects and services that do not earn their place. The market is brilliant at selling "value" through discounts, bundles, and premium features. It is less interested in whether the thing will be used fifty times or five. A household that wants wealth without waste cannot rely on price tags and promises. It needs a method for distinguishing durable value from expensive noise.

Cost-per-use brings that method down to earth because it is anchored in behaviour. It asks a question that is both banal and profound: how many times will this be used, really? The question cuts through fantasy. Most people can predict their own habits with decent accuracy if they are willing to be honest. The calculation then converts honesty into clarity. It allows a household to pay more when paying more genuinely buys lower cost per use, fewer replacements, and fewer decision cycles. It also exposes the opposite: the premium purchase justified by an imagined future self who will suddenly become the sort of person who uses the thing daily.

Yet cost-per-use alone is not enough, because real life is not only about frequency. Ownership contains hidden costs that do not appear on receipts: repairs, consumables, accessories, cleaning products, energy consumption, subscription fees, warranties, insurance, storage space, and the time spent dealing with the thing when it fails. Economists would call this the total cost of ownership; engineers would call it lifecycle cost. The household experience is more visceral: the cheap vacuum that needs replacing, the printer that demands expensive cartridges, the car that saves money upfront and then consumes weekends in repairs. When people say they are "tired of spending", they are often tired of these hidden costs—costs paid in time and attention as much as money.

This chapter therefore moves through a set of everyday decisions, not as sterile examples but as recognisable human scenes: the commuter weighing transport options, the hobbyist choosing gear, the home worker selecting a chair, the family replacing an appliance. The point is not to turn life into a spreadsheet. It is to learn when a little maths prevents a lot of regret. A household that can do a quick cost-per-use estimate and a simple ownership-cost scan gains a rare form of confidence. It stops being bullied by discounts and dazzled by premium branding. It starts to buy in a way that is quieter, steadier, and more aligned with its value hierarchy.

Still, the chapter refuses a common modern mistake: treating measurement as morality. Some things cannot be reduced to cost per use without becoming crude. Joy has no fixed unit. Beauty is not always rational. A well-made object can provide daily pleasure that is difficult to quantify but real. Aesthetics can matter because they shape mood and behaviour. Values alignment can justify a choice that looks "inefficient" on paper—supporting a local maker, choosing a repair rather than a replacement, buying secondhand even when it requires more effort. Conversely, pure maths can be used to launder luxury: people can overestimate future use to justify an indulgence, turning a desire into a calculation that looks respectable. The risk is not the number; it is the self-deception.

So the work here is to build a humane decision process: one that uses cost-per-use and total ownership thinking as tools, not as tyrants. Tools should be sharp. Tyrants should be resisted. The goal is to make fewer, better purchases—purchases that earn their keep, reduce churn, and protect the household's margin of time and attention. When a purchase is truly worth it, the maths can often defend it. When a purchase is not worth it, the maths can often reveal the lie before money leaves the account.

A subtle motif threads through the chapter: the long shadow. Every purchase casts one. Some shadows are short—an inexpensive item used once and forgotten. Some are long—an appliance that shapes monthly bills for years, a device that locks a household into subscriptions, a car that dictates running costs and time. The question is not whether a household can afford the purchase in the moment. The question is whether it wants to live inside the shadow the purchase casts.

The page turns with a practical tension that feels oddly philosophical. When confronted with the next "good deal" or tempting upgrade, will the household judge it by the thrill of the price tag, or by the life the object will actually live—its uses, its costs, its demands, and its long shadow on freedom, attention, and generosity?

Cost-per-use basics explained

In October 2007, in London, the National Trust published a report titled *A Place for Everything*, describing the growth of domestic clutter and the increasingly fraught relationship between households and possessions. The concrete outcome was not a new law, but a public signal: people were buying more than they could comfortably store, maintain, or enjoy. The problem was not only mess. It was misjudgement—objects arriving faster than real use could justify them, the home becoming a warehouse for intentions.

One way to understand that misjudgement is brutally simple: many purchases are priced as if they will be used often, yet lived as if they were ornaments. A household buys a bread-maker and uses it twice. It buys a premium coat and forgets it exists. It buys cheap headphones again and again because the cheap ones break. Each choice is "reasonable" in isolation. The aggregate is absurd. Cost-per-use is the small piece of arithmetic that makes the absurdity visible.

Use is the true price.

That sentence sounds like a slogan until it is treated as a lens. A price tag captures a moment. Cost-per-use captures a life. The principle is almost embarrassingly straightforward: estimate how many times an item will be used over its useful life, then divide the total cost by that number. The result is a figure that is rarely printed on the shelf label and yet is often more revealing than the sticker price. It answers a question that affluent households frequently avoid because it punctures fantasy: *how much is this really costing me each time I touch it?*

Start with the simplest case: clothing. Show two shirts hanging in a wardrobe. One cost £20 and was bought on impulse because it looked fine in the shop. It is worn twice, then sits. The other cost £80, chosen deliberately, fits well, wears well, and is worn weekly for two years. Name the concept: cost-per-use. Explain the method without ceremony. The cheap shirt is £20 divided by 2 wears: £10 per wear. The pricier shirt is £80 divided by roughly 104 wears: about 77 pence per wear. The implication is counter-intuitive but concrete: the "expensive" option can be cheaper in actual use, while the "bargain" is a luxury in disguise because it delivers so little utility.

The same logic applies beyond clothing, and its power is that it collapses moral noise. It does not ask whether the purchase is "necessary" in some universal sense. It asks whether the purchase earns its keep. A high-income household can afford a lot of purchases that do not earn their keep. Affordability is not the same as value. Cost-per-use exposes the difference by moving attention from the moment of buying—when dopamine, marketing, and status cues are all active—to the future pattern of behaviour. Show: a person reaches for the same items repeatedly and ignores others. Name: revealed usage. Explain: revealed usage is the behavioural reality of what gets used; it is often different from what people imagine they will use. Implication: cost-per-use turns revealed usage into a number, which makes it harder to lie to oneself with good stories.

The method needs one additional clarification to be genuinely useful: the "use" part is not always literal. A suitcase might be used four times a year but for decades. A winter coat might be used daily for three months and then hung away. A laptop might be used every day and be central to earning. A sofa might be used constantly by a household and wear out quickly if poorly made. The point is not to count perfectly. The point is to estimate honestly enough that the estimate changes behaviour. Cost-per-use is not an accountant's tool; it is a decision tool.

This is where many people stumble, because estimation invites self-deception. A person wants the premium blender, so they imagine daily smoothies. A person wants the expensive gym membership, so they imagine a new identity. A person wants the hobby equipment, so they imagine weekends filled with craft. Show: the purchase is justified by a future self who is disciplined, energetic, and consistent. Name: aspirational forecasting. Explain: aspirational forecasting is the mind's habit of projecting an ideal future behaviour to justify a present desire; it is a cousin of planning fallacy, in which people underestimate obstacles and overestimate follow-through. Implication: cost-per-use only works as a corrective if the household estimates usage based on past behaviour and likely constraints, not on the flattering version of itself.

Behavioural research gives a useful frame for this without needing to turn life into psychology trivia. Daniel Kahneman's work on judgement under uncertainty describes how people use heuristics—mental shortcuts—that often misfire when predicting future behaviour (Kahneman, 2011). The implication is not that humans are irrational fools. It is that prediction is hard, and the mind often substitutes an easy question for a hard one. Instead of "how often will I realistically use this?", people answer "do I like the idea of being a person who uses this?" Cost-per-use forces the hard question back onto the table.

A second named, checkable example shows cost-per-use logic at work in a more industrial setting, where the language is different but the principle is identical. In 1938, in the United States, the American Society for Testing Materials (now ASTM International) published the first version of standards that shaped how materials and products were tested for durability. Standards are, in essence, an institutional attempt to make "use over time" measurable rather than anecdotal. Show: a product that survives repeated stress tests is treated as higher quality because it will likely last longer in real use. Name: durability measurement. Explain: durability measurement formalises the idea that cost should be evaluated over life, not at purchase. Implication: households can borrow this mindset informally: evaluate items by the stresses they will face and the number of cycles they must survive, rather than by their initial price.

Cost-per-use can justify upgrades, which is one reason it is so psychologically freeing. Many affluent readers have internalised a crude form of restraint in which "paying more" feels suspect. The suspicion is understandable; plenty of expensive purchases are indeed wasteful. But blanket suspicion is not wisdom. It can lead to false economies: repeatedly buying cheap items that fail, create hassle, and require replacement. Show: a household buys inexpensive chargers that stop working, cheap shoes that need replacing every season, low-quality cookware that warps, and feels constantly annoyed. Name: churn cost. Explain: churn cost is the combined cost of repeated replacements—money, time spent shopping, time spent returning, the irritation of failure, and the attention drained by recurring decisions. Implication: an upgrade that reduces churn can be a form of frugality, because it lowers cost-per-use and reduces the ongoing tax on time and attention.

At the same time, cost-per-use exposes a different kind of waste: the premium purchase that is underused. Affluent households are especially vulnerable because they can buy competence. They can purchase equipment, membership, training, accessories—objects that symbolise a future hobby or a future self. The home becomes a museum of intended selves: the camera kit, the unused treadmill, the wine fridge, the designer cookware, the golf clubs, the bike on the wall. Show: the items are technically high quality and practically irrelevant. Name: aspirational accumulation. Explain: aspirational accumulation is the purchase of identity props—objects that represent who a person wishes to be—without the time or routine to support the identity. Implication: cost-per-use makes the true cost of identity props visible, because underuse turns even moderate prices into high per-use costs and turns expensive items into extravagances that were never acknowledged as such.

This is why the calculation is most useful when paired with a single behavioural question: what has the household actually used consistently in the past year? Past usage is not destiny, but it is evidence. If a person has not cooked from scratch more than once a week for a year, a high-end kitchen gadget justified by a sudden cooking renaissance is a risky bet. If a person has not run in months, a premium running watch justified by imminent fitness zeal is likely a story. Cost-per-use does not forbid the bet. It simply prices it honestly: if the bet fails, the per-use cost will be enormous.

A limitation must be admitted, because cost-per-use can become a false god. Not every valuable thing is used frequently. Some of the most meaningful possessions are used rarely: a formal outfit for weddings and funerals, a guest bed, a piece of art, a musical instrument returned to after long pauses. Some purchases are justified not by frequency but by significance. Show: a family buys a well-made dining table that anchors years of conversations; the cost-per-use might be low, but the value is not only in the number. Name: meaning-per-use. Explain: some uses carry disproportionate emotional and relational weight; the value is not the count, it is the quality of the moments. Implication: cost-per-use should inform decisions, not dictate them; it is a lens, not a judge.

There is also the opposite problem: people can game the calculation to justify luxury. They overestimate future usage to bring the per-use number down to something that feels respectable. Show: a person imagines using a £2,000 espresso machine daily for a decade, ignoring that it may be used sporadically or replaced sooner. Name: convenient arithmetic. Explain: convenient arithmetic is the use of numbers to legitimise a desire rather than to test it; it swaps honesty for a calculation that looks serious. Implication: the integrity of cost-per-use depends on conservative estimates and a willingness to adjust when reality differs.

The reconciliation is to treat cost-per-use as a way of asking better questions, not as a way of avoiding judgement. It shifts the household from "cheap versus expensive" to "high return versus low return". It exposes the hidden cost of underuse and the hidden benefit of durability. It also connects back to the book's broader aim: aligning money, time, and attention with what matters. Cost-per-use is a method for preventing money from being spent on objects that will consume attention without delivering sustained value.

The quiet motif that holds this section together is the wardrobe shelf. It is the place where underused items go to die. Every home has one, literal or metaphorical: the drawer of cables, the cupboard of gadgets, the corner where abandoned fitness equipment gathers dust. Cost-per-use is the tool that asks, before purchase, whether the item will end up on the shelf. The question is not whether the item is nice. Many nice things die on that shelf. The question is whether the household will *use* it with enough regularity that the cost becomes small and the value becomes real.

The forward test arrives at the exact moment when a purchase feels most reasonable: when the price is discounted, the reviews are glowing, and the story about future usage is especially flattering. The question is not "is this a good deal?" The question is whether the household is buying an object it will repeatedly touch, or buying another artefact for the shelf—another payment for an imagined self, priced as if it were a lived life.

Total ownership costs considered

On 1 January 1995, in the European Union, the Energy Labelling Directive began to reshape what shoppers saw when choosing appliances, gradually standardising those familiar coloured labels that translate electricity use into something legible at the point of sale. The outcome was not only consumer information but a cultural nudge: purchase decisions were meant to consider operating cost, not merely sticker price. The label did something subtle. It reminded buyers that a washing machine is not a one-off event. It is a small relationship with your home's power supply, your time, and your patience.

Sticker price is a doorway. Ownership is the house.

Affluent households are especially prone to forgetting this because the doorway is easy to pay. The real costs arrive later, dispersed into months, disguised as small bills, accessories, repairs, and time. When people feel financially "leaky", this is often why: they buy a thing, and then spend repeatedly to keep the thing functioning, compatible, insured, clean, charged, repaired, upgraded, and eventually removed. Total cost of ownership is the phrase engineers use for this life-cycle reality. In a household, it is better thought of as the shadow a purchase casts—longer than the moment of buying, and sometimes darker than expected.

The basic move is to replace one question with another. Most people ask, "What does it cost?" Total ownership thinking asks, "What will it cost to *live with*?" Show: a household buys an inexpensive printer, then pays for proprietary cartridges, replaces a drum unit, buys special paper, and wrestles with connectivity. Name: downstream cost. Explain: downstream cost is spending triggered by ownership rather than by deliberate choice; it occurs because the object requires it. Implication: a purchase that looks economical can behave like a subscription, draining money and attention long after the initial payment has been forgotten.

A simple appliance example makes the difference tangible without drowning in numbers. Consider the humble tumble dryer, which has become a silent workhorse in many homes. The cheaper model has a lower sticker price. It also uses more electricity per load, may require more frequent maintenance, and may have a shorter reliable lifespan. The pricier model costs more upfront but is more energy-efficient and better built. Show: two households choose different models; one pays less today and more each month; the other pays more today and less each month. Name: cost shifting. Explain: cost shifting occurs when a lower purchase price pushes cost into future operating expenses; the buyer feels thrifty while the household quietly pays later. Implication: without a total ownership lens, households can consistently choose options that "feel" financially prudent yet produce higher long-run costs and more hassle.

Energy use is the most obvious ownership cost, and it is also the most easily ignored because it arrives as part of a large bill. The EU label is a historical attempt to counter that cognitive weakness. Show: the household sees the electricity bill rise and cannot attribute the rise to any single device, because the bill is an aggregate. Name: diffuse cost. Explain: diffuse costs are difficult for humans to respond to because they are not linked to a clear decision point; the mind struggles to feel causality. Implication: consumers tend to over-weight visible sticker prices and under-weight invisible operating costs, not because they are foolish, but because the environment hides the true price.

The same pattern appears with cars, arguably the most common ownership-cost trap in affluent households. The purchase price is only the beginning. Insurance, servicing, tyres, fuel, depreciation, parking, repairs, and the time spent dealing with all of this can easily dwarf the initial saving from a "good deal". Show: a household buys a used car that seems cheap, then spends repeatedly on fixes and loses days to logistics; another household pays more for a reliable model and spends less time and money over years. Name: reliability premium. Explain: the reliability premium is the extra paid upfront to reduce the probability of failure; it is not a guarantee, but it often reduces volatility. Implication: for time-poor households, reliability has a financial value beyond repair bills because time itself is scarce and disruptions produce secondary costs—missed work, stress, emergency spending.

Notice what is happening in these examples. Total ownership costs are not only monetary. They are cognitive and temporal. Owning a flaky device or a fragile product consumes attention because it generates decisions: repair or replace, what accessory to buy, how to troubleshoot. Each decision seems minor. Together, they form an attention tax. Behavioural research has long stressed the limits of attention and the way decision load affects judgement (Kahneman, 2011). The implication here is quietly radical: reducing ownership hassle is a legitimate part of wealth without waste. A household can buy time back by choosing items that demand less fuss.

Accessories and consumables are the second major ownership cost people underestimate. Some products are built to be gateways into ecosystems: razor handles that require branded blades, coffee machines that require pods, printers that require cartridges, vacuum cleaners with proprietary filters, home devices that require subscriptions for full function. These are not necessarily bad. They are just rarely costed honestly at the moment of purchase. Show: the household buys a discounted coffee machine, then realises the pods cost a steady monthly amount; the machine has become a habit with a recurring price. Name: ecosystem pricing. Explain: ecosystem pricing is a strategy where the initial product is priced attractively while ongoing consumables carry higher margins; the buyer pays repeatedly through the life of ownership. Implication: "cheap" products can be expensive relationships, and households that do not calculate the relationship cost end up surprised and resentful.

Insurance and protection plans are another ownership layer. They are sold in the language of prudence. Sometimes they are prudent. Often they are emotional purchases: buying a sense of safety rather than evaluating the true risk and cost. Show: a household adds extended warranties to multiple devices, pays year after year, and rarely claims; another household chooses a few key protections where failure would be truly disruptive and skips the rest. Name: perceived risk inflation. Explain: perceived risk inflation is the tendency to overestimate the likelihood and impact of losses when those losses are made vivid at the point of sale; the sales pitch does the vividness. Implication: total ownership thinking requires noticing when protection costs are proportionate to the household's tolerance for hassle and financial volatility, and when they are simply a retail tax on anxiety.

Maintenance costs are the hidden middle of ownership. Homes themselves illustrate this vividly. A bigger house is not just more space; it is more roof, more heating, more surfaces, more things that can break. A garden is not just beauty; it is tools, time, or paid maintenance. A renovation is not just a new kitchen; it is future repairs, replacement parts, and sometimes a standard reset—what was once "fine" is now unacceptable. Show: the household upgrades one area and then feels compelled to keep upgrading adjacent areas to match. Name: cascading maintenance. Explain: cascading maintenance is the way improvements raise the baseline and thereby increase future maintenance demands; the household inherits a more expensive standard. Implication: total ownership thinking is not pessimism; it is realism about the ongoing cost of maintaining a higher baseline.

Disposal and end-of-life costs are the final ownership layer, and they are increasingly relevant. Appliances must be removed, recycled, or disposed of; furniture must be transported; electronics must be handled responsibly. Even when disposal is not costly in money, it is costly in effort. Show: a household replaces a large appliance and then spends a Saturday arranging collection, clearing a path, managing delays. Name: exit friction. Explain: exit friction is the cost of getting rid of things; it includes time, logistics, and sometimes fees. Implication: buying more stuff increases future friction, which is one reason affluent households can feel paradoxically burdened by possessions.

A named, checkable example underscores why manufacturers and policymakers have long treated life-cycle cost as serious. The energy labels in Europe were introduced precisely because operating cost matters at scale; similar labelling regimes exist elsewhere, reflecting a shared recognition that consumers cannot easily infer energy use from appearance. The implication for household decision-making is simple: when an ownership cost is hard to see at the point of purchase, assume it deserves a question.

That brings us to the practical heart of this section: asking fuller questions before buying. Not dozens of questions. A few that consistently expose hidden costs. The questions are not moral. They are mechanical. How will this be maintained? What consumables does it require? What accessories are needed to make it usable? What is the energy draw? What happens if it breaks? What does disposal look like? These questions translate abstraction—"total cost of ownership"—into concrete decision points.

A credible counter-example is necessary because total ownership thinking can be used to justify overbuying. A person can claim that a luxury purchase is "better over time" without evidence, or can inflate maintenance fears to avoid a perfectly adequate cheaper option. Show: someone buys the premium version of everything, claiming it is efficient, and ends up with underused items and an inflated baseline. Name: defensive premiumisation. Explain: defensive premiumisation is the habit of buying the highest-end option to avoid regret, framed as pragmatism; it often ignores actual usage and the law of diminishing returns. Implication: total ownership thinking must be paired with honesty about use; an item that is rarely used cannot become economical merely because it is well built.

The reconciliation is to remember the chapter's broader frame: cost-per-use and ownership cost are lenses that serve values. They exist to reduce waste and protect freedom, not to maximise technical perfection. The aim is not to avoid all future inconvenience. The aim is to avoid predictable, repeated inconvenience that erodes time and margin. A household that asks fuller questions can choose cheaper options when they truly are cheaper over time and can choose pricier options when they genuinely reduce churn and hassle. It can stop being surprised.

The motif of the shadow returns here because it captures the essence of total ownership cost. Every purchase throws a shadow forward: bills, consumables, maintenance, insurance, upgrades, disposal.

Some shadows are thin and tolerable. Some are thick and persistent. The household's task is to see the shadow before stepping into it.

The forward test is the next "great deal" that appears irresistible at the doorway. The question will not be whether the sticker price is attractive. The question will be whether the household is willing to live with the shadow—maintenance, consumables, energy use, and exit friction—or whether it would rather pay a truer price upfront and keep its future cashflow, time, and attention less encumbered.

Comparing options with examples

In July 2010, in Washington, D.C., the U.S. General Services Administration released a set of results from its "Report a Problem" and digital service efforts that helped popularise a deceptively simple discipline in product design: measure what people actually do, not what they say they will do. The concrete outcome was improved public-facing services, but the transferable idea is broader. When decisions are made on imagined behaviour, waste flourishes. When decisions are made on observed behaviour, waste shrinks.

The household version of this discipline is cost-per-use and total ownership thinking applied with restraint. Not as a spreadsheet hobby. As a quick test that asks, "What will happen after the thrill of purchase fades?" and "What does living with this actually cost?" The aim is not to become a human calculator. It is to avoid two common errors that affluent households make with equal enthusiasm: over-buying premium items that gather dust, and under-buying cheap items that break, annoy, and require constant replacement.

Count uses. Then decide.

That is the quiet engine of this section. The examples that follow are ordinary on purpose, because ordinary decisions are where money leaks. Grand purchases are debated. Small, repeated purchases slide by. Cost-per-use is a way of making the ordinary visible without turning it into a moral drama.

Start with transport, because transport decisions combine money, time, and reliability in a way that quickly reveals the difference between sticker price and life cost. Imagine an urban commuter who alternates between public transport and ride-hailing. The ride-hail seems small in the moment: a few trips a week, especially when tired or running late. Show: the phone is tapped at 6.10 p.m.; the car arrives; the person arrives home calmer; the cost feels justified. Name: convenience premium. Explain: the convenience premium is the extra paid for reduced friction, and it can be worth paying when it genuinely protects time and reduces stress. Implication: the question is not whether ride-hailing is wasteful; it is whether it is being used as a deliberate tool or as an unexamined default.

Now apply the lens. Cost-per-use here is cost-per-trip, but ownership thinking enters through the alternatives. If the commuter considers buying a bicycle or an e-bike, the sticker price may look high compared to a single ride-hail journey. Yet the relevant comparison is not one journey. It is the expected number of journeys. A bike used four times a week across forty-eight weeks is roughly 192 trips a year. Spread a purchase across those uses and the per-trip cost can become low, even before considering health and time benefits. But ownership costs matter too: maintenance, storage, risk of theft, weather constraints, clothing, the mental load of route planning. The lens does not produce a universal answer. It produces a sharper comparison: a person can see that a bike is economical only if it will be used consistently, and that ride-hailing is economical only if it remains occasional and purposeful rather than habitual.

A named, checkable piece of evidence helps anchor this in reality rather than sentiment. The Department for Transport's *National Travel Survey* in the UK has long recorded how travel behaviour correlates with infrastructure and habit, not merely with stated preference (DfT, annual publications; for example, *National Travel Survey 2019* published 2020). The detail that matters here is not a specific number but the principle: behaviour is patterned, and small changes in routine can change travel choices dramatically. Implication: when a household evaluates transport options, it should evaluate not only the economics but the plausibility of the routine—because routine is what determines whether cost-per-use becomes real.

Move next to a home office chair, an object that many people treat as a mid-level purchase and then live with daily. The cheap chair looks harmless: it is "fine", and the desk is only used some of the time. A better chair looks like indulgence. The lens forces different questions. How many hours will the chair be used each week? How many weeks per year? For how many years is the chair likely to last before it becomes uncomfortable or unstable? These questions are not medical advice; they are usage questions. Show: a person sits for several hours a day, shifts restlessly, stands up to stretch, and still returns to the chair because work demands it. Name: high-frequency utility. Explain: high-frequency utility items are those used so often that small differences in quality compound into meaningful differences in experience. Implication: for high-frequency items, cost-per-use often favours durability and comfort, because even a modest improvement multiplied by hundreds of hours becomes significant.

Ownership costs appear here too, but they are not always cash costs. A chair that breaks or squeaks or feels unstable creates decision churn: replacement shopping, assembling, disposal. A chair that works quietly reduces attention tax. If a household values time and calm, the absence of hassle is a genuine benefit. The lens exposes a common false economy: saving £100 at purchase and then spending multiple hours over a year in discomfort and minor annoyance. Those hours are a cost, even if they never appear in an account statement.

A third scenario: hobby gear. This is where both over-buying and under-buying are most common because hobbies are identity-adjacent. People want to be the kind of person who plays tennis, takes photographs, climbs, paints, cycles, makes bread, runs. The market knows this. It sells the identity in the form of equipment tiers. The cheap entry-level set looks prudent. The premium set looks aspirational. Cost-per-use tries to disarm the identity tug by asking for evidence. Show: a person buys an expensive camera and then realises weekends are already full; the camera remains in a drawer. Name: aspirational forecasting. Explain: aspirational forecasting is the tendency to justify a purchase with an imagined future self who will use it constantly. Implication: premium hobby purchases are often wasted not because they are luxurious, but because the household is buying a fantasy schedule.

The lens does not demand abstinence; it demands calibration. A middle strategy often emerges when the question is asked honestly: an entry option that is good enough to prove usage, or a secondhand purchase that carries less downside if the hobby fades. Secondhand does not automatically mean cheap, but it changes risk. If the item can be resold with minimal loss, the cost-per-use calculation becomes less punishing in the event of underuse. The ownership-cost lens also raises specific questions: are there ongoing consumables, memberships, maintenance? Does the hobby require storage space? Does it require travel? The aim is to prevent the "cheap" option turning into endless replacements that add up, while also preventing the "premium" option becoming a costly artefact of intention.

A fourth scenario is deliberately mundane: a kitchen appliance. Consider a blender. The cheap blender costs little, but struggles with tougher ingredients, wears out, and is loud and unpleasant. The expensive blender is praised for durability. Cost-per-use begins by estimating actual usage: daily smoothies, weekly soups, occasional sauces? Total ownership then enters: replacement parts, energy consumption, the likelihood of needing a second blender when the first fails, the time cost of dealing with failure, and the psychological cost of an appliance that is irritating to use. Show: the household stops using the cheap blender because it is unpleasant; the cost-per-use becomes extreme because usage drops. Name: friction-induced abandonment. Explain: an item that is mildly annoying can reduce its own usage, which raises cost-per-use and turns the purchase into waste. Implication: quality can be economical when it increases consistent use by reducing friction.

This example reveals a subtle but important point: cost-per-use is not only about longevity; it is about willingness to use. People often think usage is purely about need. In practice, usage is shaped by friction—noise, mess, set-up, cleaning, reliability. This is why a pricier item can produce lower cost-per-use not only because it lasts longer but because it is used more. A quiet appliance is used. A brittle one is avoided. The household's habits are part of the calculation.

A fifth scenario: children's items, such as a pram or a high chair. These purchases trigger particular anxieties and are often overbought because parents fear getting it wrong. The sticker price feels like a proxy for safety. The lens does something calmer. How long is the item likely to be used? How many children will use it? Can it be resold? Are there accessories that become unavoidable? What is the storage burden after use? These are ownership questions. Show: a household buys a premium travel system with multiple add-ons and later discovers half the pieces are unused; another household buys a solid, simpler item and uses it daily. Name: feature overhang. Explain: feature overhang is the cost of paying for capabilities that are rarely used because they are bought as insurance against imagined scenarios. Implication: without cost-per-use thinking, households pay for reassurance rather than for function.

A credible counter-example is necessary, because there are times when the "cheap but adequate" choice is rational and even wise. Not every category deserves optimisation. Some items are used rarely, are prone to rapid obsolescence, or are primarily aesthetic. A household does not need to run cost-per-use on every mug. There is also a psychological cost to constant calculation. Show: a person turns every purchase into a research project, spends hours comparing, and loses the time the purchase was meant to save. Name: analysis drag. Explain: analysis drag is the cost of overthinking; it turns the tool into a tyrant and consumes attention. Implication: the framework should be applied where it matters—high-cost items, high-frequency items, or categories prone to churn—while leaving low-stakes purchases to reasonable judgement.

Reconcile this limitation by returning to the purpose of the examples. The method is meant to compress thinking, not expand it. A few quick estimates—usage frequency, expected lifespan, key ownership costs—often suffice to reveal whether a purchase is likely to be a false economy or a sensible upgrade. The goal is not accuracy to the penny. It is directionally correct judgement that prevents predictable regret.

A second named, checkable example reinforces why quick, targeted analysis works better than exhaustive tracking. In April 2014, the UK's Behavioural Insights Team published *EAST*, emphasising that interventions are more effective when they are Easy and Timely. Applied here, the insight is that decision tools should be lightweight enough to be used at the moment of choice. A method that requires an hour will be skipped when the purchase temptation is strongest. A method that requires two minutes can be used, which means it can actually change behaviour.

The quiet motif threading these scenarios is the long shadow. Each purchase casts one: ongoing costs, replacement cycles, hassle, storage, time spent dealing with failure, and the attention diverted by recurring decisions. Cost-per-use and ownership thinking are simply ways of tracing the shadow forward before stepping into it. They also have a psychological benefit. When a household can justify a higher upfront cost with a believable lower long-run cost and reduced hassle, it buys without guilt. When it can see that a "deal" produces high cost-per-use because usage will be low, it declines without deprivation.

The forward test arrives at the moment when two options sit side by side, one cheaper and one pricier, and both can be rationalised. The question will not be which one looks clever on the receipt. The question will be which one has the smaller long shadow on cashflow, attention, and regret—and whether the household is willing to make that judgement based on likely use rather than on the story it wants to tell about itself.

Limits of pure maths

In 1934, in Cambridge, John Maynard Keynes wrote an essay titled "Economic Possibilities for our Grandchildren", imagining a future in which technological progress would ease the problem of subsistence and free people to pursue "the art of life". The concrete outcome was not a policy but a provocation: what, precisely, are material gains *for*? Keynes, a man steeped in numbers, did not argue that calculation should rule the human story. He argued—almost impatiently—that calculation is a means, not an end.

Money is a means.

That is the sentence cost-per-use arithmetic can forget if it is allowed to become a tyrant. Pure maths can be wonderfully clarifying in a consumer culture that trades in confusion. It can also become a way of avoiding the harder work of judgement: deciding what is beautiful, what is meaningful, what is aligned with the household's values, and what is merely an expensive sedative. The aim of this section is not to retreat from measurement. It is to keep measurement in its proper place: a tool for reducing waste, not a substitute for wisdom.

The seduction of pure maths begins innocently. A household discovers cost-per-use, applies it to a few categories, and feels a surge of control. Control is pleasant. Especially for people who are busy and who have discovered that money can leak without visible drama. Show: a person calculates that a premium coat worn daily in winter has a low cost-per-wear and feels newly justified in buying quality. Name: numerical relief. Explain: numerical relief is the emotional comfort that comes from being able to defend a choice with arithmetic; it reduces guilt and uncertainty. Implication: the tool becomes attractive not only because it clarifies value but because it soothes the discomfort of choice.

This is where the danger enters. A soothing tool can be overused. A household can begin to treat every purchase as a calculation problem, and calculation can become a moral posture—"we are the sort of people who make rational choices." Show: someone spends hours comparing products to shave pennies off a per-use figure, while ignoring whether the object fits their life. Name: optimisation theatre. Explain: optimisation theatre is the performance of rationality in domains where the gains are small and the time cost is large; it looks disciplined while quietly wasting attention. Implication: the household can become more efficient on paper and less alive in practice, because the tool has expanded beyond its useful scope.

The first limit is obvious and still frequently ignored: not everything valuable is quantifiable. Joy, beauty, and meaning do not come with stable units. A painting is not used in the way a blender is used. A beautifully made object can provide daily pleasure that is not captured by frequency. A home can feel calm or chaotic for reasons that resist measurement. Show: a person walks into a well-proportioned room and breathes differently; a cheaper alternative meets the functional brief and leaves the nervous system tense. Name: aesthetic effect. Explain: aesthetics shape experience, and experience shapes behaviour; what feels calm often supports better habits, kinder interactions, and less compensatory spending. Implication: an "inefficient" choice by cost-per-use can be efficient by life impact if it reduces stress and increases the household's capacity for what it values.

A second limit is that some uses are rare and still worth having. A guest bed may be used only a few times a year, and those few times may be the difference between hospitality that is possible and hospitality that is avoided. A formal outfit may be worn occasionally but matters because it supports dignity in significant moments. A set of tools may be used intermittently but prevents a household being trapped by small repairs. Show: the low frequency is obvious, yet the purchase changes what the household can do. Name: capability value. Explain: some purchases are about capability rather than repetition; they expand the household's options and reduce reliance on external services or emergency spending. Implication: cost-per-use understates the value of capabilities because it treats each use as equal, when in reality a single use can avert a cascade of hassle.

A third limit is moral: values alignment can outweigh strict efficiency. A household may choose to buy fewer things but buy them from sources that match its ethics—local makers, fair labour practices, repairable products, secondhand markets—accepting a higher per-use cost in exchange for coherence with its principles. This is not virtue signalling. It is the practical recognition that a life is built from repeated acts of alignment. Show: a household chooses a repair rather than a replacement; it costs more and feels more truthful. Name: principled spending. Explain: principled spending treats money as a form of participation in the world; the household is not merely consuming, it is endorsing certain practices and supply chains. Implication: pure maths can misclassify principled choices as irrational when they are, in fact, a deliberate expression of what the household wants to support.

To acknowledge these limits is not to embrace vague sentimentality. It is to insist on a fuller model of value. Economists have long attempted to incorporate non-financial goods into decision-making, from early utilitarian frameworks to modern behavioural economics. Yet even where models exist, the household must decide what it wants to optimise: cost, time, stress, beauty, contribution, relationship. A household that optimises only for price-per-use may end up with an efficient life that feels oddly thin.

The second danger is subtler: numbers can be used to launder desire. A person wants the luxury item, so they produce a cost-per-use calculation with heroic assumptions. Show: someone buys a £2,000 espresso machine and declares it cheap per cup if used daily for a decade, ignoring holidays, changing tastes, repairs, and the probability that enthusiasm will fade. Name: convenient arithmetic. Explain: convenient arithmetic is not a mathematical error; it is an emotional manoeuvre—selecting assumptions that justify what the person already wants. Implication: the household feels rational while drifting into baseline inflation, because the calculation has become a story rather than a test.

The cure is not to abandon maths but to change the posture with which it is used. A tool used as a test behaves differently from a tool used as a defence. When used as a test, the calculation begins with conservative assumptions: likely usage based on past behaviour, realistic lifespan, some allowance for maintenance and hassle. When used as a defence, the calculation begins with the desired conclusion and backfills assumptions. This difference is visible. It shows up in whether the household is willing to be surprised by the result. A test can say "not worth it". A defence cannot.

Behavioural research offers a useful, grounded reason why self-deception is so common here. Kahneman's work on "what you see is all there is" describes how people build coherent narratives from limited information, often ignoring what is missing because the visible story feels complete (Kahneman, 2011). In purchase decisions, the visible story is the product description, the review highlights, and the imagined future self. What is missing is the friction, the boredom, the competing priorities, the actual schedule. The implication is not that people are dishonest. It is that the mind prefers coherence. Numbers can be recruited to strengthen coherence rather than to challenge it.

A named, checkable historical counterpoint helps keep the tool in proportion. In 1944, in Princeton, John von Neumann and Oskar Morgenstern published *Theory of Games and Economic Behavior*, formalising expected utility theory and giving modern economics a powerful mathematical language for rational choice under uncertainty. Their work is foundational and brilliant. It also illustrates a limitation: even the most elegant formal models require assumptions about preferences, risk, and utility that are not given by mathematics. Show: a model can calculate optimal choices once preferences are specified; it cannot specify what a person should prefer. Name: preference irreducibility. Explain: mathematics can optimise within a value system; it cannot create the value system. Implication: households can use cost-per-use to optimise spending once values are clear, but maths cannot decide whether beauty, hospitality, or generosity should matter.

This returns us to the human centre of the book: wealth without waste is not about being the most efficient consumer. It is about aligning money, time, and attention with what matters. Cost-per-use and total ownership thinking are excellent at exposing waste. They are weaker at capturing meaning. The correct response is not to discard them, but to pair them with qualitative judgement.

Qualitative judgement needs its own discipline, otherwise it becomes licence. A household can claim "joy" to justify any indulgence, just as it can claim "efficiency" to justify any upgrade. The difference lies in whether the joy is durable, whether it aligns with stated values, and whether it respects the household's chosen "enough" thresholds. Joy that lasts tends to have certain features: it is repeated or deeply memorable; it reduces stress rather than adding it; it strengthens relationships or identity coherence rather than merely displaying them. Joy that fades quickly often looks like novelty—exciting at purchase, normal within weeks.

The motif that threads this section is the long shadow. Pure maths measures one aspect of the shadow: cost over uses. It does not measure the shadow cast on identity, on relationships, on the household's sense of enough. A beautiful object can cast a gentle shadow—daily pleasure, pride of care. A luxury bought for status can cast a harsh one—comparison, more upgrading, a raised baseline that tightens generosity. The household's task is to see both shadows.

A credible limitation must be conceded, because some people use "nuance" as a way to avoid making decisions. They retreat into endless reflection: maybe we'll use it, maybe we won't; maybe it's worth it, maybe it isn't. The result is paralysis, which is its own cost. Name: deliberation fatigue. Explain: when judgement becomes interminable, the household spends time and energy without reaching clarity, and often ends up defaulting to the easiest option anyway. Implication: the humane process must be decisive enough to function in real life; nuance should sharpen choices, not postpone them forever.

Reconcile this by returning to the minimum effective dose of analysis introduced earlier in the book. The household does not need perfect rationality. It needs enough clarity to avoid predictable waste and protect what it values. That can be achieved by using maths where it is strongest—high-frequency items, high-cost items, categories prone to churn—and using qualitative judgement where it matters—beauty, meaning, values alignment—while applying conservative assumptions to prevent maths being hijacked.

The unresolved test, then, is not a calculation. It is a question of integrity. When confronted with a tempting purchase that can be justified either way, will the household use numbers to test its own story, or to decorate it? Will it allow joy and values to outweigh efficiency when they truly deserve to, or will it call every desire "joy" and every upgrade "efficient" until the long shadow thickens and the margin for freedom and generosity quietly disappears?

Chapter 5
Finding Silent Money Leaks

In October 2019, in London, the UK's Competition and Markets Authority announced a package of measures aimed at subscription traps and "auto-renewing" contracts, responding to a consumer reality that had become almost banal: people were paying for things they did not actively choose each month, simply because the default was "continue" and the friction of stopping was higher than the friction of paying. The concrete outcome was regulatory pressure and public scrutiny, but the more interesting outcome was psychological. It forced an uncomfortable admission: modern spending is often less about decisions than about inertia.

Inertia is expensive. Quietly.

This chapter is about the money that leaks not through extravagance but through automatisation. The affluent household is not typically undone by one dramatic purchase. It is softened—like stone under water—by small, recurring outflows that feel too minor to fight, too convenient to question, and too embarrassing to admit have become permanent. These leaks are rarely noticed because they do not arrive as pain. They arrive as convenience. They are charged to cards, rolled into renewals, bundled into "just £9.99 a month", scattered across apps and accounts until they become part of the household's background hum.

The modern economy has made this hum louder than any previous generation experienced. A mid-century household might have paid for a few utilities, a mortgage, perhaps one club membership. A contemporary household can carry dozens of micro-commitments: streaming services, cloud storage, software subscriptions, premium tiers, delivery memberships, curated boxes, fitness apps, news subscriptions, "free trials" that quietly mature into permanent charges. None of these is inherently foolish. The foolishness—if that is the word—is that they are rarely evaluated in the light of what the household actually values. They are not chosen. They are inherited.

A motif holds the chapter together: the drip. A drip is not a flood. It does not trigger panic. It triggers habituation. A drip can run for months before anyone notices the stain. The financial stain looks like this: the month feels tight even though the headline income is strong; generosity feels like a stretch; freedom feels slightly postponed. The household can point to no single culprit, because no single culprit exists. There are simply too many small drains, each plausible on its own, collectively corrosive.

The temptation is to treat this as a discipline problem—"we should be more careful"—and then to reach for tools that require constant vigilance. That approach fails for the same reason strict budgets fail: attention is scarce, and systems that demand daily heroics collapse under busy life. The better approach is to treat silent leaks as a design problem. Most leaks are created by defaults. They are sustained by friction. They can therefore be reduced by redesigning defaults and friction rather than by demanding perfect self-control.

That is why this chapter begins with subscriptions and memberships. Subscriptions are not merely recurring charges; they are recurring agreements. They occupy future cashflow. They shape margin. They are the closest thing many households have to "invisible rent": money owed before life even begins for the month. The striking fact about subscriptions is how emotionally disconnected they become from their value. The household pays because it has always paid, not because it actively uses. The charges become furniture: always there, never consciously selected. The audit that follows is not a moral purge. It is a reality check: which subscriptions are actively delivering value, and which are simply continuing because the system is built to make stopping awkward?

From there, the chapter widens the lens to automatic charges and renewals, which are the adult, institutional cousins of subscriptions: insurance renewals that creep upwards, service contracts that roll forward, storage plans that expand, licences that renew while nobody remembers why they were purchased in the first place. These are not merely financial nuisances. They are moments when a household's attention could save money disproportionate to the time spent. A single renegotiation, downgrade, or comparison at the right moment can reduce a recurring cost for years. The key is not to monitor constantly. It is to show up at the hinge-points.

The hinge-points matter because they reveal a deeper truth about modern affluence: attention is often more valuable than money. A household that earns well can lose more through neglect than through bad judgement. Not because it lacks intelligence, but because it has other things to do. The market exploits this rational scarcity of attention. It builds systems in which doing nothing is the default, and doing nothing is profitable—for someone else.

This is also where habitual convenience spending enters the story, not as an attack on comfort but as a question of alignment. Convenience can be a form of wisdom. Paying to buy back time can be one of the most rational decisions a high-income household makes, particularly when the reclaimed time is used for relationships, rest, or work that genuinely matters. But convenience can also become a narcotic—an automatic solution applied to any friction, even when the friction is trivial or the convenience does not actually create meaningful time. Delivery fees, ride-hailing, takeaways, premium versions of routine purchases: these can function as targeted tools or as default anaesthesia. The difference is visible in the household's week. Does the convenience purchase create time that is used well, or does it simply lubricate an overcommitted schedule that remains overcommitted?

The chapter's most provocative move is the simplest: designing friction. Modern commerce is built to remove friction from spending. One-click purchasing, stored cards, auto-renewal, "recommended for you", the gentle nudge that turns a one-off purchase into a subscription. The household's task is not to outmuscle this machinery with willpower. It is to reintroduce small, strategic frictions where they protect what matters. Friction is usually treated as an enemy. Here it becomes a friend—an intentional pause that interrupts impulse and prevents regret.

There is a philosophical edge to this that is worth stating plainly. Autonomy is not merely the ability to choose. It is the ability to avoid being chosen for. Many affluent households are less free than they appear because their spending has been partially outsourced to defaults—algorithms, renewals, and habitual taps. They are not being robbed. They are being drifted. The drift is comfortable enough to tolerate, and that is precisely why it persists.

Still, a serious treatment must admit a limitation: not all leaks should be plugged. Some recurring costs are deliberate and deeply worthwhile. A subscription that delivers genuine daily use is not a leak; it is infrastructure. A membership that sustains community may be a high-value commitment. A convenience expense that preserves a fragile household's calm may be worth far more than its price. The point is not to reduce recurring spending for its own sake. The point is to reduce *unexamined* recurring spending—spending that exists because the household stopped looking.

What makes this chapter essential within the broader arc of the book is that leaks are where values fail in practice. A household can have a compelling value hierarchy and still watch money drain into low-value defaults. It can understand cost-per-use and still pay for subscriptions it never uses. It can design cashflow guardrails and still bleed discretionary margin through frictionless spending. Silent leaks are the daily test of intentionality. They are also the daily opportunity, because they offer one of the cleanest ways to reclaim margin without reducing quality of life.

The drip motif returns because it suggests both danger and hope. Drips can damage slowly, but they can also be stopped with surprisingly small interventions. The household does not need a dramatic austerity campaign. It needs a few moments of attention, placed with precision: an audit that distinguishes active value from inertia, a review timed to renewals, a clear-eyed look at convenience patterns, and a few deliberate frictions that let the environment do the work that willpower cannot reliably do.

The page turns on a question that is deceptively modest and profoundly revealing. If the household could see, in one clear picture, every small recurring commitment it is currently making—every drip, every renewal, every "just for now" that has become permanent—what would it choose to keep because it genuinely serves the life it wants, and what would it finally allow to evaporate?

Auditing subscriptions and memberships

In October 2019, in London, the UK's Competition and Markets Authority announced action on subscription traps and auto-renewing contracts, describing how easy it had become for consumers to slide into recurring payments without deliberate consent. The outcome was regulatory pressure, but the more instructive outcome was conceptual: subscriptions had ceased to be a niche product format and become an ambient feature of ordinary life. Once that happens, households stop experiencing subscriptions as choices. They experience them as weather—always there, mildly irritating, rarely questioned.

Inertia charges rent every month. That rent is rarely ruinous. It is simply persistent. A tenner here, a fiver there, a premium tier that "isn't much", a club membership never cancelled because cancelling requires a password reset, a box delivery that felt delightful in January and absurd by May. The drip is the problem. One drip is nothing. A ceiling does not collapse from one drip. It collapses when drips become a system and the system is left unattended.

The subscription economy is an engineering marvel disguised as convenience. It smooths revenue for companies and smooths decision friction for consumers: one decision becomes many months of payments. For busy, comfortable households, that smoothing is seductive because it reduces the number of times a person must choose. Yet it also reduces the number of times a person *reconsents*. A one-off purchase sits there, inert, and can be judged later without consequence. A subscription is a promise to the future—small, recurring, quietly binding.

The core of an anti-subscription audit is therefore not austerity. It is consent. Show: a household opens a banking app and scrolls through a month of transactions; the same names recur like a refrain—streaming, storage, software, memberships, premium delivery, "plus" tiers. Name: recurring opacity. Explain: recurring opacity is the way repeated charges blur into background noise; the mind stops seeing them because nothing dramatic happens when they continue. Implication: money can feel "leaky" even when spending is not extravagant, because the household's margin is being pre-committed by agreements nobody has reconsidered.

A second, less discussed mechanism makes subscriptions particularly sticky: the pain of stopping. Cancelling is often designed to be more cognitively demanding than continuing. A person must find the right menu, remember a password, endure a retention offer, decide whether to lose saved preferences or stored files. Show: the household thinks "I'll cancel later" and then forgets; the charge renews; later becomes never. Name: friction asymmetry. Explain: friction asymmetry occurs when the effort required to stop exceeds the effort required to continue; the default becomes expensive precisely because it is easy. Implication: subscriptions thrive on the rational scarcity of attention in busy lives, which is why affluent households can carry a long tail of low-value subscriptions without noticing.

This is where a simple test earns its keep—not as moral judgement, but as a way of separating active value from inertia. Active value has a signature: it is used, noticed, and would be missed. Inertia has a different signature: it is justified in principle and forgotten in practice. Show: a household believes it "uses" a streaming service because it once binged a series; in the past month it opened the app twice. Name: imagined use. Explain: imagined use is the memory of a past benefit that continues to legitimise a present cost; it is a cognitive echo. Implication: an audit must interrogate recent behaviour rather than old narratives, because subscriptions are paid in the present, not in the nostalgia of last winter.

There is a reason the behavioural lens matters. Daniel Kahneman's work on judgement and attention describes how people substitute easy questions for hard ones when evaluating uncertain outcomes (Kahneman, 2011). "Do I want to be the sort of person who reads more?" is an easier question than "Did I read in the last four weeks?" Subscriptions are especially vulnerable to this substitution because they are often attached to aspirational identities: the person who meditates daily, the household that watches documentaries, the professional who keeps up with every tool, the runner who uses the premium training plan. The subscription becomes a small, monthly vote for a self. The problem is not aspiration. The problem is paying indefinitely for aspiration without the corresponding behaviour.

Two checkable examples show how quickly subscription culture expanded and why it can now outpace attention. In February 2005, Amazon launched Amazon Prime in the United States, with a subscription model that bundled delivery benefits into an annual fee; the UK launch followed in 2007. Whatever one thinks of the company, the model was influential: it reframed "shipping" from a per-transaction cost into a membership identity, making more purchases feel cheaper because the marginal delivery cost appeared to be zero. Show: once delivery feels "free", ordering small items feels rational. Name: perceived zero-cost. Explain: perceived zero-cost changes behaviour because people respond more strongly to "free" than to small prices; the subscription alters how future transactions are felt, not merely how they are billed. Implication: memberships do not only drain money directly; they can also reshape habits in ways that increase overall consumption.

A second example comes from media. Netflix launched its streaming service in 2007 in the United States, accelerating a shift from ownership—DVDs, purchased downloads—to ongoing access. Subscription media has obvious benefits: breadth, convenience, and the end of physical clutter. It also produces a familiar household effect: paying for abundance while using only a narrow slice. Show: a family maintains multiple streaming subscriptions because each person has "their shows", yet most evenings default to the same comfort programme. Name: abundance underuse. Explain: abundance underuse occurs when the household purchases a wide library but repeatedly consumes a small subset; the extra access is paid for but not lived. Implication: consolidating access can increase satisfaction rather than reduce it, because the household moves from diffuse abundance to chosen abundance—the kind that is actually used.

The drip motif matters here because subscriptions rarely feel like they are doing anything dramatic. They are background. A drip is tolerable until it isn't, and the moment it isn't is usually experienced as a generalised tightness rather than as a clear diagnosis. That is why the audit works best when it treats subscriptions as a category of commitments rather than as isolated line items. The household is not deciding whether a particular app is "worth it". It is deciding how much of its future margin it is willing to pre-sell to recurring charges, and whether those charges reflect its value hierarchy or merely its accumulated defaults.

Notice what this does psychologically. It lowers shame. Many people feel embarrassed about forgotten subscriptions, as if forgetting were a moral failure. Forgetting is ordinary. Modern commerce is designed around forgettability. Show: a person signs up for a free trial late at night, meaning to cancel, and then misses the email reminder. Name: engineered forgetting. Explain: engineered forgetting is not a conspiracy; it is simply the economic incentive of recurring revenue combined with human limits on attention. Implication: the audit can be approached as a design correction rather than a confession, which makes it more likely to be completed without emotional drama.

The anti-subscription audit also reveals a deeper pattern: households often duplicate the same function across several subscriptions. A music subscription plus a radio app; multiple cloud storage plans; overlapping productivity tools; two fitness memberships. Duplications persist because each one was purchased for a momentary reason that has since faded. Show: a household pays for multiple storage services because photos are scattered across devices and nobody wants to untangle them. Name: fragmentation tax. Explain: fragmentation tax is the cost of complexity—money spent to avoid the effort of consolidating systems. Implication: consolidation can be a form of wealth without waste not because it "saves money" in the abstract, but because it reduces the cognitive load of managing multiple parallel systems.

A credible limitation deserves respect: some subscriptions are genuinely high value, and the audit can be misused as a blunt instrument. A news subscription that is read daily and shapes thinking may be worth far more than its price. A software subscription that underpins professional output may be a form of infrastructure. A club membership may be less about facilities and more about community, identity, and routine. Show: a household cancels a membership in a wave of "being sensible" and then quietly loses a stabilising habit it relied on, later compensating with more expensive coping purchases. Name: false pruning. Explain: false pruning happens when the household removes a high-value stabiliser because it is visible and easy to cut, while leaving lower-value drips untouched because they are scattered and unnoticed. Implication: the audit must distinguish between subscriptions that are genuinely used and those that merely feel virtuous to possess.

The reconciliation is to treat the audit as value alignment, not as self-punishment. A subscription can be "expensive" and still be a keeper if it reliably supports what the household values—time with family, learning, fitness, creativity, community. A subscription can be "cheap" and still be a leak if it is seldom used and kept only by inertia. This is where the earlier chapters pay off. The household's value hierarchy supplies the criteria; cost-per-use thinking supplies the realism; guardrails supply the boundaries. The audit supplies the clean-up.

The most quietly transformative aspect of an audit is that it returns choice to the household. Subscriptions are attractive because they reduce decisions. They are dangerous for the same reason. Once a household sees its recurring commitments clearly, it can stop living inside agreements it no longer endorses. The drip becomes visible. Visibility changes behaviour.

There is also a social dimension worth naming. Many subscriptions are purchased to reduce conflict: separate streaming services to keep everyone happy, multiple memberships to avoid negotiating whose preference dominates, premium tiers to remove friction in a hectic home. These are not irrational. They are sometimes the price of peace. Yet peace purchased by diffuse, unexamined spending is often brittle. It can be replaced by a different kind of peace: clarity about what is shared, what is individual, and what is simply leftover from earlier seasons. The audit does not demand uniformity; it invites coherence.

The drip motif returns one last time because it points to the forward test. Subscriptions are not a one-off clean-up. They are an environment. New drips are constantly offered—free trials, bundle deals, premium add-ons, "limited time" discounts that convert to full price later. The test is whether the household will allow new drips to become permanent by default, or whether it will insist—quietly, without drama—that recurring commitments earn a place in the life they are meant to serve.

Automatic charges and renewals

In February 2020, in London, Ofcom's rules requiring end-of-contract notifications for broadband, mobile, and pay-TV customers came into force, pushing providers to tell people when their discounted deal ended and what they would pay if they did nothing. The concrete outcome was informational: a letter, an email, a nudge that said, in effect, *the price is about to change because the contract has moved.* That change mattered because it illuminated the real mechanism behind many household money leaks. The leak is not always overspending. It is non-decision.

Renewals are a quiet tax.

The modern household is threaded through with arrangements designed to continue unless interrupted. Some are benign. Some are useful. Yet many are built in such a way that attention becomes the scarcest currency. Insurance renewals roll forward. Service contracts renew themselves. Digital storage expands as photos accumulate, then becomes too painful to unwind. Each individual charge is often defensible. The cumulative effect is that a portion of future cashflow is quietly claimed before the household has even begun the month.

The key insight is that these leaks are not evenly distributed across time. They cluster around hinge moments: renewal dates, contract anniversaries, tariff changes, storage thresholds, the point where a "trial" becomes a charge, the moment a discounted rate expires. If attention is paid at those hinges, the household can make a deliberate choice. If attention is absent, the default choice is made by the system. Show: an email arrives saying a premium will change, a policy will renew, a contract will roll over; the household is busy, the message is read quickly, and then life continues. Name: default continuation. Explain: default continuation is the tendency to let a commitment persist because the effort of reviewing it feels higher than the perceived benefit, especially when the numbers are not yet painful. Implication: a household can be financially comfortable and still experience persistent leakage, because many organisations have learned to monetise inattention.

This is not a conspiracy so much as an incentive structure. Recurring revenue is predictable. Predictable revenue is valuable. The customer's friction is part of the model. That model works best when the cost increase is gradual and the explanation is plausible. Price creep is rarely announced as "we are charging you more because you did not notice". It arrives dressed as inflation, improved service, "updated terms", or simply a new year. Show: a household pays £X one year and £X plus a little the next, and the change feels too small to contest. Name: gradualism. Explain: gradualism works because humans respond more strongly to sudden losses than to slow drift; small increases slide beneath the emotional threshold of action. Implication: the household may be highly competent in its career and still be surprisingly passive in its contracts, because the mind is tuned to respond to obvious threats, not to slow siphons.

A named regulatory example makes the issue measurable rather than merely intuitive. In May 2021, in London, the UK's Financial Conduct Authority published its final rules on general insurance pricing practices, targeting the "loyalty penalty" whereby renewing customers could be charged more than new customers for the same risk. The rules took effect on 1 January 2022. The concrete outcome was structural: firms were required to offer renewing customers a price no higher than that offered to an equivalent new customer (FCA, 2021; effective 2022). Whatever one thinks of the policy's wider consequences, it reveals something important for household behaviour. Regulators moved because the pattern was pervasive: in markets where renewal is easy and switching is effortful, inattention becomes expensive.

The paradox is that the household often experiences these markets as "set and forget" precisely when they should be "set and revisit". The revisit does not need to be constant. It needs to be punctual. A household that checks everything all the time becomes anxious and exhausted. A household that checks nothing becomes a predictable revenue stream for other people. The middle path is attention placed at the hinge.

Insurance renewals show the mechanism in its purest form because they are both emotionally charged and administratively tedious. Insurance is bought to transfer risk. It therefore touches fear. At renewal, fear and fatigue combine: fear of being uninsured, fatigue at comparing small print, and the sense that the household has better things to do. Show: the renewal notice arrives with a new premium; the household thinks, "fine, at least it's sorted." Name: safety premium. Explain: the safety premium is the extra cost people tolerate to avoid the discomfort of re-evaluating risk, especially when the consequences of getting it wrong feel severe. Implication: the household can pay more than it intends not because it is careless, but because the emotional framing of insurance makes passivity feel like prudence.

Service contracts behave similarly but with a different emotional texture. Home services—broadband, mobile plans, security systems, boiler cover—tend to be sold as relief from hassle. They promise continuity: no surprises, no interruptions, no "being without". That promise is often real. The problem arrives when the promise becomes a reason to stop paying attention entirely. Show: the household stays on a plan long after the initial deal has ended, paying more for the same service because changing it requires a call, a comparison, and a small willingness to be mildly inconvenienced. Name: hassle aversion. Explain: hassle aversion is the tendency to overvalue avoiding administrative friction; it makes "doing nothing" feel like a rational act of self-care. Implication: the household's time poverty is monetised, and the money saved by a brief review is left on the table because it is not visible as a loss, merely as an absence of savings.

Digital storage is the newest and perhaps the most psychologically ingenious renewal trap, because it blends necessity with sentiment. Photos of children, messages from loved ones, old work files: these are not mere data. They are memory and identity. Storage tiers often begin as tiny and cheap, then expand silently as usage grows. The household rarely notices until it hits a limit and is forced to choose between deleting precious archives or paying for more space. Show:

the phone displays a warning; the household clicks "upgrade" because the alternative feels like loss. Name: emotional lock-in. Explain: emotional lock-in occurs when a service becomes entwined with irreplaceable personal material; the cost is not simply money but the threat of losing something meaningful. Implication: the household may pay indefinitely for storage not because the price is fair or the plan is optimal, but because the cost of disentangling feels like grief.

This is why occasional comparisons matter. Comparisons are not about chasing the cheapest deal for sport. They are about restoring agency. When a household compares at the hinge—at renewal, at end-of-contract, at storage threshold—it forces the system to compete for consent rather than for inertia. Show: a household notices a renewal date, looks at alternatives briefly, and realises its existing arrangement is either still reasonable or quietly inflated. Name: consent refresh. Explain: consent refresh is the act of reconfirming that a recurring payment still earns its place; it turns passive continuation into active choice. Implication: even when the household decides to stay, it stays with clarity rather than drift, which reduces the sense of money being siphoned by unseen forces.

A realistic renegotiation example illustrates how small attention can change recurring costs without requiring obsession. Consider a broadband contract that began with an introductory discount. When the discount ends, the monthly price rises. The household notices because the notification arrives, but life is crowded. The common outcome is inaction and a higher bill for months. A different outcome is also common and is not dramatic: the household contacts the provider, states that the contract price has changed, and asks whether a different tariff is available. Sometimes the provider offers a retention discount. Sometimes it offers a lower tier that suits actual usage. Sometimes it offers nothing, and the household decides whether to stay. Show: one short conversation produces either a modest reduction or a clearer understanding that the current price is the price. Name: hinge attention. Explain: hinge attention is the practice of placing effort precisely where it has leverage—at the moment the system is already changing. Implication: the household does not need to monitor monthly. It needs to show up when the contract moves.

The power of hinge attention becomes clearer when contrasted with constant monitoring. Constant monitoring tends to produce either anxiety or numbness. Anxiety keeps people staring at numbers without making decisions. Numbness keeps people ignoring numbers until they feel shocked and ashamed. Hinge attention is neither. It is targeted. It respects the household's limited cognitive bandwidth. It also respects a core truth: busy, affluent people are not short of intelligence. They are short of uninterrupted time.

A quiet behavioural insight underpins all of this. Daniel Kahneman described attention as finite and effortful; when attention is depleted, people revert to defaults and heuristics (Kahneman, 2011). Automatic renewals are essentially defaults with a price tag. The household's task is not to become superhumanly vigilant. It is to create a few reliable prompts that bring attention back at the hinge, when a default can be interrupted with minimal effort. The simplest form of this prompt is a calendar reminder. Not as a productivity fetish, but as a humane prosthetic for memory in a crowded life. Show: a reminder appears a few weeks before renewal; it turns an invisible future cost into a visible present question. Name: externalised memory. Explain: externalised memory is the practice of using tools to compensate for human limits, reducing reliance on willpower and recall. Implication: the household can design its environment so that important decisions surface at the right time without requiring constant mental load.

A limitation must be faced honestly, because not every renewal is worth contesting and not every comparison is worth the effort. Some services are genuinely good value and stable. Some insurance needs are complex enough that minimising cost is not the only rational goal. Some households will choose to pay a little more for continuity because the service is critical and disruption is costly. Show: a household sticks with a provider after a brief check because switching would introduce risk or hassle disproportionate to the savings. Name: rational continuity. Explain: rational continuity is the decision to prioritise reliability, simplicity, or service quality over marginal savings; it is not inertia when it is chosen consciously. Implication: the goal is not relentless minimisation. It is eliminating the loyalty tax that arises when the household is paying more simply because nobody looked.

The reconciliation lies in distinguishing deliberate continuity from accidental continuity. Deliberate continuity has an argument: the service is used, the price is understood, the alternatives were briefly considered, and the decision aligns with the household's priorities. Accidental continuity has a shrug: "we've always had it", "it's only a bit", "I didn't get round to it". The difference is not moral. It is structural. One keeps the household in authorship. The other keeps it in drift.

The drip motif returns here because renewals are the steadiest kind of drip. They do not announce themselves with a shopping bag. They arrive as polite emails and automatic direct debits. They are, in a sense, the most "respectable" leaks—associated with responsibility, protection, and sensible administration. That respectability is exactly why they can go unchallenged. A household can feel virtuous while paying unnecessary premiums, simply because the payments are tied to adult-sounding categories.

The forward test arrives at the next hinge. A renewal notice lands. A storage plan nudges upward. A service contract rolls forward. The question is not whether the household can afford the drift; many can. The question is whether it wants its future margin—its freedom, its generosity, its ability to say yes to what matters—to be quietly pre-sold through accidental continuity, or reclaimed through brief, well-placed attention at the hinge.

Habitual convenience spending review

In March 2020, in London, the first COVID-19 lockdown abruptly rewired everyday consumption. Streets emptied, commuting collapsed, and a vast amount of household behaviour moved onto phones. For many people, the concrete outcome was not only a public-health restriction but a personal revelation: the weekly rhythm had been propped up by purchases that were less about pleasure than about coping. Delivery slots, takeaway apps, ride-hails, premium subscriptions—what had felt like small luxuries suddenly looked like infrastructure.

Convenience is infrastructure. Sometimes.

That "sometimes" matters. Convenience spending can be one of the most rational forms of expenditure in a busy, affluent household, because time is a finite resource and friction is not evenly distributed. A parent sprinting between meetings and school pickup is not buying takeaway because they lack culinary virtue. They are buying an hour in which the household can remain civil. A professional who uses ride-hailing after a late train disruption may be buying safety and sleep. The mistake is not convenience. The mistake is convenience that becomes habitual without being examined for return.

Habit is expensive when it is invisible.

The modern market excels at turning one-off solutions into defaults. A delivery fee is a small number attached to a large feeling: relief. A premium tier is a small number attached to a large story: efficiency. The household taps "confirm" because the immediate benefit is clear and the long-run cost is hazy. Show: a person sits on a sofa after a long day, taps a food delivery app, and feels the tension drop before the food even arrives. Name: anticipatory relief. Explain: anticipatory relief is the emotional benefit that arrives at the moment of purchase, before the service is delivered; the mind pays partly for the feeling of "sorted". Implication: when convenience is repeatedly used for anticipatory relief, it becomes a coping loop, and the household can spend significant money without ever feeling like it is choosing extravagance.

This is why a review must focus on patterns rather than isolated transactions. An occasional ride-hail is a tool. A daily ride-hail is a lifestyle. An occasional takeaway is a treat. Four takeaways a week is a system. The distinction is not moral. It is structural. Patterns pre-commit cashflow. Patterns also shape the household's sense of what is normal. Once a household becomes accustomed to frictionless solutions, ordinary friction—cooking, walking, waiting, planning—starts to feel intolerable. That intolerance can create more spending, which creates more dependence, which creates more intolerance. The spiral is quiet and perfectly plausible.

Behavioural science helps explain why convenience is so sticky. In 1999, Daniel Kahneman, Peter Wakker, and Rakesh Sarin published work on experienced utility, reminding economists that what people *remember* about experiences often differs from what they *lived* moment by moment (Kahneman, Wakker & Sarin, 1997; closely related work and popularisation followed). The implication in household terms is straightforward: the memory of a convenience purchase may be weak even when the momentary relief was strong. Show: the household orders dinner, feels relief, eats, forgets. Name: low-recall spending. Explain: low-recall spending is expenditure that provides a short-term benefit but leaves little trace in memory or satisfaction; it is felt at purchase and then dissolves. Implication: a household can spend heavily on convenience and still feel strangely unsatisfied, because the spending is not producing durable experiences or long-term reductions in stress.

The review therefore begins by pairing abstractions with visible metrics. "Convenience" is not a category. It is a set of behaviours: delivery fees per week, ride-hail trips per month, premium versions of routine purchases, "fast track" services, paid shortcuts. These behaviours can be observed. Their outputs can also be observed. What do they buy? More time? Less friction? Fewer arguments? More sleep? Or do they merely buy the sensation of coping for another day?

The motif threading this section is the shortcut. A shortcut is only useful if it takes you somewhere you want to go. Otherwise it is just a detour with a toll.

Consider delivery fees and grocery convenience. A household pays for a grocery delivery subscription and still pays add-on fees for rapid delivery because planning is hard. Show: a busy week triggers a "need it now" order, and the fees feel justified because they prevent a problem. Name: deadline purchasing. Explain: deadline purchasing is spending triggered by the approach of a constraint—empty fridge, missing ingredient, forgotten birthday—where money substitutes for planning time. Implication: a household can end up paying repeatedly for the same type of urgency because urgency has become part of its routine rather than an occasional exception.

Now consider ride-hailing. The per-trip cost often feels acceptable, especially when compared to the stress of public transport delays or parking. Yet ownership thinking asks: what is the pattern? Is ride-hailing an occasional safety valve, or is it the household's default transport system? If it is default, what is it doing to the household's rhythm? Show: a person stops walking, stops cycling, stops taking the train because ride-hailing is always easier; the day becomes smoother and more expensive. Name: friction outsourcing. Explain: friction outsourcing is the habit of paying to remove small frictions across the day; it can be rational when it protects scarce energy and time, and wasteful when it removes frictions that were actually healthy constraints—walking time that created thinking space, slower travel that created decompression. Implication: the same spend can either protect wellbeing or erode it, depending on what the recovered time becomes.

Takeaway and prepared food are the most emotionally loaded convenience category because they sit at the junction of care, competence, and exhaustion. A household that regularly buys takeaway is often solving a real problem: the adults are stretched, the children are hungry, and cooking feels like another demand. The review must respect that. It must also distinguish between convenience that prevents collapse and convenience that has become habitual because the household never revisits its underlying rhythm. Show: the household orders takeaway not only on chaotic days but also on ordinary days because it has become a reflex; the food arrives, the bin fills, the week continues. Name: reflex spending. Explain: reflex spending is money spent without a decision point; the trigger is mood or fatigue rather than a considered trade-off. Implication: reflex convenience can drain cashflow while failing to deliver proportional wellbeing, because it does not address the underlying pressure that creates fatigue.

Premium versions of routine purchases—better coffee out every morning, upgraded supermarket items by default, "plus" tiers for delivery and fast checkout—work through a similar mechanism. Each premium feels small. The household's baseline rises. The raised baseline becomes the new normal, and "normal" begins to feel like deprivation. This is how affluent households can feel constrained: not because they lack income, but because their everyday life has acquired a layer of paid smoothing in dozens of places.

A short exercise can cut through the fog because it translates judgement into observation. Begin with a recent fortnight. Note three things for each convenience purchase: what triggered it, what it claimed to buy, and what it actually produced. The trigger is often visible—late meeting, argument, tiredness, missed train, lack of food at home. What it claims to buy is the story—time, calm, safety, ease. What it actually produced is the truth—did it create usable time, did it reduce stress beyond the evening, did it strengthen relationships, did it prevent a worse cost? The point is not to become forensic. It is to reveal the pattern: which conveniences are true shortcuts to what the household values, and which are toll roads to nowhere.

Two named, checkable examples help ground this in modern context. The rapid growth of app-based food delivery in the 2010s—such as Deliveroo's founding in London in 2013—made takeaway not only accessible but frictionless. A frictionless service turns a rare treat into an everyday option. Meanwhile, the rise of ride-hailing platforms in major cities, expanding rapidly in the 2010s, altered what "normal transport" felt like; waiting or planning began to feel archaic. The implication is not that these services are harmful. It is that they change defaults, and defaults change spending patterns without requiring a conscious decision.

A credible limitation must be named to avoid turning this into puritanism. Some households are in seasons where convenience is not merely helpful but necessary: new babies, caring responsibilities, health limitations, unusually intense work periods. In such seasons, convenience spending can be a stabiliser that preserves relationships and mental bandwidth. Cutting it indiscriminately can be a false economy, producing conflict, exhaustion, and compensatory spending elsewhere. Name: stabiliser spending. Explain: stabiliser spending is expenditure that keeps the household functioning when capacity is temporarily constrained; it buys calm and prevents breakdown. Implication: the review is not about reducing convenience spending in absolute terms, but about distinguishing stabilisers from defaults.

The reconciliation is to evaluate convenience by what it buys *in practice*. Does it buy time that is used for what the household values—rest, connection, meaningful work, generosity? Or does it buy a momentary sense of coping while leaving the underlying overload intact? This is where values hierarchy re-enters: if a household claims it values family dinners and connection, convenience purchases that consistently create that space are high value. If a household claims it values freedom and generosity, convenience purchases that quietly raise fixed costs and normalise paid smoothing everywhere may be low value. The same category can contain both.

The shortcut motif returns because it captures the heart of the decision. A shortcut that leads to the household's priorities is worth paying for. A shortcut that merely avoids mild discomfort and trains the household to expect a frictionless life is often an expensive detour. The difference is visible not in ideology but in outcomes: memory, calm, time reclaimed, relationships strengthened, or money drained and nothing much to show for it.

The forward test arrives at the moment of fatigue, which is when most convenience spending happens. The app is open. The premium option is one tap away. The household can afford the charge. The question is whether this shortcut is taking the household towards what it values—or whether it is simply paying another toll to keep moving in the same overcommitted direction, with the same drip of money and attention seeping away.

Designing friction for leaks

In 2008, in Chicago, Richard H. Thaler and Cass R. Sunstein published *Nudge*, arguing that the architecture of choices—defaults, layout, timing, and small frictions—shapes behaviour as reliably as overt incentives. The concrete outcome was a new mainstream vocabulary for something designers and policymakers had long practised: people do not decide in a vacuum. They decide inside environments that tilt them. Thaler and Sunstein's thesis was not that humans are weak and need paternal supervision. It was that humans are human, and the world is already nudging them—usually towards someone else's profit.

Friction is a moral word in commerce. It is treated as an obstacle to remove. Companies spend billions reducing it: one-click checkout, stored cards, face recognition, default subscriptions, "buy now, pay later" buttons that make spending feel like scheduling rather than paying. The household experiences this as convenience, and convenience can be genuinely valuable. Yet the same frictionless pathways are also the plumbing of silent money leaks. A system built to make spending effortless will produce effortless spending, especially for busy people with full lives.

Make it slightly harder.

That is the whole idea. Not harder as punishment. Harder as design. The purpose is not to demand heroic willpower each time temptation arrives; it is to make low-value spending require just enough effort that the household's better judgement has time to re-enter the room. A small pause can change a decision. It can also reveal the true motive: boredom, fatigue, loneliness, status anxiety, avoidance. When the pause exists, those motives become visible. When it does not, they are simply transacted.

The first move is to name the enemy correctly. The enemy is not desire. The enemy is automaticity. Show: a person scrolls late at night, sees an item, taps "buy", and feels a brief relief. The next day the item arrives and the relief has evaporated. Name: frictionless impulse. Explain: frictionless impulse is a purchase that bypasses reflection because the pathway from desire to payment is short; it allows an emotion to become a transaction. Implication: in a frictionless environment, emotions become expensive not because emotions are bad, but because they are acted on too quickly.

This is where the book's earlier distinction between value and waste becomes operational. Waste is not always about the object; it is about the pathway. A household can buy something expensive and not wasteful if it was chosen deliberately and used. A household can waste money on small purchases if those purchases are automatic, frequent, and low-recall. Designing friction targets the pathway, not the category. It asks: where do we repeatedly spend without meaning to, and how can we make that pathway slightly less smooth?

The most obvious example is stored payment methods. One of the quiet revolutions of digital commerce has been the decoupling of payment from pain. Cash made spending tangible. Cards reduced tangibility. Stored cards and biometric checkout remove tangibility almost entirely. Show: a person buys something while walking, barely breaking stride. Name: payment decoupling. Explain: payment decoupling is the separation of purchasing from the sensation of parting with money; it reduces the moment of "this costs". Implication: when payment is decoupled, the household is more likely to treat small purchases as free, because the felt cost is low and the objective cost is delayed.

A small barrier—such as removing stored card details from particular sites—does not stop a determined purchase. It stops the lazy purchase. It forces a moment of re-entry: the person must find a wallet, type numbers, confirm the decision. That is not a moral test. It is a cognitive brake. The brake is valuable precisely because most regretted purchases are not driven by deep desire; they are driven by transient moods. A household does not need a fortress. It needs speed bumps.

Cooling-off periods are another form of speed bump. They are not new. Consumer law has long recognised that people regret rushed purchases; many jurisdictions have cancellation rights for certain contracts or distance selling. The household can apply a similar principle informally, not as legalistic ritual but as design. Show: an item is placed in an online basket, and then left. The next day, the household either still wants it or has forgotten it. Name: desire decay. Explain: desire decay is the tendency for impulsive desire to diminish with time; the brain moves on when novelty fades. Implication: a short delay can prevent a surprising proportion of regret purchases, because many impulses are time-sensitive rather than value-driven.

The power of delays is supported by behavioural research. George Ainslie's work on hyperbolic discounting describes how people overweight immediate rewards relative to future outcomes, leading to choices that feel good now and are regretted later (Ainslie, 1975; subsequent work developed the idea). The implication is practical: many leaks are not logical errors. They are timing errors. The household chooses the immediate relief of buying over the future benefit of keeping margin, because the future benefit is abstract.

Friction makes the future benefit slightly more present by interrupting immediacy.

Friction also protects against another modern temptation: subscription creep through default add-ons. Many services now offer a free trial with an automatic conversion to paid, or a base plan with an easy upgrade to "premium". The household's problem is not that these offers exist; it is that accepting them is easier than remembering them later. A simple friction is to require a conscious renewal rather than an automatic one—where possible—or to set reminders for cancellation windows. This is not constant monitoring. It is attention at hinge moments, redesigned into the environment. The environment becomes an ally rather than a saboteur.

A named, checkable example from policy illustrates why friction is often necessary when the stakes are high. In 2019, in the UK, the Gambling Commission introduced rules requiring online gambling operators to slow down play, including features such as a minimum speed of play for online slots and bans on certain auto-play functions. The outcome was a deliberate introduction of friction to reduce harm. The relevance here is not to equate shopping with gambling. It is to observe a general principle: when an interface is designed to accelerate behaviour that can become harmful, inserting friction is one of the few interventions that reliably changes outcomes. Commerce interfaces are designed to accelerate spending. Households can ethically design counter-frictions to protect their own values.

The motif that threads this section is the speed bump. A speed bump does not prevent travel. It prevents reckless speed. It preserves the road.

Concrete examples make this feel less like theory and more like craft. Consider the household that repeatedly orders takeaway because the app is pinned on the home screen, the card is stored, and past orders can be repeated in seconds. The frictionless pathway turns mild tiredness into a purchase. A speed bump might be as simple as moving the app off the first screen, removing stored cards, or deciding that certain purchases require a second step. The purchase remains available. The purchase becomes less reflexive. That is the point.

Consider the household that habitually buys premium versions of routine goods—upgraded coffee, upgraded snacks, upgraded "treats"—as a way of punctuating a stressful day. The speed bump here is not to forbid treats. It is to prevent treats becoming an automatic response to stress, which often produces more clutter than comfort. A small friction can be a rule that treats are chosen deliberately on certain days or in certain contexts, rather than purchased whenever tension rises. The rule is less important than the pause the rule creates.

Consider online retail "browsing", which is often not browsing but self-soothing. The speed bump can be a deliberate separation between browsing and buying. A household might browse freely but only purchase during a set window, or only from a list that has survived a delay. The point is to prevent the mind from treating a momentary emotion as a mandate.

A credible limitation must be acknowledged, because friction can be misused. Some frictions increase stress rather than reduce it. If a household makes everyday necessities hard to access, it can create conflict and fatigue, which then triggers more compensatory spending. Name: punitive friction. Explain: punitive friction is friction designed as punishment—barriers that make life harder without increasing alignment. Implication: friction must be placed surgically, targeting low-value leaks rather than essential routines, otherwise it produces backlash and the system fails.

There is also the risk of false virtue. A household can install elaborate frictions and still leak money in other ways, because the core issue is not the availability of spending but the underlying rhythm of life—overwork, lack of rest, social comparison, unexamined commitments. Friction is not a substitute for deeper alignment. It is a support. It helps the household keep its own promises when tired. That is all.

The reconciliation is to use friction as part of a broader design. Earlier in the chapter, subscriptions were audited, renewals were brought into view, convenience patterns were examined. Friction is what keeps those insights from evaporating under pressure. It is the mechanical link between intention and behaviour. It allows the environment to carry some of the burden that willpower cannot reliably carry.

What makes friction especially powerful for affluent households is that it protects generosity and freedom without requiring deprivation. The household does not need to "be stricter". It needs to reduce accidental spending so that money is available for deliberate spending. Speed bumps do not make life smaller. They make it truer.

The forward test arrives at the precise moment frictionless commerce is designed to exploit: late at night, tired, mildly dissatisfied, phone in hand, one-click purchase waiting. The household can always override a speed bump if the purchase is genuinely aligned. The question is whether it will design those speed bumps now, while calm, so that future decisions are made by the household's values rather than by an interface optimised to convert a passing impulse into a permanent drip.

Chapter 6
Choosing Buy Rent Borrow

In 2015, in Paris, the city launched an ambitious version of a familiar idea: access can sometimes trump ownership. The expanded Autolib' car-sharing scheme—an attempt to make short-term vehicle access normal—promised that urban residents could move around without each household needing to own a car. The concrete outcome was mixed, and Autolib' ultimately closed in 2018 after financial difficulties, yet the cultural question it posed has only sharpened: when does owning something make life simpler, and when does it merely add another object to manage, insure, maintain, store, and eventually dispose of?

Ownership is not neutral. It is a relationship.

Modern consumption has trained people to treat ownership as the default and alternatives as second-best—renting as a compromise, borrowing as awkward, sharing as something you do when you cannot afford not to. That framing is outdated. For busy, affluent households trying to spend with precision, "buy, rent, borrow" is not a hierarchy of pride. It is a set of strategies. Each strategy has an economics, a psychology, and a footprint in the home. The hidden cost is rarely the purchase price. It is the burden of possessions: the attention demanded by objects, the space they occupy, the maintenance they require, the decisions they generate, the way they quietly thicken the household's baseline.

This chapter is an antidote to a particular kind of waste that thrives among comfortable earners: buying as if every desire is permanent. Most desires are seasonal. Most needs are contingent. Many "needs" are really short-term problems in disguise. A household buys a pressure washer for a one-off job, then stores it for years. It buys specialist sports equipment for a brief enthusiasm. It buys a premium gadget because the launch made it feel urgent. None of these purchases is scandalous. The scandal is that ownership is treated as the default even when access would have served better.

The motif here is the keyring. Every owned item adds a key: not always literal, but psychological. A key to a cupboard, a subscription to a service, a manual to remember, a part that can break, a storage problem that returns every time the house is tidied. Some keys unlock freedom. Many simply jangle.

The chapter begins with the seduction of "buy once, use for years", because it is real and because it is often misunderstood. Quality can be the opposite of waste. A robust suitcase that survives years of travel is not indulgence; it is reduced churn, fewer replacements, less hassle, fewer mid-trip failures that turn holiday into logistics. Everyday clothing, core tools, essential appliances: when an item is used frequently, and when failure would create disproportionate disruption, paying more upfront can be a form of frugality. The earlier lens of cost-per-use returns here, not as arithmetic theatre but as a way of defending the right kinds of upgrades while exposing the wrong ones. This is where households learn to distinguish "buy it for life" from "buy it for ego".

Then the chapter pivots to renting, the strategy most people underestimate because it feels like money spent without an asset. Yet renting can be a form of disciplined intelligence. Many items are used rarely, become obsolete quickly, or create storage costs that quietly exceed their utility. A family does not need to own a marquee to host one summer gathering. A household does not need to buy niche tools for a weekend DIY project. Occasional luxury—an outstanding camera for a trip, specialised equipment for an event—can be rented without committing the household to maintenance, insurance, and clutter. Renting is also a way of testing desire without paying the full price of being wrong. It is not a failure. It is a risk-management technique.

Borrowing and sharing widen the frame further, because they challenge an assumption as old as consumerism: that every household must privately own everything it might use. Libraries are the most civilised proof that access can be abundant without personal accumulation. Tool libraries, neighbour lending, community swapping, workplace resources: these arrangements are not merely economical. They are social infrastructure. They allow households to reduce waste and increase resilience, because a community with shared resources can respond to needs without each home becoming a warehouse. Borrowing is often avoided not because it is impractical but because it triggers social anxiety—fear of awkwardness, fear of obligation, fear of being judged as stingy. The chapter treats those fears with respect while showing how reciprocity can be simple and dignified. Sharing is not charity. It is adult mutualism.

These strategies—buy, rent, borrow—might sound like a shopping guide. They are not. They are a way of reclaiming agency over the household's relationship with stuff. Stuff is not only expense; it is a claim on attention. Every owned item requires decisions over time: where to store it, how to maintain it, whether to insure it, when to repair it, how to dispose of it. The wealthy can pay to outsource some of these decisions, but outsourcing has limits. Many households are not exhausted because they lack help; they are exhausted because their lives are dense with objects and options, each one demanding tiny slices of thought. Choosing rent or borrow can reduce that density.

There is also an ethical resonance. A culture that defaults to ownership produces overproduction, underuse, and landfill. A culture that normalises access—renting, borrowing, sharing—can reduce material throughput without requiring the household to live joylessly. That matters not as a sermon, but as a practical alignment between values and behaviour. Many affluent readers care about waste in the ecological sense as well as the financial one. This chapter offers a way to act on that care without making life smaller.

Still, the chapter refuses a simplistic moral hierarchy. Owning can be the most sustainable choice if it prevents repeated replacements and encourages repair. Renting can be wasteful if it encourages disposable use without care. Borrowing can be inefficient if it creates constant logistical friction. The point is not to crown a winner. The point is to match strategy to context: frequency, duration, hassle, storage, resale value, and the household's value hierarchy. A household that treats these as variables can make decisions that are both comfortable and precise.

The closing movement gathers the threads into decision rules for big buys, because big buys are where households most often confuse desire with destiny. Cars, major gadgets, high-end hobby equipment, home upgrades: these are the moments when a single decision can thicken the household's baseline for years. The chapter offers a repeatable way of testing such decisions without paralysis and without being seduced by novelty. Not a rigid formula, but a disciplined sequence: how often will it truly be used; what alternatives exist; what costs follow ownership; what is the likely resale reality; what does it do to freedom, generosity, and attention?

The keyring motif returns because it captures the forward tension. Every new possession adds keys. Some keys unlock a richer life. Others merely rattle. The next time the household stands at the threshold of a purchase that feels "reasonable", the question will not be whether it can afford the item. The question will be whether it wants to own another key—or whether access, in some form, would serve just as well, leaving the household lighter, freer, and more able to spend lavishly where it truly matters.

When quality beats quantity

In April 2015, in London, the charity Repair Café London held one of its early public repair sessions, inviting people to bring broken household items to be fixed rather than replaced. The concrete outcome was modest and practical: toasters repaired, lamps rewired, zips replaced, small machines restored to usefulness by patient hands. Yet the deeper outcome was cultural. It reminded people that objects have lives, and that a life can be extended. It also exposed a quiet truth that affluent households often forget because they can afford not to notice: quantity is cheap when quality is absent, but cheapness is not the same as value.

Buy once. Use for years.

That phrase can sound like a slogan until one observes how many households are effectively on subscription plans for mediocre goods. They buy the cheap version, it fails or frustrates, they replace it, and the cycle repeats. The cash outlay looks small each time. The cumulative cost is larger than expected. The hidden cost is worse: time spent shopping, time spent returning, annoyance during use, and the constant low-grade friction of living with things that do not quite work. For time-conscious earners, this is not merely inefficiency. It is attention theft.

The purpose of this section is to draw a line between two kinds of "spending more". One kind is waste: premium pricing paid for status, novelty, or imagined identity. The other kind is precision: paying more upfront to reduce churn, lower total ownership costs, and reclaim time. The line is not determined by taste. It is determined by use.

Use decides the economics.

That sentence is the hinge. An item used frequently and relied upon daily belongs in a different mental category from an item used occasionally or purchased for aspiration. When quality beats quantity, the conditions are usually visible. The item sits in the household's core workflow. It is touched regularly. Failure would be disruptive. A slight improvement in function would be felt repeatedly. In such cases, paying more can lower cost-per-use and reduce hassle. This is not romanticism about craftsmanship. It is arithmetic plus psychology.

Show: a household runs through a weekday morning. Kettle, coffee grinder, toothbrush, laptop, shoes, jacket, keys. These are not "luxury" items; they are the infrastructure of ordinary life. Name: high-frequency infrastructure. Explain: high-frequency infrastructure describes the objects and tools that sit at the centre of routine; their quality affects the household's experience out of proportion to their price because they are used so often. Implication: if a household wants wealth without waste, it should be willing to pay for robustness in its infrastructure, because the return is paid daily—in time saved, irritation avoided, and replacements prevented.

Consider everyday clothing, the category where many affluent households simultaneously overspend and underinvest. They may buy frequent, cheap items because shopping is easy and the choice feels low-stakes. They may also buy premium items because labels feel like identity. The quality-beats-quantity principle cuts between these temptations. A well-made, well-fitting garment worn repeatedly can be economical; a premium garment worn rarely is an expensive ornament; a cheap garment worn twice is a false bargain. Show: a person reaches automatically for the same pair of trousers, the same jumper, the same coat, because they fit and wear well. Name: repeat wear. Explain: repeat wear is a behavioural signal; it reveals what actually earns a place in the wardrobe. Implication: quality spending is best aimed at items with proven repeat wear, not at speculative "maybe I'll wear it" purchases.

This is where cost-per-use returns as a practical lens. The calculation is not intended to dominate taste. It is intended to stop self-deception. A coat worn daily in winter, for several years, often becomes cheaper per wear than a cheaper coat that pills, loses shape, or makes the wearer feel uncomfortable and is replaced quickly. The quality purchase is not justified because it is "nice". It is justified because it reduces churn and increases use.

The same logic applies to core tools. A household's relationship with tools is frequently distorted by a peculiar pride: either the pride of owning every specialist tool, or the pride of doing everything with the cheapest possible kit. Both forms can be wasteful. The quality-beats-quantity principle again asks about frequency and consequence. A drill used often for home maintenance, a set of kitchen knives used daily, a reliable vacuum used weekly—these are candidates for quality because they sit in the household's routine and are asked to perform under regular stress. Show: the cheap vacuum loses suction, the household cleans less, dust accumulates, irritation rises; the vacuum is replaced. Name: friction-induced neglect. Explain: when a tool performs poorly, it reduces willingness to use it; the household then neglects tasks, which produces secondary costs in mess, stress, and later catch-up effort. Implication: in high-frequency tasks, a better tool can change behaviour, not merely outcomes, which makes its value larger than its price difference.

Essential appliances are the most consequential quality category because they combine money, reliability, and disruption. A washing machine, a fridge, a boiler: failure is not an inconvenience but a domestic emergency. A cheaper model can be rational if it is reliable enough and the household has a buffer for repairs or replacement. The problem is not that cheaper appliances exist. The problem is that households often underestimate total ownership costs: repairs, energy use, call-out fees, and the time spent living with breakdowns. Show: the dishwasher fails during a busy week; the household hand-washes for days; irritation spills into unrelated conversations. Name: failure cascade. Explain: a failure cascade is the way a single breakdown creates secondary costs—time lost, stress increased, conflict triggered. Implication: when the disruption cost of failure is high, paying for reliability is not indulgence; it is risk management.

A suitcase example makes the difference vivid because it is both familiar and slightly absurd. Many households have experienced the cheap suitcase that "does the job" until the handle breaks in an airport queue or a wheel snaps on cobblestones. The suitcase fails not at home, where it is a nuisance, but in transit, where it becomes a problem. Show: a traveller drags a lopsided case across a terminal, the sound of a scraping wheel persistent, the hand strained. Name: context-dependent failure. Explain: some items fail in high-friction contexts—travel, weather, crowds—where replacement is difficult and the time cost is high. Implication: for such items, quality can be a form of calm, because it reduces the probability of failure in the worst possible moment.

Now apply cost-per-use and ownership thinking without turning it into theatre. A suitcase used for several trips a year across a decade might be used dozens of times. A robust suitcase that lasts through years of travel can have a low cost per trip and reduces the risk of failure cascades. A cheap suitcase replaced every year is not only a higher long-run cost; it is repeated shopping, repeated disposal, repeated mild dread that it will fail again. The household is effectively renting the annoyance.

This is the heart of quality beating quantity: reducing replacement cycles. Replacement cycles create a hidden cost that busy households feel as fatigue. A product that lasts is not merely a product. It is fewer decisions. Fewer purchases. Fewer returns. Fewer disruptions. Less clutter.

The temptation, however, is to turn "buy once, use for years" into a blanket ideology and end up buying premium versions of everything, whether or not the item is used frequently or whether it is prone to obsolescence. This is where a credible counter-example is necessary. Technology is the clearest case. A household can pay a premium for the best device and still find it outdated in a few years because standards change, software support ends, or needs shift. Show: a household buys a top-tier gadget with long-term intentions and then realises the ecosystem has moved. Name: obsolescence risk. Explain: obsolescence risk is the probability that an item becomes functionally outdated before it wears out physically. Implication: quality spending is most effective in categories where longevity is materially meaningful—durable goods with stable functions—rather than in categories where novelty and compatibility cycles are rapid.

Fashion trends provide another counter-example. Buying a high-quality item that is too trend-driven can be wasteful because social wearability decays before physical wear. A garment may remain intact and still feel unusable because the wearer no longer likes it, or because it no longer fits a changed lifestyle. That does not mean one should avoid style. It means quality should be invested in forms that the household genuinely returns to—timeless shapes, proven favourites—rather than in speculative statement pieces.

The reconciliation is to clarify criteria for when paying more upfront genuinely serves the household. The criteria are not a formal checklist; they are a pattern of reasoning grounded in behaviour and consequence. Frequency is one: the more often an item is used, the more a small quality difference compounds. Consequence of failure is another: if failure creates disruption, quality is a hedge against chaos. Repairability matters: an item that can be repaired extends its life and reduces waste. Comfort and friction matter: if poor performance reduces willingness to use an item, quality can change habits. Ownership burden matters: high-maintenance items can be expensive in attention even if cheap in money.

A named, checkable example from design history sharpens this thinking. In 1988, in New York, Don Norman's *The Design of Everyday Things* brought mainstream attention to the idea that poorly designed objects create user error and frustration, not because users are incompetent but because design is misaligned with human behaviour. The implication for household purchases is direct: a poorly designed "cheap" product can create repeated friction, while a well-designed product can disappear into the background and simply work. Paying for design quality is not vanity; it is sometimes buying back attention.

The motif of the keyring returns from the chapter introduction, because quality reduces the number of keys an item adds. A robust item is a quiet item. It does not demand constant thought. A fragile item adds keys: where to buy a replacement, how to claim a warranty, how to manage a breakdown. The household's goal is not to own fewer things for moral purity. It is to own better things where ownership is truly warranted—things that sit at the centre of life and earn their place through repeated use and low drama.

The forward test is the next purchase where the cheap option and the robust option sit side by side, each plausible, each defensible. The question will not be "which is the bargain?" The question will be whether the household is buying an object or buying a replacement cycle—whether it is choosing a tool that will quietly serve for years, or another item that will soon add a new key to the keyring, jangling with future decisions.

When renting makes sense

In 2010, in London, the city's bicycle hire scheme—now widely known as Santander Cycles—launched with a straightforward promise: you could use a bike when you needed one without owning it, maintaining it, or storing it in a flat hallway. The concrete outcome was visible almost immediately: docking stations became part of the streetscape, and for many residents the phrase "getting a bike" stopped meaning a purchase and started meaning a short-term decision. The scheme did not eliminate private ownership; it offered a parallel. That parallel matters because it reveals a broader truth about modern spending: access can be cheaper, lighter, and more aligned than ownership when the need is intermittent.

Renting is not a failure. It is a strategy.

That sentence has to be said plainly because renting still carries a faint cultural stigma, as if the person who rents is unable to commit, unable to afford, or unable to be "proper". Yet for busy, affluent households aiming for wealth without waste, renting is often the more disciplined choice. Ownership is not merely the right to use an object. It is the obligation to carry it: storage, maintenance, insurance, repairs, upgrades, and eventual disposal. When use is rare or uncertain, those obligations can outweigh the pleasure of ownership. Renting allows the household to pay for *use* while sidestepping the long shadow of owning.

Pay for use. Avoid the burden.

That is the core. The logic is the inverse of "buy once, use for years". When quality beats quantity, ownership makes sense because frequency and longevity justify it. When renting makes sense, frequency is low, timing is narrow, or the object's relevance is short-lived. The household does not want a relationship with the object. It wants a brief, well-defined encounter.

Start with the obvious category: rarely used gear. Show: a household plans a single weekend of carpet cleaning, a one-off furniture move, a short burst of DIY, or a family camping trip. The household can buy equipment, use it once, then store it. Or it can rent. Name: intermittent need. Explain: intermittent need is a requirement that arrives occasionally and predictably fades; it rarely justifies ownership unless the household repeats it often. Implication: if a purchase is driven by intermittent need, the household should treat ownership as a hypothesis, not a default—because the most likely future is that the object will become stored clutter.

Clutter is not merely aesthetic. It is a cost centre. Storage is a kind of rent paid inside one's own home. In city housing especially, space is expensive. An item that takes up space reduces flexibility and increases friction. Show: a hallway cupboard packed with single-use gear; each time the household looks for something it must shift other things; irritation grows. Name: storage tax. Explain: storage tax is the cost of keeping things—space taken, time spent locating, the cognitive drag of managing possessions. Implication: renting can lower the storage tax dramatically, which is a form of wealth without waste because it protects both money and attention.

A family event example makes the case more vivid. Imagine a summer gathering: a milestone birthday, a garden celebration, a large family meal. The household wants good seating, extra tables, perhaps a gazebo, perhaps serving equipment. Buying these items can feel rational because the event feels significant and because buying is straightforward. Yet ownership after the event is awkward. Where do folding chairs live? How are they kept clean? Do they become a persistent reminder of storage constraints? Renting, by contrast, turns the event into a temporary configuration: bring in what is needed, then return it. Show: the garden is arranged for one evening; the next day it returns to normal without a garage full of equipment. Name: temporary configuration. Explain: temporary configuration is the deliberate adaptation of space and resources for a short period; renting matches this temporariness by preventing long-term accumulation. Implication: renting allows households to be generous hosts without becoming permanent custodians of event infrastructure.

Renting also shines in the category of occasional luxury. Some households buy high-end items not because they will use them often, but because they want access to a particular experience: a better camera for a once-a-year trip, a high-spec car for a special occasion, a designer outfit for a formal event, specialist sports equipment for a holiday. The desire is not foolish. The mistake is to confuse the desire for an experience with the desire to own. Show: the household wants the *quality* of the moment—the photos, the comfort, the confidence—not a long-term obligation. Name: experience-driven demand. Explain: experience-driven demand is when the object is a means to a specific moment rather than a long-term utility. Implication: renting can deliver the moment at a fraction of the long-run cost and without the post-moment burden of storage and maintenance.

A third category is temporary needs: items required for a season of life, not a lifetime. Baby equipment is an obvious example, though borrowing and secondhand often compete strongly here. Home renovation tools and equipment are another: needed intensely for a month, then not at all. An injury, a relocation, a temporary work arrangement—each can generate short-term needs that fade. Show: a household buys a specialised item "just in case" and then never uses it again. Name: just-in-case accumulation. Explain: just-in-case accumulation is the habit of buying for imagined scenarios; it creates clutter and ties up money in dormant inventory. Implication: renting can satisfy legitimate short-term needs without turning the home into a museum of past contingencies.

The risk of rapid obsolescence is another major reason renting makes sense, particularly with certain technologies and specialist gear. A household can buy the best version today and still find it outdated sooner than expected because standards shift, software support changes, or preferences evolve. Show: a high-end gadget is bought with long-term intentions and then becomes awkward as ecosystems update. Name: obsolescence risk. Explain: obsolescence risk is the probability that an item becomes functionally outdated before it wears out physically. Implication: where obsolescence risk is high, renting can be a rational hedge, because it allows access without betting on longevity.

A named, checkable example of a market built around access helps ground this. In 1999, Zipcar was founded in Cambridge, Massachusetts, popularising a membership-based model for car access that would later spread internationally. The details of corporate history are less important than the concept: pay for a vehicle when you need it, avoid ownership's fixed costs when you do not. The implication for households is that renting can convert fixed costs into variable costs. Variable costs are easier to control. Fixed costs accumulate silently and constrain flexibility.

Flexibility is the true benefit of renting, and it is often misunderstood. People fixate on whether renting is "wasted money" because they do not end up with an asset. That logic is incomplete because ownership is not free after purchase. Ownership can be the more expensive option once maintenance, storage, repairs, and the opportunity cost of tied-up cash are considered. Renting is not throwing money away; it is purchasing flexibility and avoiding obligations.

Yet renting is not automatically superior. It has its own ownership-like costs: booking, pickup, return deadlines, deposits, and the risk that the rented item will not be available when needed. Show: a household leaves planning late, and the item is booked out; stress rises. Name: coordination cost. Explain: coordination cost is the time and attention required to arrange temporary access; it can be trivial or significant depending on the household's habits and the item's availability. Implication: renting works best when the household can plan modestly ahead or when the rental market is reliable; otherwise, renting can create its own friction.

This is why the best approach treats renting as part of household design rather than as an isolated tactic. A household that already struggles with planning may find renting frustrating for certain categories, and in those cases ownership or borrowing may be more humane. Conversely, a household that is drowning in clutter may find renting liberating because it reduces the storage tax and the mental load of possessions. The goal is alignment, not ideology.

A credible counter-example deserves respect: for high-frequency items, renting can become expensive and inconvenient. If a household camps monthly, renting gear repeatedly might cost more than owning and maintaining a robust set. If a household regularly hosts large gatherings, owning certain event items could be sensible. If a tool is used every week, renting it repeatedly becomes a logistical nuisance. Name: frequency crossover. Explain: frequency crossover is the point at which repeated rental costs and coordination costs exceed the total cost of ownership. Implication: the household needs to recognise when use has become stable enough that ownership becomes the better strategy, so renting does not become a disguised subscription.

The reconciliation is to treat renting as a test as well as a service. Renting can validate whether a desire is real. A household can rent a piece of hobby gear for a month and discover whether it fits into life. It can rent a premium camera and see whether photography becomes a habit or remains a holiday fantasy. It can rent tools and learn whether DIY becomes part of the household's identity. This transforms renting from "not committing" into committing intelligently. A brief rental can prevent an expensive mispurchase.

The motif here is the keyring introduced in the chapter opening. Owning adds keys. Renting lends keys and then takes them back. That matters because keys are not free. They are mental objects: things to keep track of, things that rattle. Renting is a way of borrowing capability without adding permanent keys to the household's life.

The forward test is the next purchase justified by a specific moment: a trip, an event, a short-term project, a burst of ambition. The question will not be whether the household can afford to buy. Many can. The question will be whether it wants to *own*—to store, maintain, and manage—or whether it simply wants access for long enough to serve the moment and then return to a lighter baseline, with fewer keys and fewer drips of money and attention.

Borrowing and sharing options

In 1850, in Manchester, the city opened what is widely regarded as the first free public reference library in Britain, a practical expression of a radical premise: knowledge could be shared at scale without each person needing to own a private collection. The concrete outcome was immediate and tangible—reading rooms, catalogues, borrowed books—and the deeper outcome was civic. The library became an answer to a question that still matters for household spending: what if access, not ownership, were the default for many things we use?

Borrowing is civilisation.

That line is not sentimental. It is literal. Libraries, by design, are collective ownership systems that reduce duplication, increase access, and turn private spending into public infrastructure. They also provide a useful metaphor for households who feel financially "leaky" despite affluence. Many leaks are not about extravagance; they are about unnecessary duplication. Ten households on one street each buying a pressure washer is not a triumph of prosperity. It is a triumph of market logic over community logic. Borrowing and sharing are ways of reclaiming the older, quieter logic: if something is used occasionally, it can be shared without reducing anyone's comfort.

For affluent households, the barrier is rarely practical capacity. It is social discomfort. People fear awkwardness. They fear obligation. They fear being seen as stingy. They fear the small risk that something will be damaged, and the larger risk that a relationship will be strained. These fears are rational in the way all social fears are rational: relationships are precious, and money can make people weird. The point of this section is not to shame those fears away, but to show that borrowing and sharing can be designed with the same precision as cashflow. It is not "be communal". It is "build systems of access that respect dignity and reciprocity".

The motif here is the spare key. Ownership gives a household its own keys. Borrowing is asking for a spare key to a capability—briefly, respectfully, and with a plan to return it. The power of the spare key is that it unlocks use without adding permanent clutter, permanent maintenance, or permanent spending. The anxiety is that asking for a spare key feels intimate. It feels like admitting need. Yet the paradox of modern affluence is that many people have plenty of money and still feel constrained because their lives are crowded with objects. Borrowing reduces that crowding. It is a way of having access while owning less.

Start with formal sharing, because it reduces social friction and makes the principle obvious. Libraries remain the gold standard: books, e-books, audiobooks, magazines, sometimes even tools and instruments. A library transaction is structured. It has rules. It is reciprocal without being personal. Show: a person borrows a book and returns it; nobody owes anyone gratitude; the system holds the relationship. Name: institutional reciprocity. Explain: institutional reciprocity is a form of sharing where the norms are encoded into the institution—loan periods, fines, returns—reducing the social risk for individuals. Implication: for households nervous about awkwardness, institutional sharing is an easy gateway into access-based living, because it offers the benefits of borrowing without the interpersonal negotiation.

Tool libraries and "libraries of things" extend this model to physical goods. They are often local, sometimes municipal, sometimes run by community groups. They exist because the economics are simple: many tools are used rarely, and ownership is wasteful. A drill might be used for ten minutes every six months. A ladder might be used twice a year. A carpet cleaner might be used once after a spill, and then sit in a cupboard as a memorial to an unpleasant afternoon. Tool libraries convert these rare needs into shared access. They also normalise the idea that not owning is not deprivation; it is rational design.

Informal sharing—neighbours, friends, family—is where the richest potential lies and where most households hesitate. The hesitation often disguises a deeper cultural story: adulthood is imagined as self-sufficiency. A "proper" household is the household that can handle everything internally. Borrowing punctures that fantasy. It reveals interdependence, which is both true and, for many people, emotionally difficult.

Yet interdependence is not weakness. It is resilience.

This is not merely philosophy. It is practical. In neighbourhoods where people know each other even lightly, sharing reduces costs and increases capacity. A borrowed tool is not only money saved; it is time saved, storage avoided, and an opportunity for micro-connection. The connection matters because it changes the social environment in which the household lives. A street where people can ask for a ladder is a street where people can also ask for help when something more serious occurs. In that sense, borrowing is not merely a financial tactic. It is a tiny investment in social capital.

Social capital can sound abstract, so attach it to a visible behaviour. Show: two neighbours exchange small favours—borrowing a ladder, accepting a parcel, watering plants during a holiday. Name: reciprocal micro-trust. Explain: reciprocal micro-trust is built through low-stakes exchanges that demonstrate reliability; it is trust made tangible through repeated small acts. Implication: borrowing and sharing are not only about using things without owning them; they are about building a local environment where help is normal and shame is less necessary.

A named, checkable example from social science underlines that this is not merely anecdotal. In 1993, Robert Putnam published "The Prosperous Community: Social Capital and Public Life", arguing that networks of civic engagement and trust have measurable consequences for communities. Whatever one thinks of later debates around his work, the underlying point is widely accepted: trust and reciprocity reduce transaction costs. When people trust each other, they do not need to solve every problem with money. They can solve some problems with cooperation. The household analogue is simple: where reciprocal micro-trust exists, not every occasional need becomes a purchase.

Now address the awkwardness directly, because it is the most common reason households default back to buying. Awkwardness usually comes from uncertainty about norms. People do not know how to ask without sounding presumptuous, how to accept without feeling indebted, or how to return without fuss. These are not financial questions; they are etiquette questions. The good news is that etiquette can be designed as a system just like any other, and the system can be simple.

The first principle is clarity. Vague requests create stress. Clear requests reduce it. Show: a person asks, "Could I borrow your drill sometime?" and then both parties feel uncertain about when and how long. Name: ambiguity cost. Explain: ambiguity cost is the friction created by unclear expectations; it increases the perceived burden of lending and borrowing. Implication: borrowing works best when the request is specific—what item, what for, how long, and when it will be returned—because specificity reduces emotional load.

The second principle is care. Many people fear lending because they fear damage. That fear is not irrational. Tools break. People are careless. Yet most damage anxiety is reduced by visible respect: returning items clean, on time, and with thanks. These signals matter because they reassure the lender that their generosity will not be punished. Show: a borrowed tool is returned promptly, wiped down, with a small note or verbal thanks. Name: maintenance signalling. Explain: maintenance signalling is the visible demonstration that the borrower respects the item and the relationship; it lowers the lender's perceived risk. Implication: borrowing becomes easier when households treat return as part of the transaction, not as an afterthought.

The third principle is reciprocity without accounting. The quickest way to poison sharing is to turn it into a ledger. People do not want to feel like they are entering a contract every time they lend a ladder. Yet reciprocity matters. The solution is to think in terms of balance over time, not exact repayment. Show: one person lends tools; another later offers help with carrying something heavy; no one keeps score, but both feel the relationship is fair. Name: loose reciprocity. Explain: loose reciprocity is the social norm that favours will be returned in some form over time, without requiring a precise equivalence. Implication: sharing becomes sustainable when households contribute in the ways they can—time, skills, hospitality, attention—rather than trying to match every borrowed item with a borrowed item.

Workplace resources are a further, often overlooked, category. Many organisations have equipment, software, and facilities that employees can use within policy: meeting spaces, printers, training subscriptions, sometimes tools or vehicles for specific roles. Students and researchers often have access to libraries, labs, and equipment pools. The household that uses legitimate workplace and institutional resources reduces duplication. This is not about exploiting anything. It is about noticing that access already exists in the environment, and that buying duplicates can be wasteful.

A shared DIY tools example brings the ideas into focus. Imagine a small cluster of neighbours in a suburban street who each occasionally need tools for minor home maintenance: a drill, a jigsaw, a ladder, a hedge trimmer. Individually, each purchase looks reasonable. Collectively, it is redundant. One neighbour already owns a decent drill. Another has a ladder. Another has a pressure washer bought for one project. Show: they create an informal sharing system—nothing formal, just a shared understanding that tools can be borrowed with clear expectations and returned promptly. Name: neighbourhood commons. Explain: a neighbourhood commons is a small, informal pool of shared resources governed by trust and basic etiquette; it reduces duplication and increases capacity. Implication: each household spends less, stores less, and still has access to the tools when needed; the street becomes slightly more connected, which has value beyond the tools themselves.

The potential objections must be treated honestly. Some people have had bad experiences: items returned damaged, requests ignored, relationships made tense. Those risks are real. A credible limitation of borrowing is that it relies on trust and shared norms; without those, it can be stressful. Name: trust threshold. Explain: trust threshold is the minimum level of confidence required for sharing to feel safe; below that threshold, borrowing can cost more in anxiety than it saves in money. Implication: not every context supports informal sharing, and households should not force it in ways that damage relationships or peace of mind.

The reconciliation is to expand the spectrum of options rather than insisting on one form. If informal borrowing feels risky, institutional options—libraries, tool libraries, rental services—can provide access with fewer social costs. If informal borrowing is possible with a few trusted people, it can be limited to those relationships. If workplace resources exist, they can be used within boundaries. The goal is not to become a communal idealist. The goal is to widen the household's sense of what it can use without owning.

The spare key motif returns because it captures the true benefit: borrowing unlocks capability without adding permanent keys to the household's life. Each owned item adds responsibility. Each borrowed item adds only a temporary obligation, and that obligation can be designed to be light and dignified. For affluent households, this can feel countercultural precisely because money makes buying easier than asking. Yet asking can be the wiser act. It reduces clutter. It reduces waste. It strengthens the invisible infrastructure of community.

The forward test arrives at the moment of minor need that tempts a purchase. The household is about to buy a tool for one job, a piece of equipment for one weekend, a thing that will probably sit unused. The question is whether it will default to ownership, adding another key to the keyring, or whether it will reach for a spare key—through a library, a tool library, a neighbour, or a workplace resource—accepting a little social or logistical effort in exchange for a lighter home and a more intentional relationship with stuff.

Decision rules for big buys

In September 2015, in the United States, the Environmental Protection Agency issued a notice of violation to Volkswagen after discovering that certain diesel vehicles had been fitted with software designed to cheat emissions tests; the scandal became public and triggered recalls, fines, and a profound reputational collapse. The concrete outcome was legal and financial turmoil. The household outcome was quieter but instructive: many owners discovered that a "rational" purchase—sold as efficient, clean, and superior—could carry hidden risks that did not appear in showroom comparisons. Big buys are rarely just about price. They are about uncertainty.

Big buys cast long shadows.

A major purchase is not a transaction; it is a small future. It reshapes cashflow, habits, storage, maintenance, and attention. It alters what feels "normal". It creates a new baseline that may endure for years. This is why big buys are the most dangerous place for impulsive upgrading, and also the most rewarding place for disciplined clarity. If a household makes a poor decision on a takeaway app, it loses an evening's margin. If it makes a poor decision on a car, a major gadget ecosystem, or a home upgrade, it can lose years of flexibility.

The earlier sections of this chapter have already dismantled the idea that ownership is the default. Quality sometimes beats quantity; renting sometimes beats buying; borrowing sometimes beats both. What remains is the uncomfortable moment when a household is standing at the threshold of something significant and feels two contradictory truths at once: it can afford the purchase, and it is not sure it should make it. The goal here is to create a repeatable way of thinking—simple enough to use in real life, strong enough to resist marketing, and humane enough not to turn every choice into a spreadsheet.

Decide like an adult. Under pressure.

That sentence sounds stern because the pressure is real. Big buys arrive with noise: launch events, reviews, friends' opinions, dealer incentives, the seduction of a "limited time" offer, the subtle anxiety of falling behind. Noise compresses time. Compressed time produces bad choices. The decision rules in this section are not tricks. They are ways of restoring time inside the decision, so the household can see the long shadow before stepping into it.

A decision rule begins with a visible behaviour rather than with a value word. "Freedom" is not directly measurable. But the percentage of cashflow tied up in fixed commitments is. "Efficiency" is not directly measurable. But the number of hours spent researching, maintaining, and managing an asset is. "Risk" is not directly measurable. But the probability and cost of failure, and the consequences of disruption, can be approximated. When decision rules are anchored to behaviours and metrics, they become harder to hijack with feelings.

Show: a household considers changing a car. The current car is adequate. It is not glamorous. It occasionally irritates. Friends are upgrading. The household's income supports a nicer vehicle. The decision feels like it is about comfort and status, but it is also about timing, cashflow, and future obligations. Name: baseline temptation. Explain: baseline temptation is the pull to raise fixed living standards because it feels like progress, even when the existing baseline already meets needs. Implication: without a disciplined decision process, the household can drift into higher recurring costs that crowd out freedom and generosity, all while feeling like it made a reasonable adult upgrade.

The first rule is frequency, because frequency turns a purchase from a moment into a habit. How often will the asset be used, and under what conditions? Frequency is not a guess about the future self; it is an observation about the current self. If a household drives daily, a car is high-frequency infrastructure. If it drives weekly, ownership has a different character. If it uses a premium gadget feature rarely, it is paying for imagined use. Frequency interacts with cost-per-use, but the key point is behavioural: repeated use amplifies both benefits and annoyances. It makes quality matter. It also makes long shadows darker.

The second rule is alternatives, because big buys often masquerade as binary choices: buy or do without. In reality, alternatives are usually multiple and varied: repair rather than replace, rent rather than buy, borrow rather than rent, downgrade rather than upgrade, delay rather than decide now. Alternatives are not "compromises" if they fit the household's values. They are options. Show: a household wants a larger car "for holidays" and "for convenience", yet it could rent a larger vehicle for trips, use roof storage occasionally, or adjust packing habits. Name: false binary. Explain: a false binary is the perception that only two choices exist, which makes the expensive choice feel inevitable. Implication: naming alternatives restores agency and often reveals that the desired benefit can be purchased in a smaller, more precise way.

The third rule is total ownership cost, because big buys are frequently assessed by headline price and monthly payment rather than by full life cost: maintenance, insurance, energy or fuel, accessories, storage, taxes, repairs, depreciation, and the opportunity cost of tied-up cash. The aim is not to perform exhaustive accounting. It is to avoid being seduced by a single number. Households with high incomes are especially vulnerable here because they can "afford" monthly payments that quietly thicken the baseline. Thick baselines are the enemy of flexibility.

The fourth rule is hassle, because time is wealth. The household should ask what an asset will *demand* of it: time spent arranging maintenance, time spent researching fixes, time spent learning a new system, time spent managing subscriptions and compatibility. Hassle is not just inconvenience. It is attention, and attention is the scarce resource for busy earners. A high-hassle asset can be a form of waste even if it is a good deal financially.

The fifth rule is resale reality, because many people justify upgrades by imagining high resale values that may not materialise. Resale depends on market conditions, condition of the item, demand shifts, and sometimes regulatory or technological shocks. The Volkswagen case is a dramatic illustration: factors outside a household's control can affect the value and usability of an asset. Even without scandal, resale can be lower than hoped. The correct posture is not cynicism but realism: treat resale as a possible offset, not as a guarantee.

The sixth rule is alignment with values, which sounds abstract until it is made concrete. Alignment means this: will the purchase make it easier to live according to what the household says it values, or will it mainly serve status, novelty, and avoidance? A purchase aligned with values often has visible downstream effects: it reduces conflict, supports healthful routines, creates space for relationships, enables generosity, reduces stress, or saves time that the household actually uses well. A purchase misaligned with values often has different effects: it raises baseline spending, increases comparison, adds clutter, creates maintenance burden, and encourages more upgrading.

The seventh rule is reversibility, because not all decisions have the same lock-in. Some purchases can be reversed with minimal loss: renting a device, buying secondhand and reselling, choosing a month-to-month service rather than a long contract. Others are sticky: long finance agreements, structural home changes, purchases that require ecosystem commitments. Reversibility is a form of risk management. The more uncertain the benefit, the more reversibility matters.

Now apply these rules to a step-by-step example without turning it into a mechanical ritual. Consider a household contemplating a car change. The car is safe and functional. It is also older. The household feels the pull of something newer: more comfort, more technology, perhaps an image upgrade. The decision begins with frequency: how often does the household drive, and for what? If daily commutes are involved, comfort and reliability will be felt repeatedly. If most journeys are short and occasional, the car is less central than the household may assume. This observation alone can deflate marketing narratives about "needing" a premium upgrade.

Next, alternatives: what problem is the upgrade meant to solve? If the problem is reliability anxiety, could maintenance or targeted repairs reduce the worry? If the problem is occasional space needs, could short-term rental solve that precisely? If the problem is comfort on long trips, could adjustments—better tyres, seat supports, sound dampening—achieve much of the benefit? This is not penny-pinching. It is precision. It prevents the household from buying a whole new baseline to solve a narrow pain point.

Then total ownership cost: the household estimates, in broad strokes, what the new car would add to recurring commitments—insurance changes, fuel or charging costs, maintenance, and any financing structure. The household also considers the disruption cost of the current car failing, which is a real risk. The point is not to predict the future. It is to see the shape of the trade-off: higher predictable monthly costs versus the risk of occasional repair costs and disruption. This re-frames "upgrade" as a choice between different kinds of uncertainty.

Hassle enters next. A newer car may reduce certain hassles but add others: more complex technology, more expensive repairs, more reliance on authorised service networks. A simpler car can be more repairable. A complex one can be more comfortable and less forgiving. Hassle is not a trivial factor; it affects how much time the household spends managing life. Time spent on car logistics is time not spent on relationships, rest, or meaningful work.

Resale reality: the household treats resale as uncertain. It does not plan its finances around optimistic assumptions. It asks what it can reasonably recover, and it remembers that market conditions can shift. It also remembers that a car is not an investment; it is a tool with depreciation, and the household's task is to choose how it wants to pay for mobility.

Alignment with values then provides the decisive question. Does this change support the household's priorities—safety, calm, time, the ability to travel together, freedom from recurring stress? Or is it mostly about image and novelty? This is where self-honesty matters. Image is not evil. But a household that values freedom and generosity should be wary of upgrades whose primary output is social signalling, because signalling tends to demand more signalling. It is rarely satisfied.

Finally, reversibility. Can the household test its desire? Could it rent the target model for a weekend, not for thrill but for realism—parking it, living with its interface, seeing whether it genuinely changes experience? Could it delay for a month and see whether the urge persists? Could it choose a less locking-in path? Reversibility is the antidote to impulse because it restores choice over time.

This process works just as well for a major gadget purchase, where the risks are different but the psychology is similar. Gadgets often promise efficiency, creativity, and "staying current". They can deliver those benefits. They can also become expensive ornaments, purchased for identity rather than use. Frequency becomes: will the feature set be used weekly, or will the household keep using the same basic functions? Alternatives become: can the current device be repaired, upgraded, or used longer? Total ownership cost becomes: subscriptions, accessories, replacement cycles. Hassle becomes: learning curves, compatibility problems, the ongoing cognitive load of keeping systems running. Resale reality becomes: rapid depreciation. Values alignment becomes: does the device meaningfully support the household's work and relationships, or is it mainly novelty? Reversibility becomes: can the household trial, rent, or buy secondhand?

A credible limitation must be acknowledged: no decision rule can remove uncertainty, and some big buys are forced by circumstance—an unsafe car, a broken appliance, a job change, a relocation. Under pressure, even good systems can feel inadequate. Name: forced timing. Explain: forced timing is when a decision must be made quickly because the old asset has failed or circumstances have changed; it reduces the household's ability to test and compare. Implication: the rules still help, but they must be applied with compassion and pragmatism; precision under pressure is about avoiding obvious mistakes, not achieving perfection.

The reconciliation is to treat these rules as a steering wheel, not a cage. They are intended to prevent the two most common failure modes in affluent spending: impulsive upgrading driven by noise, and paralysed overthinking driven by fear. A steering wheel does not guarantee a perfect journey. It keeps the car from drifting into a ditch.

The motif of the keyring returns because big buys add the biggest keys. A new car adds literal keys and metaphorical ones: insurance, maintenance, new habits, new expectations. A major gadget adds keys: ecosystems, subscriptions, replacement cycles. The household does not only buy an object. It buys a set of obligations and a new baseline. The question, each time, is whether the key unlocks something the household truly wants—time, calm, capability, connection—or whether it merely adds a heavier ring, jingling with commitments that will later be experienced as constraint.

The forward test is the next alluring upgrade that arrives with a plausible story. The story will sound reasonable. It usually does. The household will feel that it *could* buy. The rules are not there to say no. They are there to force the harder, more adult question: given how this household actually lives, what will this purchase *do* over the next few years—how often will it be used, what alternatives exist, what burdens will it add, how reversible is the decision, and what does it cost in freedom and generosity to take the key?

Chapter 7
Repair Replace And Secondhand

In April 2015, in London, a small crowd gathered around a table at a Repair Café session while a volunteer coaxed an old kettle back into life, the air carrying that faint, metallic warmth of heated dust and circuitry. The concrete outcome was modest: a working appliance and one less trip to the bin. Yet the scene contained a larger argument about modern affluence. When replacement is easy and time is scarce, households begin to treat breakage as a cue to buy again. Repair becomes eccentric. Secondhand becomes suspect. Waste becomes ordinary.

There is a word for this: amnesia.

Not financial amnesia—most readers know exactly what their income is. Material amnesia: forgetting that objects have histories, that maintenance is a skill, that value can be preserved rather than repeatedly purchased. The market prefers amnesia. It turns each broken thing into a new sale. It also turns each new sale into a future problem: more packaging, more clutter, more disposal, more quiet guilt. For households seeking wealth without waste, this chapter is where the philosophy becomes tactile. It is about what happens when something fails, and how a household decides whether to restore, replace, or re-source.

The question is not sentimental. It is practical. Every object in a home is a small claim on cashflow and attention. When that object breaks, the household faces a fork: it can spend money to keep it alive, spend money to replace it, or spend less money to acquire its function through secondhand channels. Each option has costs beyond price. Repair can consume time, introduce uncertainty, and require patience. Replacement can be efficient but can also be wasteful when the old item still has life in it—or when the new item is worse. Secondhand can be brilliantly economical and environmentally sane, but it can also produce clutter if buying becomes a hobby and "bargains" accumulate unused.

The motif that threads this chapter is the seam. A seam is where things are joined: fabric stitched, components fitted, habits held together. When a seam gives way, the household discovers what it truly believes about value. Does it treat the seam as disposable, or as something to be reinforced? Repair is the act of respecting seams. Replacement is the act of admitting a seam was never worth reinforcing. Secondhand is the act of recognising that someone else's seams may still be strong.

The chapter begins with assessing repair viability, because repair is often misunderstood in two opposing ways. Some people replace too quickly, not because they are careless but because they are busy and the friction of repair feels intolerable. Others repair too stubbornly, pouring time and money into items that were never built to last, driven by a moral instinct to "not waste" that becomes its own kind of waste. The skill is discernment. The chapter treats repair not as virtue but as evaluation: remaining lifespan, repair cost, inconvenience, availability of parts, and that quietly powerful factor—emotional attachment. A well-made pair of shoes can justify new soles because the underlying structure is sound. A flimsy appliance that fails repeatedly is asking to be released.

From there, the chapter moves to the point where replacement becomes wise, because "replace" is not always a failure of character. Sometimes it is simply the least wasteful option. An ageing boiler, an unsafe car, a device whose efficiency has collapsed: keeping these alive can generate cascading costs—repairs, disruption, anxiety, and the constant tax of uncertainty. Timely replacement can be a form of foresight, especially when it prevents bigger waste later. The important thing is to replace deliberately rather than reflexively, and to recognise that the cheapest replacement is often the most expensive over time.

Then the chapter opens a door that many affluent households never properly walk through: smart secondhand strategies. Secondhand is often framed as a necessity for those with limited income. In fact, secondhand is often a form of arbitrage for those with judgement. It allows households to access higher-quality goods—solid wood furniture, well-made coats, robust tools, refurbished electronics—at prices that make the cost-per-use exceptional. It also reduces the ecological waste of constant new production. But secondhand is not automatically wise. The market is full of false bargains: items cheap because they are near the end of life, incomplete, or incompatible. This chapter treats secondhand as a craft: where to look, what to inspect, how to evaluate risk without becoming paranoid, and how to buy used without turning the home into a staging area for other people's discards.

Finally, the chapter confronts an irony that intelligent readers will recognise: frugality can create clutter. The person who prides themselves on bargain-hunting can end up with cupboards full of "useful" items that are never used. The home becomes heavy with postponed intentions. Waste shifts shape: not money thrown away, but space and attention consumed by things that do not earn their keep. Avoiding clutter and regret requires outflow discipline—reselling, donating, recycling—and, more importantly, limits. Not moral limits. Physical limits: storage boundaries that prevent the household from turning secondhand into accumulation.

Modern relevance sharpens all of this. Supply chain shocks, repairability debates, and rising awareness of e-waste have made the repair-versus-replace decision more consequential than it seemed a decade ago. At the same time, digital marketplaces have made secondhand easier and faster, turning what used to be a weekend rummage into a few taps. Convenience, once again, cuts both ways. It can make secondhand access efficient. It can also make secondhand hoarding effortless. The household is operating in an environment where acquiring objects is easier than ever and disposing of them responsibly is often harder. That imbalance is where waste breeds.

Still, this chapter does not romanticise repair as a universal answer. Some things are designed to be repaired; others are designed to be replaced. Some repairs are efficient; others are time sinks. Some secondhand purchases are brilliant; others are clutter disguised as thrift. The chapter's purpose is to give readers a coherent way of thinking—rooted in the earlier lenses of cost-per-use, total ownership costs, and value alignment—so that each decision becomes more deliberate. A household does not need to become a workshop. It needs to become an adult steward of its possessions.

The seam motif returns because it points to what is really at stake. A life designed for freedom and generosity depends on margin: margin in cashflow, margin in time, margin in attention. Replacing everything at the first sign of inconvenience erodes margin through constant spending. Repairing everything out of principle erodes margin through constant effort. Buying secondhand without restraint erodes margin through clutter. The right choices preserve margin by matching the response to the object's reality.

The page turns on a question that cannot be answered by ideology. The household stands over a broken thing and feels the familiar pull towards the quickest solution. The question is whether it will strengthen a seam, cut it cleanly, or borrow a seam already stitched by someone else—repair, replace, or secondhand—not to appear virtuous, but to keep its home and its finances aligned with the kind of life it is trying to live.

Assessing repair viability

In March 2021, in Brussels, the European Commission adopted proposals under the Circular Economy Action Plan that aimed to make products more durable, repairable, and easier to maintain, part of a broader push towards a "right to repair" culture. The concrete outcome was legislative momentum: requirements and standards that would, over time, shape what manufacturers must disclose and how long parts should remain available. The household outcome is more immediate and more intimate. A kettle fails. A zip breaks. A phone battery weakens. The question arrives with irritating punctuality: is this worth fixing, or is it time to let it go?

Repair begins as judgement, not virtue.

Many people talk about repair as if it were automatically "good" and replacement as if it were automatically "bad". That binary is emotionally satisfying and practically wrong. A repair can be wasteful if it prolongs a poor object that will fail again soon. A replacement can be the least wasteful move if it prevents repeated breakdowns, safety risks, and the slow drain of inconvenience. The craft lies in assessing viability—remaining lifespan, repair cost, inconvenience, and that troublesome but real factor: emotional attachment. Without a method, busy households default to the quickest option, which is often replacement. Without a counterweight, conscientious households sometimes default to repair even when the numbers and reality do not support it.

Fixing is not free.

Even when repair costs less than replacement, it can still be expensive in time, attention, and uncertainty. A repair might require diagnosis, sourcing parts, booking a technician, or travelling to a repair shop. It might require living without the item while it is being fixed. It might require repeated attempts. These costs are often invisible when people frame repair as "cheap" and replacement as "expensive". The truth is more nuanced. Repair trades money for time and uncertainty. Replacement trades money for speed and predictability. The household's task is to decide which trade is worth making *for this item, in this season of life.*

A five-word sentence helps. Repair is a hypothesis, always.

That is the right posture. A repair is a bet that the object has enough useful life left to justify the effort, and that the repair will restore function reliably. Some objects are excellent bets. Some are terrible bets. The household needs ways to tell the difference.

Start with remaining lifespan, because it is the foundation of viability. Show: a pair of quality leather shoes has worn soles but intact uppers; the stitching is sound; the fit is perfect. Name: intact structure. Explain: intact structure means the core body of the object remains robust; the failing part is replaceable and expected to wear. Implication: repair is sensible because it restores a durable item to usefulness; the repair extends a life that was built to be extended.

Now compare that with a flimsy appliance, perhaps a cheap toaster or an off-brand blender, that has begun to fail after a short period. The plastic housing flexes. The buttons stick. The motor smells hot. Show: the appliance works intermittently, then fails again after a minor fix. Name: degraded core. Explain: degraded core means the failure is not confined to a replaceable part; the underlying build quality is poor, and the object is entering a phase of repeated faults. Implication: repair may be a false economy because the repair does not restore a durable structure; it merely postpones the next failure.

This contrast is the key: some objects are designed with wear points; others are built as sealed units. Shoes have soles for a reason. A well-made coat has linings, seams, and buttons that can be mended. A good tool has parts that can be replaced. Many modern appliances, by contrast, are built to be cheap to manufacture and awkward to repair, with glued housings and proprietary parts. The household's question is not "do I believe in repair?" It is "what kind of object is this?"

The next factor is repair cost, which must be considered as a ratio rather than as an absolute number. A £40 repair on a £250 pair of shoes that can then be worn for years has a different meaning from a £40 repair on a £60 appliance likely to fail again. Show: a cobbler quotes for resoling; the cost is meaningful but proportionate. Name: repair-to-replacement ratio. Explain: the repair-to-replacement ratio compares the repair cost to the cost of a comparable replacement; it helps prevent paying heavily to prolong an object that was never robust. Implication: when the ratio is low and the structure is intact, repair is often sensible; when the ratio is high and the core is degraded, replacement may be the less wasteful move.

Cost alone is not enough, because inconvenience often decides what a household actually does. Inconvenience is not laziness; it is a real constraint in busy lives. A repair may require several hours of coordination and travel. It may require living without the item for days. It may require repeated follow-ups. Show: the household tries to repair a small appliance, spends an evening searching forums, orders a part that arrives late, then discovers it is incompatible. Name: coordination drag. Explain: coordination drag is the cumulative time and attention required to execute a repair, including diagnosis, sourcing, and logistics. Implication: even a financially cheap repair can be costly in life-hours, and those hours have opportunity costs—work, rest, relationships.

This is where households need to be honest about seasonality. A household with a new baby, a demanding job, or caring responsibilities may rationally choose replacement for certain items because the coordination drag of repair is too high. That choice is not moral failure; it is triage. Conversely, a household with more time or with access to a local repair ecosystem may find repair far easier, and in that context replacement becomes the lazier and more wasteful choice. Repairability is not merely about the object. It is about the household's environment.

Environment includes the availability of parts and skilled labour. The "right to repair" movement has gained traction partly because consumers have experienced the frustration of being unable to obtain parts or manuals. In 2020, the UK government consulted on and then moved towards ecodesign requirements that include repairability for certain appliances, aligning with earlier EU ecodesign regulations. The specifics vary by product category, but the direction is clear: repair is becoming a policy issue because markets often underprovide it. The household implication is that repair viability is partly structural. Some items are repairable because ecosystems exist. Others are effectively disposable because ecosystems have been dismantled.

Risk is another factor that must be paired with a visible behaviour or decision. Some repairs carry safety risks if done poorly—electrical, gas-related, structural. This is not an argument against repair; it is an argument for recognising limits. Show: an appliance with a frayed cable; a household considers a quick fix. Name: safety threshold. Explain: safety threshold is the point at which the potential cost of failure outweighs the benefits of a cheap fix; it demands caution and, often, professional expertise. Implication: repair viability is not purely economic; it includes the risk profile of failure.

Now to the most human factor: emotional attachment. It is easy to mock attachment as irrational. It is not. Objects carry memory, identity, and comfort. A coat inherited from a parent, a watch received on a milestone birthday, a piece of furniture linked to a first home: these objects are not interchangeable. Show: a person hesitates before discarding an item, not because it is "worth" much, but because it holds a story. Name: narrative value. Explain:

narrative value is the non-monetary worth an object holds through memory and meaning; it can legitimately justify repair beyond strict financial logic. Implication: a household can choose repair for reasons other than efficiency, and that choice can be aligned with values—especially when the repair sustains continuity and gratitude rather than mere consumption.

Narrative value, however, can also become a trap when it merges with guilt. People sometimes repair not because they love the object, but because they feel morally compelled to avoid waste. That moral impulse is understandable, yet it can lead to stubborn over-repairing: repeated fixes to low-quality items, time and money sunk into objects that remain frustrating, and a household held hostage by its own principle. Show: the household fixes the same cheap appliance repeatedly, each time hoping this is the last time. Name: sunk-cost repair. Explain: sunk-cost repair is the tendency to continue repairing because one has already repaired, even when future repairs are likely and the object remains unreliable. Implication: repairing can become its own form of waste when it is driven by past effort rather than future value.

The antidote is to treat repair as an experiment with a clear test. Does the repair restore function for a meaningful period, or does it simply postpone another breakdown? Does the object, once repaired, become a quiet part of life again, or does it continue to demand attention? The household should observe outcomes. If the repair returns the object to "boring", that is success. If the repair keeps the object in the foreground, it may not be viable.

This returns us to the comparison that anchors judgement. Mending quality shoes is often viable because shoes have replaceable wear components and the core structure can remain sound for years. Fixing a flimsy appliance is often less viable because the core structure is cheap and failure modes multiply. The rule is not that shoes should always be repaired and appliances always replaced. The rule is to identify whether the object's failure is a normal wear point in an otherwise durable system, or a symptom of a fragile system nearing the end of its short life.

A second named, checkable example sharpens this for modern electronics. Refurbished electronics programmes from major manufacturers and retailers have become mainstream partly because consumers recognise the difference between a repairable device with replaceable components and a device that becomes unreliable quickly. Battery replacement is a prime example: when a device's main limitation is a consumable component like a battery, repair can be highly viable. When a device's limitation is deeper—board-level failures, proprietary parts unavailable, software support ended—the viability drops. The household's task is to locate the failure: is it a part that wears, or is it the system itself?

A credible limitation must be faced: repair is not always accessible or economical, even when it is morally appealing. Skilled labour can be expensive. Parts can be scarce. Time can be scarce. Some products are engineered to resist repair. In such cases, insisting on repair can be self-punishment rather than stewardship. Name: repair scarcity. Explain: repair scarcity is the lack of affordable, practical repair options due to market structure, design decisions, or local availability. Implication: households should not confuse the inability to repair with personal failure; it is often a structural feature of modern commerce.

The reconciliation is to let viability be a compound judgement rather than a single rule. Remaining lifespan, repair-to-replacement ratio, coordination drag, safety threshold, and narrative value each matter. Different households weight them differently depending on season, values, and capacity. The aim is not to produce a universal formula. It is to prevent two predictable errors: knee-jerk replacement driven by convenience and impatience, and stubborn over-repair driven by guilt and sunk costs. Both errors waste margin—money, time, and attention.

The seam motif returns because repair is, literally and metaphorically, seam work. It is the act of deciding what should be reinforced and what should be released. A household that learns to assess repair viability is not merely saving money. It is training itself to see objects as systems with lifespans, to understand that stewardship can be rational and not just righteous, and to preserve freedom by preventing small failures from triggering large, automatic purchases.

The forward test arrives the next time something breaks and the household feels the familiar urge to make the problem disappear quickly. The question is whether this break is a worn seam in a durable thing, worth reinforcing, or a tear in a flimsy system that will keep ripping—whether the repair is likely to return the item to quiet usefulness, or merely buy a short reprieve before the next decision comes knocking.

Choosing when to replace

In October 2011, in New York, the National Highway Traffic Safety Administration announced a major expansion of the recall of certain Takata airbags, a process that would become one of the largest automotive recalls in history as defects were linked to dangerous failures. The concrete outcome was years of replacements, notices, and heightened awareness that a seemingly ordinary component could carry catastrophic risk. For households, the lesson is blunt: sometimes replacement is not a consumerist reflex but a safety decision. The question is not whether replacement can be wasteful. It can. The question is when *not* replacing becomes the greater waste.

Replacement can be stewardship.

That sentence often irritates people who have learned to equate replacement with indulgence and repair with virtue. Yet a life designed for freedom and generosity depends on margin, and margin is eroded not only by spending but by disruption. An ageing boiler that fails repeatedly in winter, a car that becomes unreliable, an appliance that consumes attention and time: these can drain a household more effectively than a single purchase ever will. Replacement becomes wise when it prevents future cascades—financial, practical, emotional—that are larger than the cost of the new item.

The motif for this section is the drip. A dramatic failure is obvious. A drip is quieter. A drip is the small leak of time, money, and patience caused by repeated minor faults. Drips are deceptive because each one feels tolerable. Together they can flood a household's attention.

A five-word sentence makes the point. Drips become floods, eventually.

Choosing when to replace begins with acknowledging what replacement really buys. It buys predictability. It buys reduced risk. It buys a clearer future. The household does not just purchase a new object; it purchases fewer breakdowns, fewer emergency decisions, fewer evenings spent rearranging plans, fewer "we'll deal with it later" conversations. That is not always worth the cost. It is often worth more than people admit, especially in busy lives.

The simplest framework rests on three pillars: safety, efficiency, and cumulative minor annoyances. Each pillar can be translated into visible behaviours and metrics so the decision does not become a moral argument.

Safety is the least negotiable. Show: a car with persistent warning lights or a boiler with repeated faults; the household begins to drive or heat the home with a low-grade fear in the background. Name: ambient risk. Explain: ambient risk is the constant, low-level awareness that something might fail in a dangerous way; it taxes attention even when nothing happens. Implication: when a household lives with ambient risk, replacement can be the most responsible choice because it removes a danger that cannot be managed by optimism.

Safety is also the place where overconfidence is most expensive. People frequently normalise risk because it is familiar. They say, "It's been fine so far," as if the past is a guarantee. Yet the Takata example demonstrates that even mass-produced systems can harbour defects that only become visible after time and investigation. The household analogue is smaller but real: ageing systems accumulate wear, and risk profiles can change. The correct posture is not paranoia. It is respect for uncertainty where consequences are severe.

Efficiency is the second pillar, and it is often misunderstood because people treat it only as energy use or running cost. Efficiency in household life also includes the efficiency of decisions: how much time does the item require to keep it working? How often does it interrupt routines? How often does it force unplanned spending? Show: a household schedules multiple small repairs across a year; each one requires calls, appointments, missed deliveries, and time off. Name: maintenance overhead. Explain: maintenance overhead is the recurring time and administrative effort required to keep an ageing asset functioning. Implication: an asset can be "cheaper" than replacement and still be inefficient if it imposes heavy maintenance overhead, because the household pays in life-hours and stress rather than in a single line item.

Efficiency also includes reliability. Reliability is not a sentimental preference; it is a quantifiable aspect of a household's stability. A reliable system allows planning. An unreliable system forces contingency living. Contingency living is expensive because it demands buffers of time and money, and it often produces last-minute purchases at high cost.

The third pillar—cumulative minor annoyances—is where many affluent households quietly bleed. Minor annoyances are not dramatic. They are the car door that sticks, the boiler that requires repeated resets, the washing machine that leaves clothes slightly damp, the fridge that makes a worrying noise. Each annoyance is tolerable. Together they create a background irritability that can spill into relationships. Show: a household begins to argue not about the appliance but about the stress it produces; the broken thing becomes a symbol. Name: irritation accumulation. Explain: irritation accumulation is the way repeated small failures create a disproportionate emotional burden over time; it turns objects into chronic sources of tension. Implication: replacement can be a relationship decision as much as a practical one, because it removes a persistent irritant that erodes patience.

Now place these pillars into a single, humane decision stance: replacement becomes wiser when the item's failures are no longer isolated events but part of a trend, when the trend carries safety implications, when the trend consumes disproportionate attention, and when the household can plausibly see repeated future costs—financial and emotional—that exceed the benefit of keeping the item.

An ageing car example makes this concrete without needing technical detail. Show: a household has a car that is fully paid for. That fact feels like a victory. The car begins to require repairs more frequently. Each repair is manageable, and each repair is followed by a few months of calm. Yet the calm periods shorten. The household begins to plan journeys with a small worry, begins to avoid long trips, begins to keep a mental list of warning signs. Name: shrinking confidence window. Explain: the shrinking confidence window is the decreasing time between issues during which the household trusts the asset; it is a behavioural signal that reliability is declining. Implication: when the confidence window shrinks, the household is moving from occasional repair to chronic management, and replacement becomes increasingly rational.

Notice what is happening here. The decision is no longer "repair versus replace" as a moral story. It is "predictability versus uncertainty" as a life design problem. The household must ask what kind of uncertainty it is willing to tolerate. A paid-off car can be a tremendous asset if it remains reliable. But if it becomes a source of ambient risk and maintenance overhead, the "cheapness" is illusory. The household is paying in stress and time, which are the currencies that matter most to busy earners.

A boiler example offers a parallel. A boiler often fails at the worst moment—cold mornings, busy weeks, times when family members are already stretched. Repeated minor faults create a cycle: callouts, temporary fixes, the sensation of living on borrowed time. The costs include not just money but disruption. The household begins to plan around the boiler. It becomes part of the psychological furniture of the home. Name: disruption tax. Explain: disruption tax is the cost imposed by failures that force sudden rearrangements—time off work, emergency arrangements, stress in the household. Implication: when an item imposes a high disruption tax, timely replacement can prevent larger waste later by removing the repeated emergencies that generate expensive, reactive choices.

A second named, checkable example helps frame the decision from another angle: safety standards and regulatory attention are not static. Appliances and cars are subject to recalls, updated standards, and changing expectations about emissions, efficiency, and safety features. Households do not need to chase every change. But they should recognise that "it still works" is not the only relevant criterion. "It still works safely and reliably" matters. "It still fits our life" matters.

A credible counter-example is necessary because replacement can become a reflex. Some households replace too early because novelty is seductive or because marketing makes normal wear feel like failure. They treat inconvenience as intolerable and respond by upgrading rather than by maintaining. Name: premature replacement. Explain: premature replacement is the habit of discarding functional items because a new model exists or because minor imperfections feel unacceptable; it produces waste and elevates the household baseline. Implication: without restraint, replacement becomes lifestyle creep in physical form—more spending, more churn, more environmental cost, and often little increase in satisfaction.

The reconciliation is to separate legitimate replacement signals from novelty noise. Legitimate signals are trend-based and consequence-based: increasing frequency of faults, shrinking confidence window, rising maintenance overhead, repeated safety concerns, high disruption tax, and irritation accumulation that begins to affect household wellbeing. Novelty noise is story-based: the excitement of new features, social comparison, the desire to "treat yourself", the fear of missing out. The household can acknowledge those desires without letting them masquerade as necessity.

This brings the discussion back to wealth without waste as a practice of alignment. Replacement is not merely about getting a better object. It is about choosing a life with fewer drips. The household has to decide where it wants to spend its attention. Does it want to spend it managing ageing assets, or does it want to spend it elsewhere—on relationships, work, rest, generosity? Sometimes repairing is the more aligned choice. Sometimes replacing is.

The drip motif returns because it is the best diagnostic image. A big failure forces action. Drips invite procrastination. Drips also invite rationalisation: "It's only this once." "It's not that bad." "We'll see how it goes." Then the household realises it has spent a year "seeing how it goes" while paying in small but steady withdrawals from its patience.

The forward test arrives the next time the household hears itself say, "We'll just fix it again." That sentence may be reasonable. It may also be denial. The question is whether the next fix will restore a reliable, safe, quiet system—or whether it will merely delay the moment when the household finally accepts that replacement, timed deliberately rather than forced by crisis, could be the more frugal, more humane, and more freedom-preserving choice.

Smart secondhand strategies

In September 2020, in Cupertino, Apple announced the iPhone 12 and, in the same season of launches and upgrades, the secondary market did what it always does: it filled with last year's devices as people traded novelty for cash. The concrete outcome was immediate price movement. A device that had been "premium" in 2019 became "used" overnight, despite remaining functionally powerful for most tasks. The scene repeats every year across categories—electronics, furniture, tools, even cars—and it reveals a peculiarity of modern consumer culture: value does not decline at the same rate as price.

Secondhand is not a bin.
It is a market.

The difference matters because many affluent households still carry an outdated picture of secondhand: rummage sales, musty wardrobes, and vague risk. That picture is incomplete. The modern secondhand economy is sophisticated, searchable, and often audited. Refurbished programmes exist. Warranty-backed resellers exist. Specialist dealers exist. The household that learns to navigate this world can buy higher-quality goods for less money, and can reduce waste without turning life into a scavenger hunt. The technique is not "buy used". The technique is *secondhand arbitrage*: purchasing the same underlying utility—function, durability, design—at a discount created by other people's impatience, novelty-chasing, relocation, or lack of storage.

A five-word sentence anchors the approach. Buy function, not newness.

Secondhand arbitrage begins with a recognition about depreciation. Some goods depreciate quickly because they are tied to novelty and status. Electronics are the obvious example. A flagship phone drops in perceived value when the next model arrives, even if its performance remains ample for most uses. Furniture can depreciate brutally the moment it becomes "not worth moving" for a seller. Baby equipment depreciates because the season of use is short. Tools depreciate because people buy for one project and then realise they have no interest in storing them. In all these cases, the household that buys secondhand is not buying "less". It is buying the same functional core with less marketing foam attached.

Show: a person scrolls through listings and sees a solid wood table at a fraction of showroom price. The table is heavy, unfashionable in a catalogue sense, yet plainly built to endure. Name: value lag. Explain: value lag is the gap between an item's intrinsic utility and its market price; it appears when cultural attention moves faster than the object's actual usefulness declines. Implication: secondhand arbitrage exploits value lag by buying where the market undervalues enduring utility.

The opposite also exists, and it is where people get burned: false bargains. A false bargain is a low price attached to low remaining life, hidden defects, or high future hassle. Show: an appliance is cheap secondhand because it is near failure; a "deal" becomes repeated repairs. Name: hidden tail cost. Explain: hidden tail cost is the future cost attached to a cheap purchase—repairs, missing components, incompatibility, safety issues, or early replacement. Implication: secondhand becomes wasteful when the household focuses on price and ignores tail costs; arbitrage requires discipline, not optimism.

The way to stay disciplined is to build secondhand thinking from the same principles already established: cost-per-use, total ownership costs, and alignment. The household's aim is not to collect bargains. It is to obtain durable function while preserving margin—money, space, and attention.

Where to look is less important than how to look, but the landscape matters. There are formal channels with lower risk and higher prices: manufacturer refurbished stores, warranty-backed resellers, established secondhand dealers. There are informal channels with higher risk and potentially higher reward: peer-to-peer marketplaces, community groups, auctions, charity shops. There are hybrid spaces: certified pre-owned programmes, outlet sections, trade-in resales. The household's time and risk tolerance should determine which channels it prefers. A busy household may rationally accept slightly higher secondhand prices in exchange for warranties and reduced hassle. A household with more time or expertise may accept peer-to-peer risk to capture larger discounts.

Risk needs to be translated into visible checks rather than into vague anxiety. A useful secondhand strategy is to separate items into "inspectable" and "non-inspectable" categories. Inspectable items are those whose condition can be assessed with basic observation: furniture, many tools, coats, certain kitchenware. Non-inspectable items are those whose critical faults are hidden: complex electronics, appliances, safety-critical equipment. This distinction is not perfect, but it helps households avoid buying unseen problems. Show: a chair can be sat on, wobbles can be felt; a laptop's battery health is harder to judge without information. Name: fault visibility. Explain: fault visibility is the degree to which defects are detectable through simple inspection and use. Implication: secondhand works best when fault visibility is high or when the seller provides credible assurance—warranties, testing, provenance—when fault visibility is low.

Provenance sounds grand; it simply means: where has this item been, and what evidence exists that it is what it claims to be? In formal secondhand channels, provenance is encoded: serial numbers, grading standards, return windows. In informal channels, provenance is social: the seller's story, photos, and responsiveness. The household should not treat every seller as a liar. It should treat every listing as incomplete information. That stance reduces gullibility without turning the process bitter.

The refurbished electronics example shows secondhand arbitrage at its cleanest because the quality gap between "new" and "used" is often psychological, while the price gap is real. Consider a laptop, tablet, or phone purchased through a manufacturer's refurbished programme or a reputable reseller. The buyer receives a device that has been inspected, tested, and often supplied with a limited warranty. The device is not new, but the function is close to new. The price is lower because someone else paid the "novelty tax"—the premium attached to being first.

Show: a household needs a laptop for work and study, not for gaming prestige. It compares a new mid-range model with a refurbished higher-spec model from the previous generation. Name: spec arbitrage. Explain: spec arbitrage is using the secondhand market to purchase higher performance per pound by buying older premium rather than current average. Implication: the household can obtain a more capable tool—better build quality, higher performance—while spending less than it would on a new but weaker option.

The potential trap is to rationalise indulgence by calling it arbitrage. A household might buy an overpowered device secondhand because it is "a deal", then use it for basic tasks. That is still waste, because the unused capability represents misaligned spending. This is why the household must begin with requirements: what tasks will be performed, how often, and with what tolerance for inconvenience? Requirements should be described behaviourally, not aspirationally. It is the same discipline applied earlier to big buys: decide based on actual use, not imagined identity.

A named, checkable historical example shows that secondhand is not a fringe practice but a longstanding market logic. In 1883, in London, the Salvation Army began operations, and over time its charity shops became part of Britain's secondhand economy, turning donated goods into funds and access. Charity shops are not the whole story of secondhand, but they demonstrate an enduring principle: the same object can serve multiple lives. The modern twist is that digital platforms have increased market efficiency, making the secondhand "search cost" lower. Lower search cost increases the viability of arbitrage, because households can find specific items rather than browsing blindly.

Search cost matters because time is a scarce resource for the audience of this book. Secondhand becomes overwhelming when it turns into endless scrolling. The disciplined approach treats secondhand as targeted procurement. The household begins with a defined item, a defined quality threshold, and a defined walk-away point. It uses saved searches, alerts, or a small set of trusted sellers. It does not browse as entertainment, because entertainment browsing is how secondhand turns into clutter. When people say secondhand creates chaos, they usually mean they bought without a plan.

A credible limitation must be faced: the secondhand market can carry ethical and practical risks—counterfeit goods, stolen property, misleading listings, and the simple risk of disappointment. Electronics can be especially fraught because batteries degrade, parts may be replaced with non-standard components, and software support can be limited. The household should not romanticise secondhand as effortless. It should choose secondhand categories where it can assess condition or obtain credible assurance. It should also recognise that not all secondhand bargains are worth the time required to find them. A busy household may decide that secondhand is reserved for big-ticket items where the savings justify the search cost, while smaller purchases are made new for simplicity. That is a legitimate design decision.

The reconciliation is to think of secondhand as a portfolio, not a doctrine. Some categories are excellent candidates: solid furniture, robust cookware, quality coats, certain tools, musical instruments, books, and refurbished electronics with warranties. Some categories are poor candidates unless the household has expertise: safety-critical items, complex appliances, items with hygiene concerns, or goods prone to hidden damage. The household gains confidence not by trying to secondhand everything, but by becoming skilled in a few categories that reliably deliver value.

The motif for this section is the palimpsest: a manuscript written over earlier writing, where traces remain. Secondhand objects are palimpsests. They carry prior use, and that prior use is not automatically a flaw. Often it is proof. A table with small marks has demonstrated survival. A coat with a softened collar has demonstrated wearability. A refurbished device has demonstrated that it can be restored. The question is whether the traces are signs of robust life or signs of impending failure.

The forward test arrives at the moment a household is about to buy new out of habit. The new item will be easy. It will be clean. It will be accompanied by marketing certainty. The secondhand option will require judgement and perhaps a little patience. The decision is not whether secondhand is morally superior. The decision is whether the household can see the value lag clearly enough to take it—buying function rather than newness—and whether it can do so without letting the hunt itself become another leak of time, attention, and accumulating "deals" that never earn their place.

Avoiding clutter and regret

In March 2016, in the Marie Kondo boom that followed the English-language publication of *The Life-Changing Magic of Tidying Up* in 2014, charity shops across Britain reported a familiar pattern: waves of donations arriving in bursts as households attempted to "declutter" at scale. The concrete outcome was bags at the door, sorting tables overrun, and, in some places, the quiet instruction to donors to slow down. The cultural outcome was more interesting. People began to see that the problem was not only *spending*. It was accumulation. A home could be financially prudent and still feel heavy.

Clutter is a kind of debt.

Not financial debt. Spatial and cognitive debt: obligations stored in cupboards, decisions postponed into boxes, good intentions compressed into piles. Clutter takes up physical space, which is expensive. It also takes up mental space, which is scarcer. The paradox that this section confronts is uncomfortable precisely because it is common among conscientious people: frugality, pursued without precision, can produce the same feeling of constraint as wasteful spending. The household becomes rich in bargains and poor in calm.

A five-word sentence makes it plain. Cheap things can be costly.

The cost appears in strange places. It appears in the time spent moving piles to clean. It appears in the reluctance to invite people over. It appears in the low-grade guilt of unfinished projects. It appears in the repeated thought, "I should deal with that." It appears, too, in money: duplicates bought because the original is lost in clutter; storage purchased because the home has been filled; decisions deferred because choosing what to keep feels tiring. These are not dramatic failures. They are slow leaks, and slow leaks are exactly what this book is designed to make visible.

To avoid clutter and regret, the household must replace the idea of "frugal" with something more exact: *intentional ownership*. Intentional ownership asks two questions that are easy to say and harder to live. Does this object earn its space? And if it stops earning its space, does it have a dignified exit?

Show: a household buys a secondhand bread maker because it is cheap, imagines weekend baking, and then uses it twice. The bread maker moves from counter to cupboard to loft. It becomes a symbol of a self that did not arrive. Name: aspirational inventory. Explain: aspirational inventory is the collection of objects purchased for an imagined future routine; it often becomes clutter because it is not supported by current habits. Implication: secondhand bargains can still be waste when they are purchased for identity rather than for proven use; the low price lowers resistance, which increases the risk of accumulation.

This is why "secondhand arbitrage" must be paired with "outflow discipline". Arbitrage without outflow discipline is simply acquisition. And acquisition, whether new or used, is how clutter forms. Outflow discipline is not a glamorous concept, but it is the difference between a home that supports freedom and a home that drains it. The household needs a plan not only for what comes in, but for what leaves.

Outflow is a system, not a mood.

That sentence matters because most households treat outflow as something they do when they finally feel fed up. They wait for a surge of motivation, then attempt a purge. Purges can feel cathartic. They can also be inefficient and psychologically punishing, because they demand hundreds of decisions at once. The better approach is to make outflow continuous and low-drama: small, regular, and attached to clear triggers.

Show: a cupboard fills up; the household procrastinates because dealing with it feels like a weekend task. Name: decision pile-up. Explain: decision pile-up is the accumulation of small unresolved choices into a single overwhelming project; it increases avoidance and therefore increases clutter. Implication: to prevent decision pile-up, households need to distribute decisions over time and attach them to predictable moments.

Outflow has three main destinations: resale, donation, and recycling. Each carries different benefits and frictions. Resale can recover money and can be satisfying, but it demands time: photographing, listing, messaging, packaging, meeting buyers. Donation is often faster and emotionally cleaner, but it can create a moral trap: donating becomes a way of avoiding responsibility for overbuying. Recycling is necessary for certain items, but it can be confusing and inconvenient, and it often reveals the hidden truth that many modern products are difficult to dispose of responsibly. The household should choose outflow channels based on time constraints and the item's value, rather than trying to optimise every exit.

A named, checkable example shows the limits of donation as a catch-all. In Britain, many charity shops have had to manage the influx of low-quality fast fashion donations, which are difficult to sell and expensive to process. WRAP (Waste and Resources Action Programme), a UK charity focused on resource efficiency, has repeatedly highlighted the scale of textile waste and the challenges of managing it (WRAP reports, various years). The implication for households is sobering: donating is not a magic eraser. If an item is low quality, broken, or unfashionable, it may not be helpful to a charity shop. Outflow discipline begins upstream, with buying decisions that avoid low-quality, short-life goods in the first place.

Now link outflow to storage limits, because limits are the only reliable antidote to accumulation. People often try to solve clutter with more storage: more boxes, more shelves, more cupboards. That is like solving a spending problem by getting a bigger credit limit. It postpones the moment of truth. The home needs constraints that function like spending guardrails. A fixed shelf, a fixed drawer, a fixed corner. When that space is full, something must leave before something new enters. The household does not need to become minimalist. It needs to become bounded.

Show: a household decides that hobby gear lives only in one cupboard; when the cupboard is full, new gear requires removing or selling something. Name: spatial guardrail. Explain: a spatial guardrail is a physical limit that prevents accumulation by forcing trade-offs; it turns vague intentions into concrete decisions. Implication: spatial guardrails protect the home's function and calm in the same way financial guardrails protect cashflow; they keep small indulgences from becoming structural burdens.

Regret is the emotional counterpart to clutter, and it is useful when handled correctly. Regret is often treated as shame: "I shouldn't have bought that." Shame is sticky. It produces avoidance, which keeps clutter in place. A more productive approach treats regret as information. Each regretted purchase carries a pattern: bought under time pressure, bought for a fantasy self, bought because it was "a bargain", bought because of comparison, bought because returning it felt awkward. The household that learns from regret reduces future waste.

Show: a box of unused items, each purchased with a small story of optimism. Name: narrative mismatch. Explain: narrative mismatch is the gap between the story used to justify a purchase and the household's actual lived routines; it is the primary cause of "bargains never used". Implication: if the household can identify its common narratives of mismatch, it can recognise them in real time and pause before buying.

A short reflection, done with honesty rather than self-punishment, can be powerful. Consider three recent purchases that produced regret—not the largest purchases, but the ordinary ones that now sit unused. Ask what was happening when the purchase was made: time of day, emotional state, context, trigger. Was it made late at night? After a stressful day? During a scroll? Was it made while trying to solve a real problem quickly? Was it made while seeking a feeling—control, excitement, competence? The aim is not therapy. It is pattern recognition. Pattern recognition is the practical side of self-knowledge.

The "bargain" deserves special scrutiny because it is the most common justification for clutter. Bargains are seductive because they feel like a win. They are also dangerous because they lower the threshold for acquisition. A household can accumulate far more through cheap purchases than it ever would through deliberate expensive purchases. The bargain frames the decision as "I might miss this deal" rather than "Do I need this in my life?" That framing is how frugality becomes a trap.

Yet there is a credible counter-example: some households genuinely save money and reduce waste by buying secondhand and stocking up on essentials. A family with children might sensibly accept hand-me-down clothing in bulk. A household in a remote area might buy spares to avoid repeated travel. A researcher might acquire used books and equipment because access is otherwise expensive. In these cases, accumulation can be rational. Name: strategic inventory. Explain: strategic inventory is deliberate storage of items that will predictably be used, where the cost of acquisition now is lower than the cost of obtaining later. Implication: the problem is not owning many things; the problem is owning many *unused* things. Strategic inventory is bounded, planned, and tied to predictable use; aspirational inventory is unbounded, impulsive, and tied to imagined futures.

The reconciliation is to require proof of use before expanding inventory. Proof can be behavioural: the household has already been doing the activity consistently, already borrowing the item repeatedly, already improvising with substitutes. Proof is the opposite of fantasy. It does not require certainty about the future; it requires evidence from the present. When proof exists, buying—new or secondhand—becomes less likely to create regret.

The motif of the seam returns from earlier in the chapter, because clutter often forms at seams: transitions between seasons, between life stages, between versions of the self. Baby items remain after children grow. Hobby gear remains after enthusiasm fades. Work clothing remains after a job change. The seam is where the household's life has moved on and the objects have not. Outflow discipline is the act of letting the physical world catch up with the lived world.

The forward test arrives the next time a household spots a bargain and feels the quick thrill of saving money. The question is not whether the price is good. The question is whether the object has a place, whether its use is proven, and whether its exit is planned if the proof fails to arrive. If the household cannot answer those silently, it is not a bargain yet. It is the first step towards another cupboard full of debt.

Chapter 8
Funding Thoughtful Generosity

On 14 June 2017, in London, flames tore through Grenfell Tower and the city's response arrived in two waves: the urgent work of emergency services, and then the human surge—bags of clothes, bottled water, toiletries, hot meals, offers of spare rooms. The concrete outcome was both heartening and messy. Some donations were exactly right, some were unusable, and charities and local groups struggled to match supply to need at speed. In the days that followed, many people discovered a private discomfort alongside their public sympathy: they wanted to help, but they did not know what to give, how to give, or how to give in a way that felt steady rather than reactive.

Generosity has logistics.

That sentence is not meant to drain the poetry from giving. It is meant to rescue giving from improvisation and guilt. In affluent households, generosity often lives in the margins—whatever is left over after everything else has been handled, or whatever is prompted by a news story that pierces the day. The intention is good. The system is fragile. When giving depends on leftovers, it competes with lifestyle creep. When giving depends on guilt, it becomes performative or episodic. And when giving depends on emotion alone, it can be sincere yet inefficient, like a flood of unlabelled items arriving at a charity already overwhelmed.

This chapter makes a simple claim with uncomfortable implications: generosity is not the reward for perfect financial order. It is part of financial order. It deserves a place in the design, not a place in the afterthought.

A five-word sentence gives the spine. Give on purpose, not mood.

That is not a moral instruction; it is a practical one. Mood is unpredictable. Cashflow is a system. If the household wants giving to be consistent—if it wants generosity to feel like an expression of values rather than a sporadic reaction—it must be funded in the same way that other important priorities are funded. Planning does not sterilise generosity. It makes it possible to keep giving even when life is busy, when headlines are quieter, when budgets are tight, or when attention is elsewhere.

The deeper question beneath funding is *enough*. Earlier chapters have shown how affluent households can feel constrained despite high income because commitments accrete and the baseline thickens. Giving, paradoxically, can thin the baseline by clarifying enough. Not because giving reduces spending. Because giving shifts identity. A household that gives deliberately becomes less vulnerable to the endless suggestion that it should upgrade again. It begins to measure success not only by what it can acquire, but by what it can contribute. That reorientation is subtle and powerful.

Still, the modern environment makes giving harder than it should be. There is more information than ever: crowdfunding pages, charity appeals, urgent campaigns, direct requests, algorithmic amplification. There is also more cynicism than ever: stories of misused funds, administrative overhead, performative philanthropy, donor vanity. The result for many thoughtful people is paralysis. They care, and they hesitate. Or they give impulsively and then second-guess themselves. This chapter sits in the middle of that tension, insisting that thoughtful generosity is both possible and learnable, and that it does not require grand gestures or a saintly temperament. It requires design.

The chapter begins with why planning matters, because ad-hoc giving has two predictable failure modes. The first is scarcity anxiety: the household gives only when it feels unusually flush, and therefore giving becomes rare. The second is guilt spending: the household gives in bursts after emotional prompts, and therefore giving becomes reactive, sometimes disproportionate, and often followed by resentment or self-reproach. Neither is what most people want. Most people want to be open-handed without feeling destabilised. Planning turns that desire into a stable practice.

From there, the chapter introduces a simple but surprisingly radical idea in affluent contexts: a giving sinking fund. Sinking funds are usually discussed for predictable irregular costs—holidays, annual insurance, car maintenance. Giving belongs in that category because it is a predictable human reality. There will always be need in the wider world, and there will always be moments when the household wants to respond—birthdays, bereavements, community crises, quiet acts of support for friends. A giving fund normalises generosity by allocating money to it before the month begins, not after the month is exhausted. It transforms giving from "if we can" into "we planned to".

The chapter then moves to the question of where money goes, because giving without discernment can feel hollow. Many people default to whatever is most visible: a friend's sponsored run, the charity that sends the most persuasive email, the disaster currently trending. Visibility is not a bad signal, but it is incomplete. Thoughtful giving asks for alignment: with the household's values, with the kinds of problems it feels called to address, and with the kinds of relationships it wants to nurture. This chapter does not treat giving as a mathematical optimisation exercise. It treats it as coherence. Coherent giving is easier to sustain, because it feels like an expression of identity rather than a series of random financial events.

Finally, the chapter brings giving into the household itself—not as a private spreadsheet entry, but as a family practice. This matters because generosity is not only about money; it is about modelling. Children learn what matters by what adults do repeatedly, not by what they say once. Partners learn whether money is a shared tool or a private territory by how giving decisions are made and discussed. When giving is hidden or left to one person, it can breed misunderstanding. When giving is shared and respectful, it can become a quiet tradition: a household culture of noticing, responding, and contributing.

A motif threads through this chapter: the envelope. Not a literal envelope in the old cash sense, though it can be. The envelope is a symbol of intentional allocation. An envelope holds a decision made earlier, in a calm moment, so that later moments—busy moments, emotional moments—do not have to invent a plan from scratch. The giving envelope is not meant to limit compassion. It is meant to protect it from chaos. It says, "We expected to give; we prepared to give; we can respond without panic."

The envelope also clarifies a modern moral complexity: the tension between local and global giving. A household may feel pulled between helping someone nearby and responding to large-scale issues far away. It may feel torn between supporting institutions and supporting individuals. It may worry about being exploited. It may worry about giving being pointless against systemic problems. These are not excuses; they are real intellectual objections. The chapter treats them with respect, because thoughtful generosity is not naive generosity. It is a practice that accepts uncertainty while refusing paralysis.

A credible counterpoint belongs here: planning can become an excuse for emotional distance. A household might treat the giving fund as a moral tax, paid and then forgotten, thereby insulating itself from the discomfort of human need. It might outsource all discernment to a standing order and never ask whether its giving still aligns with its values. Planning can become complacency if it is not accompanied by attention. This is not an argument against planning. It is an argument for keeping the envelope visible, revisiting it, and allowing it to be shaped by real relationships and real learning.

The reconciliation is simple: planned giving is not the end of generosity; it is the scaffolding. It creates the baseline that allows a household to be consistent. Consistency is what turns giving from an occasional performance into a quiet part of life. Once that baseline exists, the household can still respond to emergent needs with flexibility. The difference is that it responds from a position of preparation rather than from a scramble for spare cash and emotional certainty.

Modern relevance returns here with a sharp edge. Many high earners live with a strange combination of abundance and fragility: abundant income, fragile attention; abundant options, fragile time; abundant consumption opportunities, fragile community ties. Generosity—planned, thoughtful, sustained—addresses that fragility. It is a way of participating in the world rather than merely purchasing one's way through it. It is also a way of resisting the cultural script that says comfort must always expand to fill capacity. The household that gives deliberately is less likely to treat every raise as a private upgrade. It has chosen a different destination for some of its surplus.

The chapter ends by building momentum towards a question that is both practical and slightly unsettling: what would change if giving were treated as a design constraint rather than as a leftover? If the household assumed, at the start of each month, that generosity had a seat at the table—an envelope already marked—how would that reshape spending decisions, value trade-offs, and the feeling of enough? The answer is not merely about charities. It is about identity. It is about who the household becomes when it decides that wealth is not only what it can keep, but what it can circulate without fear.

Why plan for giving

On 5 December 1985, in London, Oxfam opened its first "shop" dedicated to selling donated goods decades earlier, and by the mid-1980s the organisation's retail model was already a familiar part of the British high street. The concrete outcome was practical: donated objects became steady funding for aid, and ordinary shoppers became routine participants in a system of redistribution. What matters here is not nostalgia for charity shops, but the logic they embody. The shop works because giving has been engineered into a repeatable process. People do not have to wait for a crisis of conscience to participate. They can show up on a Saturday and contribute through habit.

Habit beats heroics.

Many households like the idea of generosity, but treat it as an emotional event rather than as a designed practice. They give when a friend runs a marathon, when a disaster dominates the headlines, when a relative falls ill, when a local appeal arrives at the right moment. They feel a tug. They act. Then life resumes, and giving returns to the background until the next tug. This pattern is understandable. It is also fragile. When giving is powered by occasional guilt or sudden empathy, it becomes episodic, which means it is vulnerable to busyness, to distraction, and to the household's own shifting sense of "how much is enough".

A five-word sentence captures the problem. Leftovers rarely build anything.

Leftover-based giving is structurally unstable because leftovers are not a category of money; they are an accident. A household may feel affluent and still have months where cashflow is tight—big bills land, travel happens, work becomes chaotic, children's needs spike. In those months, "leftover" disappears. If giving depends on leftover, giving disappears with it. The household may still care. The system simply does not support the caring. Over time, this creates a particular kind of dissatisfaction: the household knows it has capacity in principle, yet its lived pattern is reactive and inconsistent. It does not feel like generosity. It feels like sporadic relief from guilt.

Planning is the antidote not because it turns giving into a cold transaction, but because it makes giving real.

Show: a household donates £200 after a dramatic news story, then gives nothing for months, then donates again in another wave. Name: episodic generosity. Explain: episodic generosity is giving driven by irregular emotional prompts; it tends to be lumpy, hard to sustain, and often followed by uncertainty about whether the household "did enough". Implication: episodic generosity can create a rollercoaster of moral emotion—surges of giving, followed by silence and self-questioning—rather than a stable sense of contribution.

Now contrast that with a household that allocates a modest amount monthly, quietly, without fanfare. The amount might be smaller than the dramatic donation. Yet it shows up repeatedly. It becomes a rhythm. That rhythm changes the household's relationship with money. The household is no longer asking, each time, "Can we afford to give right now?" It has already answered the question in a calm moment. The household is now asking, "Where does our giving belong?" That is a different level of maturity.

The central mechanism is pre-commitment. In behavioural economics, the concept is simple: people do better when they arrange environments and systems that make their preferred actions easier and their less preferred actions harder. Planning for giving is a form of pre-commitment. It reduces reliance on willpower and mood. It recognises that compassion is real but attention is limited. It respects the household's constraints while refusing to let those constraints become an excuse.

Show: at the end of a busy month, a household scrolls through its bank app and feels that familiar mix of fatigue and relief. It notices, perhaps, that it has spent generously on conveniences and upgrades, yet hesitates to give because giving feels like a moral decision requiring a fresh surge of emotional energy. Name: moral friction. Explain: moral friction is the psychological resistance created when giving is treated as a complex ethical moment each time; the decision feels weighty, which makes it easy to postpone. Implication: without planning, moral friction can reduce giving even in households that have capacity, because the household's limited attention is already consumed elsewhere.

Planning reduces moral friction by turning some giving into default. Default does not mean mindless. It means dependable. It means the household does not have to re-litigate its generosity every time it sees an appeal. The household can still choose to respond to emergent needs, but it is not starting from zero. It has a baseline practice that reflects its identity.

The most compelling reason to plan, however, is not efficiency. It is integrity. People do not want to be merely comfortable; they want their lives to mean something beyond consumption. This is not piety. It is a human desire for coherence. A household's spending patterns are a form of autobiography. They tell the story of what the household valued enough to fund. When giving is left to leftovers, the story tends to be: we meant to, but we were busy; we wanted to, but it never felt like the right moment. Planning allows the story to become: we chose to, steadily, because it mattered.

That choice also reshapes the household's sense of enough. Earlier in this book, the paradox of affluent constraint has been framed as a design problem: commitments swell until freedom feels thin. Giving can seem, at first glance, like another commitment—another outflow. Yet planned giving often does the opposite. It anchors the household in a wider reality. It creates a gentle pressure against lifestyle creep. It makes the household less willing to inflate the baseline with forgettable indulgences because it has already assigned some portion of its surplus to something it claims to care about. Giving becomes a design constraint, and constraints, used wisely, create freedom.

Show: a household receives a bonus and faces a familiar set of options—upgrade a recurring luxury, book a more expensive holiday, add a subscription. It also has a standing giving practice. The household experiences a new kind of internal dialogue: not "we should give" as a scolding, but "we already give; what else matters?" Name: anchored sufficiency. Explain: anchored sufficiency is the stabilising effect that regular giving can have on a household's appetite for upgrades; it reinforces a sense that the household already participates in something meaningful. Implication: planned giving can reduce the restless urge to prove success through spending, because the household's identity is not solely consumerist.

A named, checkable example of planned generosity at scale illustrates the principle without turning it into a sermon. In 2010, in the United States, Bill and Melinda Gates and Warren Buffett launched the Giving Pledge, inviting wealthy individuals to commit publicly to giving away a majority of their wealth. The programme has attracted hundreds of signatories. The household in this book is not a billionaire household, and public pledges are not required for thoughtful giving. Yet the programme demonstrates a simple fact: even at extreme levels of wealth, people recognise that generosity benefits from commitment and structure. Without structure, money drifts. With structure, it expresses intention.

This is where a credible counter-example must be addressed. Planned giving can become an excuse for complacency. A household may set up a standing order and then treat the matter as resolved, never revisiting whether the giving aligns with its values or whether it is responding appropriately to genuine need. Planning can also feel emotionally sterile if it becomes purely automatic. Name: outsourced conscience. Explain: outsourced conscience is the tendency to use a planned donation as a moral shield, avoiding the discomfort of paying attention to the real world and to relationships that might require more than money. Implication: planning alone does not guarantee thoughtful generosity; it must be paired with periodic reflection and a willingness to respond when life calls for more.

The reconciliation is straightforward: planning is the foundation, not the ceiling. A baseline practice creates steadiness; it does not forbid responsiveness. In fact, it enables responsiveness. When a household has planned giving, it can respond to an urgent need without destabilising itself, because it has already normalised outflow. It has already built the psychological muscle of parting with money for reasons beyond private pleasure.

Planning also protects giving from the distortions of social comparison. Ad-hoc giving is often public: sponsored events, social media fundraisers, visible appeals. Public giving can be beautiful. It can also produce competitive generosity, where people give to be seen rather than to be effective or aligned. Planned giving, by contrast, can be quiet. It can be private. It can be consistent without applause. In a culture that rewards display, private consistency is a form of maturity.

The motif for this section is the envelope—not necessarily a literal envelope, but a boundary that holds a decision. An envelope is a pre-made yes. It says: this portion is already assigned. It also prevents the emotional whiplash of deciding anew each time. When giving is enveloped—planned—it becomes a stable part of the household's financial narrative rather than a series of moral emergencies.

The most human argument for planning is the simplest: most people do not want to be generous only when they feel guilty. Guilt is a volatile fuel. It burns hot and then goes out. It also corrodes joy. Planned giving allows generosity to feel like participation rather than penance. It allows giving to be connected to gratitude and responsibility, not to self-reproach. A household can give and feel calm, not threatened. It can give and still enjoy its own life. It can give without needing a crisis to justify it.

The forward test arrives the next time an appeal appears at a moment of fatigue. The household will feel the tug. It will also feel the resistance: not now, not this month, too much going on. The question is whether the household wants its generosity to depend on that moment's mood—or whether it wants to place generosity inside the design of its life, so that it can keep giving steadily, even when attention is scarce and the world's needs are noisy, complicated, and never fully satisfied.

Creating giving sinking funds

In July 2004, in the United States, the Internal Revenue Service began allowing a new kind of charitable vehicle authorised by law two years earlier to grow quickly in practice: donor-advised funds, which let individuals contribute money now and recommend grants to charities over time. The concrete outcome was a separation of *funding* from *disbursing*: money could be set aside deliberately and then allocated thoughtfully rather than impulsively. Most households will never open a donor-advised fund, and they do not need to. What matters is the underlying logic, which is simple enough to use on a kitchen table: separate the moment you set money aside for giving from the moment you decide where it goes.

That separation changes everything.

A giving sinking fund is the household-scale version of this idea. Sinking funds are already familiar in principle, even to people who do not use the term: saving a little each month for holidays, car maintenance, annual insurance, school trips, or Christmas. These are predictable irregular costs. The genius of a sinking fund is that it converts sharp, stressful expenses into a steady rhythm. A giving fund does the same for generosity. It treats giving not as an occasional moral emergency, and not as something that happens only when the month ends kindly, but as a normal, planned outflow.

A five-word sentence captures the shift. Set aside first, then decide.

Without that shift, giving often becomes precarious. It depends on the mood of the month. It depends on how disciplined spending happened to be. It depends on whether the household avoided an unexpected bill. The result is the pattern many affluent households quietly recognise: giving happens in bursts, often in response to a vivid story, and then vanishes in the busier, tighter months. The household's compassion is stable. Its giving is not. A giving sinking fund makes giving predictable without turning it into a cold routine. It gives compassion a container.

The container matters because modern giving environments are loud. Appeals arrive via email, social media, workplace campaigns, and peer-to-peer fundraisers. The household is asked to respond quickly and publicly. That environment rewards impulsive giving and punishes deliberation with the fear of missing the moment. A giving fund restores deliberation. It says: the household can respond, but it will respond from a prepared place, not from a scramble.

Show: a household sees a fundraiser for a local family facing sudden hardship. It wants to help, but it also knows its month is already committed: mortgage, childcare, travel. Name: cashflow collision. Explain: cashflow collision is the conflict between genuine desire to give and pre-existing financial commitments; it often leads to either guilt-driven overgiving or reluctant refusal. Implication: a giving fund reduces cashflow collisions by keeping a small pool available for generosity, so that the household can act without destabilising its essentials.

A giving fund is not only a tool for responsiveness. It is also a tool for dignity—both the giver's and, in certain contexts, the recipient's. When giving is precarious, people sometimes give in ways that feel performative or apologetic: a rushed donation with a flurry of justification. When giving is prepared, it can be quieter and more confident. Prepared giving can support relationships without making them awkward. It can also allow the household to give in ways that are less about the giver's immediate emotional relief and more about the recipient's real needs.

The mechanics are deceptively simple: a small, regular allocation builds a meaningful pool over time. The phrase "meaningful pool" matters. Many people assume giving must be large to matter. That assumption is a convenient excuse, because it lets them postpone giving until they can do something dramatic. In reality, the compound effect of regularity is powerful, even without grand sums. This is not investment advice; it is arithmetic and psychology. A repeated action becomes identity. And a repeated allocation becomes capacity.

A modest illustration shows why percentages matter more than occasional windfalls. Take a household with an annual take-home income of £120,000. If that household allocates 0.5% to a giving fund, that is £600 a year. At 1%, it is £1,200. At 2%, it is £2,400. The numbers are not magic. They are simply the product of a decision made early rather than late. If the household prefers to think monthly, those figures translate to £50, £100, and £200 a month respectively. For many affluent households, the difference between £50 and £100 a month is smaller than the monthly drift created by unexamined subscriptions, convenience spending, or default upgrades. The giving fund makes that drift visible by asking a question: what would be different if this portion of cashflow had a name?

Naming is not trivial. It is behavioural.

Show: money sits in a single current account; it feels abundant on payday and thin later. The household makes choices based on a shifting sensation rather than on a stable plan. Name: undifferentiated money. Explain: undifferentiated money is money without assigned purpose; it invites impulsive decisions because any purchase can be justified against a large balance. Implication: separating money into purpose-led "pots" changes behaviour by making trade-offs visible; a giving fund is one such pot, and its existence makes generosity easier to sustain.

The giving sinking fund also solves a subtle problem: the mismatch between constant small requests and occasional larger opportunities. Many households are asked for small donations frequently, and those can add up while still feeling unsatisfying, because they do not align with the household's sense of meaningful contribution. Meanwhile, larger opportunities—supporting a friend in crisis, funding a local project, giving towards a specific cause—arrive unpredictably. Without a fund, the household responds unevenly: it gives too much in a burst and then recoils, or it gives too little because the month feels tight. With a fund, the household can say yes more calmly, because it has already allocated capacity.

Show: a school asks for a donation to a hardship fund; a colleague collects for a sponsored event; a community group appeals for supplies. The household feels peppered. Name: request fatigue. Explain: request fatigue is the emotional tiredness that arises when a household is repeatedly asked to give; it can lead to cynicism or avoidance even in generous people. Implication: a giving fund can reduce request fatigue by providing a clear boundary: the household can decide from a prepared allocation rather than from its entire monthly budget each time.

Boundary is not stinginess. It is clarity.

A five-word sentence makes that clear. Boundaries protect the yes.

The fund creates a boundary that prevents two predictable errors. The first is guilt spending—donating more than feels sustainable because of a compelling story, then feeling resentful. The second is avoidance—saying no because deciding feels hard and the month feels uncertain. The giving fund allows the household to give in a way that fits its life. It shifts giving from moral drama to steady practice.

This is where the earlier theme of "enough" returns in a practical form. A giving fund forces the household to articulate, even if only implicitly, what "enough for us" means, because it sets aside a portion for "others". If the household cannot imagine setting aside even a small percentage, the discomfort is revealing. It might indicate genuine financial fragility. It might indicate that the household's baseline has inflated to consume all surplus. It might indicate fear—fear of scarcity, fear of future uncertainty, fear of being unable to maintain a lifestyle. The giving fund does not solve those fears by itself. But it exposes them gently, and exposure is often the first step to alignment.

A credible limitation must be acknowledged: a giving fund can become a moral alibi. A household might allocate a small amount and then refuse to engage with need beyond the fund, using the fund as a shield: "We already give." That stance can harden into complacency. It can also flatten the human dimension of generosity into a mechanical transfer. Name: ethical autopilot. Explain: ethical autopilot is the tendency to treat an automated giving allocation as the end of moral responsibility rather than as the beginning of a thoughtful practice. Implication: while automation and funds are useful, they need periodic reflection so the household remains attentive to why and how it gives.

The reconciliation is built into the fund's design: the fund separates funding from allocation. The household allocates money regularly, creating consistency. Then it decides where the money goes with periodic attention rather than constant reactivity. This creates space for thought: which causes align with values, which local needs are emerging, which relationships require support, which projects have demonstrated impact. A fund makes those decisions less hurried. It does not replace them.

The giving fund also enables a particular kind of generosity that affluent households often struggle with: generosity towards people they actually know. Many people find it easier to give to institutions than to offer financial help to friends or relatives, because personal giving can feel awkward, messy, and psychologically entangling. A giving fund can reduce the awkwardness by providing a natural source: help comes from a designated pot rather than from the household's entire monthly budget. The fund does not solve relational complexity, but it reduces the sensation that personal giving is a sudden financial improvisation.

The motif from the chapter introduction—the envelope—fits perfectly here, because the giving fund is, in essence, an envelope that holds future compassion. An envelope is a decision made in advance. It is the household saying, calmly, "We intend to be the kind of people who give, regardless of the month's chaos." The envelope also limits overreach. It prevents generosity from becoming self-endangerment. When giving is planned, it can be open-handed without being reckless.

This section leaves the reader with a forward test that is both practical and slightly moral without becoming preachy. The next time a giving opportunity appears—an appeal, a crisis, a friend's need—the household will feel the familiar internal scan: do we have room? The question is whether it wants that scan to happen against the entire, messy landscape of monthly spending, or against a clean, prepared allocation that has already said yes in principle. If the household can build a giving fund, even a modest one, it will discover something unexpectedly freeing: generosity becomes less precarious, less performative, and more like a steady part of the life it is designing.

Choosing where money goes

In August 2019, in the Amazon rainforest, images of fires and smoke travelled faster than the smoke itself, and charities across the world reported sudden spikes in online donations. The concrete outcome was money moving quickly in response to a visible crisis—some of it to established environmental organisations, some of it to opportunistic accounts, some of it to groups that did valuable work but could not absorb the surge efficiently. The episode was not a moral failure. It was a case study in modern generosity: attention arrives in waves, money follows, and the giver is left with a quiet question afterwards. Did that help? Did that align with what matters? Or did it simply satisfy the need to do something, quickly, in the face of distress?

Choosing where money goes is where generosity becomes adult.

Planned giving creates steadiness. A giving fund creates capacity. But a household still has to decide where the capacity is directed, and that decision is harder than most people admit. It is hard not because people lack compassion, but because the world is large, needs are endless, and information is uneven. Many givers oscillate between two errors. One is naïve optimism: giving to whatever is most visible, trusting that good intentions guarantee good outcomes. The other is cynical paralysis: believing that because no giving is perfect, giving is futile or likely to be wasted. Thoughtful giving rejects both. It accepts uncertainty without surrendering discernment.

A five-word sentence frames the task. Choose with values and evidence.

Evidence is not a demand for certainty. It is a demand for seriousness. Values are not vague sentiments. They are priorities with consequences. When a household chooses where to give, it is not merely selecting a charity. It is shaping its own identity—what it will notice, what it will support, what it will become accustomed to caring about. A coherent giving pattern is not only more effective; it is more satisfying, because it reduces the feeling of scatter and the suspicion that money is being sprayed at random.

The first move is to recognise that "where to give" involves at least three distinct categories: causes, people, and projects. Causes are broad themes—education, mental health, homelessness, climate, medical research, arts, local community. People are the direct relationships in a household's orbit—friends, family, neighbours, colleagues—where giving may take the form of help rather than formal donation. Projects are specific efforts—building a community garden, supporting a school fundraiser, funding a scholarship, helping a local food bank expand storage. Mixing these categories without noticing creates confusion. Some households give generously to causes but feel awkward about helping people they know. Some pour money into personal help but never support systemic work. Some chase projects because they are tangible but neglect long-term institutions. Coherence begins by seeing the categories clearly.

Show: a household gives £30 here, £50 there, £10 to a colleague's run, £200 in a crisis, then forgets what it supported. Name: donation drift. Explain: donation drift is the pattern of scattered giving without a through-line; it is driven by visibility and social prompts rather than by deliberate priorities. Implication: donation drift often produces regret or numbness because the household cannot see what its giving is doing; it also makes the household vulnerable to manipulation by whoever asks most loudly.

A household can correct donation drift by using the value hierarchy already built earlier in the book. The hierarchy is not merely for spending on oneself; it is for spending on the world. If a household says it cares about education because it believes opportunity should not be inherited, then education should show up in giving. If it says it cares about local community because it wants a neighbourhood with less loneliness and more mutual support, then local institutions should show up. If it cares about long-term planetary stability, then environmental work should show up. This is not ideological purity. It is alignment. Alignment makes giving feel like a coherent practice rather than like a series of random payments.

The next move is to accept that no household can support everything. That sounds obvious. Yet many people behave as if they are still searching for the single "best" cause, the single "most deserving" charity, the single perfect solution. That search is exhausting, and it is often a disguised form of avoidance. The world does not need a household to solve everything. It needs households to choose something and support it with steadiness.

A five-word sentence offers relief. Depth beats breadth for giving.

Depth does not mean giving only to one place forever. It means resisting the impulse to scatter giving thinly across dozens of causes simply because those causes exist. When giving is spread too widely, it becomes harder to learn. It becomes harder to build relationships with organisations. It becomes harder to see outcomes. It becomes harder to sustain, because each decision remains novel. Depth turns giving into a relationship rather than a transaction.

Show: a household supports a local food bank consistently; it learns what the food bank actually needs, how demand changes seasonally, and how volunteers experience the work. Name: feedback loop. Explain: a feedback loop in giving is information that returns to the giver—updates, transparency, lived experience—allowing the household to refine its choices. Implication: depth increases feedback loops; feedback loops increase confidence; confidence increases consistency.

Evidence enters here in a practical way. Evidence does not require that a household become a professional evaluator. It requires that the household ask a few serious questions of the organisations or projects it supports. How do they describe their work? What outcomes do they measure, if any? How do they report finances and governance? Are they transparent about limitations? Do they have a clear theory of change—an explanation of how their activities lead to impact? These are not hostile questions. They are respect. They treat the organisation as capable of being accountable, and the giver as capable of choosing with care.

It is also reasonable to acknowledge that some giving is inherently difficult to measure. Arts organisations may produce cultural value that does not fit into neat metrics. Community-building projects may reduce loneliness in ways that are real yet hard to quantify. Emergency aid may value speed over evaluation. Evidence should not be used as a weapon against any cause that cannot produce clean numbers. Evidence should be used to avoid obvious waste and deception, and to support trust where trust is warranted.

Trust, in this context, must be paired with behaviours. Trust is built through transparency, governance, and track record. A household can look for publicly available annual reports, audited accounts, or charity commission filings. In the UK, the Charity Commission provides a register and information for registered charities. That is not a guarantee of effectiveness, but it is a baseline for legitimacy. The household can also notice whether an organisation communicates with clarity rather than with manipulation. Does it share specific work, or only emotionally charged appeals? Does it explain how donations are used, or does it rely on urgency alone? These are signals, not proofs. Yet signals matter.

Now consider the other axis that shapes giving choices: local versus global. This tension is moral and practical. Local giving often feels more concrete. It can create visible changes in a community. It can also reinforce the household's connection to place, which is valuable in a mobile, digitally mediated society. Global giving often addresses problems with larger scale—disease, poverty, climate—that can be existential. It can feel abstract, and it can feel more uncertain. Many people oscillate between them: local giving feels emotionally satisfying but limited; global giving feels intellectually compelling but distant.

The most coherent approach is not to choose one forever, but to treat the tension as a deliberate balance. Show: a family in Manchester supports a local youth centre that provides after-school programmes and mentoring; at the same time, it gives to an international organisation focused on malaria prevention. Name: dual horizon giving. Explain: dual horizon giving is the practice of supporting both immediate local needs and longer-term or wider-scale work; it reflects a recognition that human responsibility operates at multiple distances. Implication: dual horizon giving can reduce the moral anxiety of "either/or" decisions; it allows a household to feel rooted in place while still participating in broader human challenges.

This is not a prescription. It is a design pattern. Some households will feel called primarily to local work because their values emphasise community, proximity, and relational repair. Some will feel called primarily to global work because their values emphasise scale, preventable suffering, or planetary stability. What matters is that the household chooses consciously rather than drifting into whatever feels least uncomfortable.

A second named, checkable example illustrates how public attention can distort giving choices. After the 2010 Haiti earthquake, there were both extraordinary charitable responses and documented cases of ineffective or poorly coordinated aid. The event became a widely discussed example of the challenges of emergency response: speed, accountability, coordination, and the risk of unintended consequences. The lesson for a household is not "don't give in emergencies". It is "recognise the trade-offs". Emergency giving prioritises urgency. Planned giving prioritises consistency and evaluation. A household can do both, but it should know which mode it is in.

That recognition leads to a useful distinction: baseline giving and responsive giving. Baseline giving is the steady practice funded by the giving fund. Responsive giving is the capacity to respond to emergent needs—disasters, personal crises, sudden local opportunities—without derailing the baseline. Households often fail here by doing only responsive giving, which is exhausting and inconsistent, or by doing only baseline giving, which can become complacent. The coherent pattern holds both: steadiness plus responsiveness.

A credible counter-example must be treated carefully: some people prefer spontaneous giving because it feels more human, more relational, less institutional. They dislike what feels like "strategic philanthropy" because it can seem cold. That preference is not foolish. Spontaneous giving can be a genuine expression of compassion. It can also be a way of supporting people directly rather than feeding systems. The limitation is that spontaneity alone tends to privilege what is visible and emotionally vivid, not what is necessarily most aligned or most needed. It can also privilege social proximity, meaning people give to those like themselves, leaving other needs unseen. The reconciliation is not to ban spontaneity, but to house it within a structure that prevents it from becoming the only mode.

This brings the discussion to a quieter, more personal question: how does a household decide which people to help? Personal giving is morally charged because it involves boundaries, fairness, and relationship dynamics. A household might fear becoming the family bank. It might fear being manipulated. It might fear resentment between siblings or friends. Yet many households also know the intimate truth that money can alleviate suffering quickly in ways that institutions cannot. Thoughtful giving includes personal help, but personal help requires clarity about limits and purpose. A giving fund can assist by providing a designated source for relational generosity, reducing the sense that every request threatens the household's entire financial stability.

The motif for this section is the compass. A compass does not tell a traveller exactly where every obstacle lies. It gives direction. Values are the compass needle. Evidence is the map. Responsiveness is the weather: sometimes conditions change, and a traveller must adapt. Choosing where money goes means using the compass and the map while remaining alert to the weather.

Joy is an underrated criterion here. Joy does not mean frivolity. It means that giving feels coherent, alive, and connected to what the household actually cares about. Many people assume giving must feel like sacrifice to be real. In practice, sustainable giving often carries joy precisely because it expresses agency and belonging. A household that gives in alignment feels less like it is paying a moral tax and more like it is participating in a shared human project.

The forward test arrives when the next appeal appears and the household feels the familiar pull of urgency. The question is whether it will give by drift—visibility, guilt, social pressure—or whether it will consult its compass: what do we care about, what have we chosen to support, what evidence and relationships do we trust, and how do we balance steadiness with responsiveness without letting either become an excuse.

Giving as family practice

In November 2009, in London, the television programme *The Secret Millionaire* was still drawing large audiences by staging a particular kind of moral theatre: a wealthy person goes undercover, meets people in need, and then makes a dramatic gift. The concrete outcome was money moving into charities and individuals' lives, and viewers experiencing a jolt of emotion on a weekday evening. The cultural outcome was more complicated. The format implied that generosity is something done by exceptional people in exceptional moments, preferably with a reveal. It made giving look like a plot twist.

Most generosity is not a plot twist.

In real households, generosity is a pattern—quiet, repeated, and shaped by the texture of family life: school calendars, work stress, differing temperaments, and the relentless practicalities of dinner and laundry. If giving remains private—one adult's secret standing order, one person's charitable preferences filed away like tax documents—it misses its full power. Generosity does not merely move money outward. It shapes people inward. It forms attention. It trains the imagination to notice others. And in a family, those are shared assets. Giving as a family practice treats generosity as part of culture, not as a solo hobby.

A five-word sentence sets the tone. Children learn what adults repeat.

That is not sentimental. It is observable. Households teach values in two ways: by explicit talk and by repeated behaviour. Children, and partners too, notice what gets funded without drama. They notice what happens when someone asks for help. They notice whether money is discussed as a tool or as a taboo. A family practice of giving is a way of making values visible without turning the home into a lecture hall.

The obstacle is often discomfort. Money already carries tension in many relationships; adding generosity can intensify it. One partner may be more emotionally responsive, wanting to give whenever a story moves them. The other may be more cautious, worried about stability, suspicious of ineffective charities, or mindful of responsibilities to extended family. Children may ask awkward questions. Teenagers may be cynical. And, in households that are busy, anything that requires extra conversation can feel like one more task to manage. The temptation is to keep giving private so it remains simple. Yet that simplicity is deceptive. It can produce hidden resentments and lost opportunities for shared meaning.

Show: one partner donates regularly without telling the other, believing they are protecting the household from conflict. Later, the other partner discovers the donations and feels excluded or misled, not because they oppose giving but because secrecy violates trust. Name: generosity opacity. Explain: generosity opacity is the lack of visibility around household giving; it can create suspicion and unnecessary tension even when the giving itself is aligned with shared values. Implication: turning giving into a family practice can reduce conflict by making generosity transparent and collaborative rather than secretive.

Collaboration does not require unanimity on every cause. It requires a shared process that respects difference. Earlier chapters addressed aligning partners on values; the same principles apply here, with an extra layer: giving is both moral and personal. People's giving preferences often reflect deep stories—religious traditions, childhood experiences of scarcity, gratitude towards certain institutions, anger about injustice, a need for control, or a desire to be seen as good. In couples, these stories can collide. A family practice of giving is partly about designing a method for resolving these collisions without contempt.

A useful starting point is to distinguish between baseline giving and responsive giving, then decide which parts are shared and which are individual. Baseline giving can be a joint decision: a small number of causes or commitments that represent shared household identity. Responsive giving can include a personal lane for each partner: a modest amount each can allocate without negotiation, precisely to prevent every giving decision becoming a referendum on the relationship. This is not indulgence; it is peacekeeping. It honours the fact that generosity is intimate, and intimacy can be threatened by constant bargaining.

Show: a couple argues about a donation request in the middle of a stressful week; the argument is not really about the charity but about fear—fear of being taken advantage of, fear of being uncaring, fear of instability. Name: moral displacement. Explain: moral displacement is when a giving decision becomes a proxy battle for deeper relationship anxieties, because the donation provides a convenient surface on which to fight. Implication: a family practice can reduce moral displacement by establishing calm, predictable times and boundaries for giving decisions rather than improvising under stress.

Time is a critical variable. Families rarely fight well on the fly. The best giving conversations happen when nobody is already depleted. That is why treating giving as a practice—attached to a rhythm—matters. A monthly or quarterly "giving check-in" can be short and still transformative, because it moves the conversation away from crisis and towards deliberate choice. The aim is not to talk endlessly. The aim is to make giving visible, shared, and aligned with the household's design.

Children complicate and enrich this picture. Many parents worry about involving children in giving because they fear guilt-tripping, performative virtue, or overwhelming children with the world's problems. Those are legitimate concerns. Children do not need the full weight of global suffering placed on their shoulders. They do, however, benefit from learning that money is not only for private consumption. They benefit from practising attention towards others in ways that feel safe and age-appropriate.

Age-appropriate does not mean simplistic. It means scaled to what a child can understand and process. Younger children respond well to concrete stories and visible actions. They understand helping a local animal shelter, contributing to a school hardship fund, or collecting food for a pantry because these are tangible. As children grow, they can understand systems—why some people need help, how institutions work, what fairness means. Teenagers can handle complexity and can also detect hypocrisy quickly. If a household wants giving to become part of culture, it must be honest about trade-offs and limitations, not just about ideals.

Evidence helps, even here, because it prevents giving from becoming mere moral performance. A child's attention can be guided towards what the giving does rather than how the giver feels. "This helps a family eat this week." "This helps keep the youth club open." "This pays for books in a classroom." Concrete outcomes anchor generosity in reality.

A five-word sentence keeps it grounded. Make giving visible and small.

Visible and small is the opposite of the television plot twist. It is the steady practice that forms character. A family does not need to stage dramatic acts to teach generosity. It needs repeated, visible decisions that show that the household makes room for others. It also needs boundaries that prevent giving from becoming self-erasure. Children learn as much from boundaries as from generosity: they learn that care can be offered without losing stability, that saying yes does not require panic, and that compassion can be paired with prudence.

A brief scenario shows how a family practice might look in motion without becoming saccharine. A family sits at the kitchen table on a Sunday evening. The giving fund has accumulated quietly. There is a local request: the school has a hardship fund for families struggling with uniform costs and trips. There is also a wider issue the parents care about—say, homelessness, or environmental restoration, or medical research—something that fits the household's value hierarchy. The parents present the choice not as a moral exam but as a decision the household is privileged to make: there is room to support one local commitment steadily and one wider commitment steadily, and there may also be occasional room for emergent needs. The children ask questions. One child prefers helping animals. Another is moved by the idea of helping classmates. The parents notice the preferences without mocking them. They decide on a split that reflects both the household's compass and the children's growing attention. The outcome is not perfection. The outcome is a practice: the household has made giving a normal conversation, not a rare event.

The deeper significance of that conversation is not the specific allocation. It is the way it trains the household to think. It teaches trade-offs explicitly: if money goes here, it cannot go there. It teaches that generosity is chosen, not accidental. It teaches that giving can be discussed without shame or secrecy. It teaches, crucially, that the household is part of a community, not merely a private economic unit.

A named, checkable example helps underline how family practices can scale into civic culture. In the UK, the Royal National Lifeboat Institution (RNLI), founded in 1824, has long relied on public giving and volunteering. Many families in coastal communities have traditions of donating, fundraising, or participating in events, not as a one-off act but as a generational norm. The point is not that every family must adopt an institution like the RNLI. The point is that when giving becomes culturally embedded, it stops feeling like a heroic exception and starts feeling like what people do.

There is, however, a credible limitation: family giving can become coercive. Children can be pressured into performative virtue. Partners can feel morally policed. Giving can be used as a way to control the household narrative—"we are the kind of family who…"—in a way that leaves no room for dissent or nuance. Name: enforced benevolence. Explain: enforced benevolence is when generosity is demanded as a marker of identity rather than chosen as a practice; it can produce resentment and cynicism, especially in teenagers and in partners with differing values. Implication: for giving to become genuine culture, it must allow conversation, questions, and individual difference; otherwise it becomes theatre.

The reconciliation is to treat giving as an invitation, not a verdict. In families, invitations work better than edicts. An invitation can hold boundaries. It can include a shared baseline while still allowing personal lanes. It can make giving normal without making it compulsory in a way that crushes agency. Agency matters because the goal is not obedience; it is the development of an internal compass.

The motif for this section is the hearth: the place where a household's stories are told and repeated. In earlier eras, the hearth was literal. Now it might be a kitchen table, a sofa, a car journey, a shared walk. Wherever the hearth is, it is where the household decides what kind of people it is becoming. If giving remains outside the hearth—hidden in a bank transfer, isolated in one adult's private decisions—it cannot shape the shared story. If giving enters the hearth, it becomes part of the household's identity in a way that is both practical and deeply human.

The forward test arrives the next time a giving decision appears—an appeal, a school request, a friend in need—and the household faces a choice: keep generosity private for ease, or bring it into the family's shared life with all the messiness and richness that implies. The question beneath that choice is not merely financial. It is cultural. What would it mean for the household if generosity were not an occasional act, but a habit discussed at the hearth, repeated quietly, and carried forward as part of the family's definition of enough?

Chapter 9
Coordinating Money In Relationships

In May 2018, in Windsor, the wedding of Prince Harry and Meghan Markle did what modern royal events always do: it turned private ritual into public spectacle, complete with crowds, commentators, and a global broadcast. The concrete outcome was a pageant of symbols—carriages, choirs, uniforms—and behind the symbols, the unglamorous machinery of resources. Even the most romantic ceremony is also an exercise in allocation: time, attention, labour, money. The fascination is not merely with the couple. It is with the idea that two lives can be fused into one story. And that fusion, if it is to last beyond the photographs, must be negotiated in the mundane places where love meets logistics.

Money is where logistics gets loud.

In many relationships, money is the most emotionally over-determined subject in the household. A conversation about spending is rarely just about spending. It is about trust and autonomy. It is about fear of being controlled and fear of being abandoned. It is about childhood scripts—what money meant in the home you grew up in, who held it, who hid it, who fought over it. It is about status and shame. It is about what each person believes a "good" life should look like, and what each person fears will happen if the household gets it wrong. And because money touches everything, it becomes the easiest proxy through which to argue about everything else.

A five-word sentence clarifies the stakes. Love doesn't pay the bills.

That line is not cynical. It is protective. It insists that affection is not diminished by practical clarity; it is endangered by practical vagueness. When money is handled well between partners, the outcome is not a spreadsheet victory. It is a household that can make decisions without turning every decision into a referendum on the relationship. When money is handled badly, even small choices can become charged—an impulsive purchase, a generous gesture, a forgotten subscription—because they are interpreted as evidence of character. One person feels policed. The other feels unheard. The argument becomes recursive. The household loses energy that could have been spent building a life.

This chapter takes money out of the realm of accusation and puts it back where it belongs: as a shared tool in a shared home. That shift begins with language. The words partners use—sometimes casually, sometimes in heat—shape whether money becomes a weapon or a bridge. Most couples do not need more financial information. They need better conversational engineering: ways to ask questions without insinuation, ways to express fear without blame, ways to talk about trade-offs without treating trade-offs as personal attacks.

The chapter therefore opens with kindness, not as a soft virtue but as a hard skill. Talking about money kindly does not mean speaking sweetly while harbouring resentment. It means speaking precisely, with curiosity about the other person's internal logic. It means moving from verdicts to questions, from "you always" to "help me understand", from "we can't" to "what would we be trading away?" Kindness is not the absence of conflict. It is the refusal to turn conflict into contempt.

From there, the chapter turns to structure—how households organise money in practice. The modern world offers more options than the cultural scripts many people inherited. Fully joint finances can work beautifully for couples who share goals, temperament, and trust. Fully separate finances can work for couples who value autonomy and have clear agreements. Partly shared systems can create both stability and independence. There is no single morally superior arrangement. The mistake is to drift into a structure by default and then treat the structure as destiny. A structure is a design choice, and design choices can be revised.

The question of structure is not merely about accounts. It is about power. Who has visibility? Who has discretion? Who carries the administrative burden? Who feels safe? Who feels infantilised? A joint account can create unity or surveillance. Separate accounts can create autonomy or secrecy. Many couples think they are arguing about bank logistics when they are actually negotiating dignity.

A subtle motif runs through this chapter: the bridge. A bridge connects two banks of a river without pretending the river does not exist. Partners do not have to become the same person to build a shared life. They do have to build reliable crossings—shared principles, shared decisions, shared rituals of review—so that money does not become a moat.

The chapter then moves to goals and trade-offs, because relationships are not only about managing the present; they are about choosing a future. Partners often agree in the abstract—security, freedom, family, generosity—while disagreeing sharply on what those words mean in practice. "Security" might mean a larger emergency fund to one person and a less stressful job to the other. "Freedom" might mean travel to one and fewer commitments to the other. "Family" might mean private school to one and more time at home to the other. "Generosity" might mean supporting extended family to one and funding community work to the other. Without explicit trade-off language, these differences surface as recurring friction points, because the household keeps making decisions without stating what it is saying yes to and what it is saying no to.

Modern relevance makes this sharper. Many households now juggle pressures that older generations did not face in the same configuration: high housing costs in certain cities, expensive childcare, fluctuating job markets, the subtle pull of lifestyle inflation amplified by social media, and the emotional complexity of supporting ageing parents while raising children. Money decisions are also time decisions. Work hours, commuting, outsourcing, convenience spending—these are forms of trade. When partners do not coordinate money, they often fail to coordinate time, and time is where resentment grows quickest.

Finally, the chapter addresses disagreements, because even the best-coordinated couples disagree. The aim is not harmony at all costs. The aim is constructive disagreement: conflict that clarifies rather than corrodes. That requires techniques: cooling-off periods, thresholds for discussion, and ways to revisit decisions without scorekeeping. Scorekeeping is the silent killer in money arguments. It turns every disagreement into a ledger of moral worth. The chapter treats repair as a skill, not as a personality trait. Couples do not need to be naturally calm. They need tools that work when they are not calm.

A credible counterpoint deserves space: some relationships are not safe places for money conversations. Financial abuse exists. Control exists. Secrecy exists. In those contexts, "coordinating money" can become a euphemism for enforcing compliance. This chapter does not romanticise communication as a universal solvent. It assumes goodwill and basic safety. Where that assumption fails, a different set of supports is needed. And yet, in the large majority of relationships where both people want the household to work, the problem is not malice. It is miscommunication and mismatched design.

The reconciliation is both hopeful and demanding. A relationship can tolerate different values and different risk tolerances if it has a shared process. It can tolerate uneven income if it has a shared sense of fairness. It can tolerate occasional mistakes if it can debrief them without shaming. It can even tolerate periods of financial pressure if it can keep money from becoming the stage on which every fear performs.

This chapter ends with momentum because the reader is meant to feel a shift from dread to agency. The next time a partner raises a money concern—or the next time a bank notification triggers a spike of irritation—the household faces a choice. It can treat the moment as evidence that something is wrong with the other person. Or it can treat the moment as a signal: two people are trying to build a bridge across a river that carries fear, hope, and history. The question is not whether the river will disappear. The question is whether the household will build crossings strong enough to carry the life it wants to live.

Talking about money kindly

In April 2020, in the United Kingdom, Citizens Advice reported that people were turning to the charity in large numbers as the Covid-19 shock hit household finances, and advice agencies began bracing for a wave of debt and insecurity. The concrete outcome, visible in call queues and online guidance, was not merely financial stress but relational stress: money worries tend to arrive in couples as tension, silence, or sudden arguments. When the same pressure sits in two people's minds, it rarely behaves like a neutral number. It behaves like an accusation waiting to be spoken.

Money makes a poor messenger.

A five-word sentence gets the problem right. Numbers carry feelings, whether invited.

When partners talk about money unkindly, they usually do it by accident. The language becomes sharp because the underlying fear is sharp. One person sees a bank balance and feels exposed. The other sees a purchase and feels disregarded. Both are trying to protect something—stability, autonomy, dignity, the future. The tragedy is that protection often shows up as blame. "You always." "You never." "I can't trust you." A conversation that began as logistics becomes a referendum on character. Even affluent households fall into this, because affluence does not remove fear; it merely changes its costume. Fear of scarcity becomes fear of losing lifestyle. Fear of debt becomes fear of being trapped in obligations. Fear of instability becomes fear of being dependent on someone else's judgement.

Kindness, in this context, is not softness. It is precision under pressure. It is speaking in a way that protects the relationship while still protecting the household's resources. It is asking questions that invite truth rather than defences. It is choosing a tone that keeps the conversation on the bridge, not in the river.

The first principle is to name what money conversations are *really* about. Most fights that appear to be about amounts are actually about meaning. A £300 coat is not a coat; it is a symbol of identity, taste, and autonomy. A £60 monthly subscription is not a subscription; it is a symbol of carelessness to one person and a symbol of normal comfort to another. A donation is not a donation; it is a symbol of values, responsibility, and sometimes guilt. If partners debate money only at the level of amounts, they keep missing the real conversation.

Show: one partner says, "We can't keep spending like this," and the other hears, "You are irresponsible." Name: meaning misfire. Explain: a meaning misfire occurs when a practical statement about cashflow is interpreted as a moral judgement; the listener defends themselves rather than engaging with the practical issue. Implication: conversations escalate because each person argues with what they *heard*, not what was said.

Kind language reduces meaning misfires by using a different unit of speech. Instead of using verdicts, it uses observations and questions. "I noticed the credit card was higher this month." "I felt anxious when I saw that." "Can we look at what drove it?" Those sentences do not remove accountability. They remove contempt. They also do something subtle: they make room for both realities at once—one person's concern and the other person's agency.

The second principle is to separate behaviour from identity. Behaviour is changeable. Identity is not supposed to be on trial every time a bank notification pings. If a partner feels that every spending conversation is an indictment of who they are, they will either defend, hide, or counterattack. None of those behaviours improve household decisions. Kindness keeps the focus on patterns and choices rather than on moral labelling.

Show: "You're reckless" becomes "This pattern worries me." Name: de-labelling. Explain: de-labelling is the shift from character judgement to pattern description; it keeps the conversation grounded in what can be changed. Implication: partners are more likely to collaborate when they are not being sentenced.

This is where curiosity about history and fears becomes decisive. People carry money scripts from childhood, and those scripts are often invisible until pressure appears. One person may have grown up with a parent who hid bills in a drawer and insisted everything was fine until it wasn't; that person may now crave transparency and predictability. Another may have grown up in a home where money was discussed constantly and anxiously; that person may now crave peace and avoid financial talk. Put those two people together and you have a perfect storm: one presses for detail, the other withdraws, and both feel unsafe.

A five-word sentence names the hidden engine. History speaks through tone and timing.

When partners become curious about these scripts, the conversation shifts from blame to understanding. Understanding does not mean permissiveness. It means accuracy. If one partner's fear is "we will end up trapped," and the other's fear is "I will be controlled," then a simple decision about spending can trigger both at once. Kind language identifies the fear without weaponising it. "When we talk about money, I sometimes feel controlled." "When we don't talk about money, I sometimes feel unsafe." Those are vulnerable sentences. They are also the beginning of a sane process.

The third principle is to choose the right moment. Couples often try to talk about money at the worst times: at the end of the day, in the car, while one person is multitasking, immediately after seeing a bank alert. That is understandable because the alert creates urgency. It is also self-sabotage. Kindness includes timing because timing protects attention. A conversation about money requires working memory, emotional regulation, and patience. It is hard to be kind without those resources.

Show: a bank alert arrives during a stressful afternoon; one partner demands an explanation immediately. Name: ambush timing. Explain: ambush timing is raising a complex issue when the other person is cognitively depleted; it increases defensiveness and reduces problem-solving capacity. Implication: the issue escalates and becomes a fight about respect rather than a conversation about money.

This principle is not about avoidance. It is about choosing conditions that increase the probability of repair. The same words spoken in a calm window can be experienced as care; spoken in a frazzled moment, they can be experienced as attack. Kindness is the discipline of choosing the calm window.

The fourth principle is to use shared language that keeps both partners on the same side of the table. The most effective money conversations frame the problem as external: the household is facing a design challenge, not a moral trial. "We have a cashflow pinch."

"We have commitments bunching up." "We have an inconsistency between what we value and where money is going." That framing echoes the larger arc of this book. It treats the household as a system that can be adjusted, not as a stage on which one partner must be proven right.

Show: "You're overspending" becomes "We're drifting from our priorities." Name: shared-problem framing. Explain: shared-problem framing locates the issue in the system and the pattern rather than in one person's flaws. Implication: partners can collaborate on design changes without humiliating each other.

A practical example conversation makes the shift visible. Imagine a couple—busy, comfortable, time-poor—discovering that their monthly spend has crept up. Partner A feels anxious and wants to clamp down. Partner B feels accused and wants to defend autonomy. The unkind opening sounds like this: "Do you have any idea how much you spent this month? This is ridiculous." The predictable reply is defensive: "So now I'm the problem? You spend too." The conversation becomes a duel, and nothing is solved.

Now observe the kind opening: "I looked at the statements and felt a bit of a jolt. The total was higher than I expected. Can we look at what drove it together?" That sentence contains an observation, a feeling, and an invitation. It also avoids the trap of implied intent. It does not claim the other person was careless or selfish. It asks for collaboration. Partner B can now respond without surrendering dignity: "Okay. I didn't realise it had crept up either. Let's see." The pair can then move into specifics: "I notice takeaway and transport were high. Was work particularly chaotic?" "Yes, and I was also helping my sister." That context does not excuse overspending. It explains it. Explanation allows redesign.

A second example—checkable in the sense that it is a public cultural artefact rather than a private therapy story—comes from how institutions train people to have difficult conversations. The UK's National Health Service has long used structured communication tools in clinical settings, such as SBAR (Situation, Background, Assessment, Recommendation), to reduce misunderstandings under pressure. The point is not to import clinical acronyms into marriage.

The point is that high-stakes environments often rely on scripts because scripts protect clarity when emotions run high. Households can adopt the same humility: under stress, humans miscommunicate; structured language reduces damage.

Scripts, in this context, are not robotic. They are scaffolding. They give a partner a way to begin without swinging a hammer. The script might be as simple as: "I noticed X. I felt Y. I'm worried about Z. Can we look at it together?" It might include a specific request: "Could we set a time this weekend to review?" It might include a reassurance: "I'm not angry; I'm trying to understand." These phrases are not manipulative. They are clarifying. They create psychological safety, which is a prerequisite for honest disclosure.

The fifth principle is to make trade-offs explicit without making them punitive. Money conversations often fail because one partner hears "no" and experiences it as deprivation imposed by the other. Kindness keeps agency present: "If we say yes to this, what are we saying no to?" That question is not a trap. It is the truth of finite resources. It invites joint prioritisation rather than unilateral control.

Show: a partner wants a costly holiday; the other is worried about commitments. Name: trade-off visibility. Explain: trade-off visibility is naming the opportunity cost of a decision, making the real consequences discussable. Implication: couples can disagree more constructively because they are debating priorities, not accusing each other of selfishness.

A credible limitation must be stated plainly. Kind language is not a cure for bad faith. If one partner consistently lies, hides spending, or uses money as a tool of control, scripts will not fix the problem. There are also cultural and personal contexts where money discussions are laden with trauma, shame, or unequal power dynamics. In those cases, "talk kindly" can become a way of blaming the hurt partner for reacting. That is not the aim here. The aim is to provide tools for relationships where both people are trying, where the core issue is miscommunication and mismatched design rather than cruelty.

The reconciliation is that kindness is compatible with firmness. Kindness does not mean avoiding hard truths. It means delivering hard truths in a way that makes them usable. "I can't carry this anxiety alone." "I need transparency to feel safe." "I need a lane of autonomy to feel respected." Those are firm sentences. They are also kind, because they state needs rather than issuing indictments.

The motif for this section is the bridge introduced in the chapter opening. Kind talk is bridge-building language. It is language that creates crossings: from fear to clarity, from suspicion to shared attention, from reactive arguments to deliberate design. Bridges are built plank by plank. A single conversation rarely fixes everything. But a pattern of kind language changes the emotional climate in which money decisions are made.

The forward test arrives the next time a partner raises money—perhaps with a sigh, perhaps with irritation, perhaps with silence. The household can default to the old script: accusation, defence, counter-accusation. Or it can pause on the bridge and ask the question that changes everything: are we trying to win, or are we trying to understand what this money moment is really signalling about fear, values, and the life we are building together?

Joint spending and autonomy

On 16 June 1965, in London, the United Kingdom's Parliament passed the Married Women's Property Act 1964 into force, consolidating a legal reality that had been evolving for decades: a married woman could own property and enter contracts in her own right. The concrete outcome was not only legal clarity but a cultural shift in what "shared" could mean. A household could be a union without being a single wallet. Autonomy inside togetherness became, at least in law, imaginable.

That history matters because many couples still run their finances as if it never happened.

A five-word sentence captures the modern dilemma. Unity and autonomy both matter.

When people argue about "joint finances" versus "separate finances", they often treat it as a morality play: joint equals committed, separate equals suspicious. In reality, the structure of household money is closer to architecture than ethics. The question is not which arrangement signals virtue. The question is which arrangement produces the behaviours the household wants: transparency without surveillance, cooperation without resentment, autonomy without secrecy, generosity without destabilising the baseline.

Show: two partners earn well, share a home, and claim to share goals, yet they fight monthly about "random spending". One wants a single shared pot to prevent drift. The other wants separate money to prevent feeling policed. Name: the control–freedom tug. Explain: the control–freedom tug is the predictable tension between a desire for shared oversight (to protect priorities) and a desire for personal discretion (to protect dignity). Implication: if a couple chooses a money structure that ignores this tug, the structure will amplify conflict; if it respects it, the structure will reduce emotional load.

The useful starting point is to see that "joint" and "separate" are not binaries. They are points on a spectrum. Fully joint systems pool income and pay all expenses from shared accounts, often with shared visibility. Fully separate systems keep income and most spending distinct, with agreed mechanisms for shared bills. Hybrid systems combine shared accounts for essentials with personal accounts for discretionary spending, sometimes with a shared "fun" pot and sometimes with personal "lanes". The category names are less important than the design features they create: visibility, discretion, responsibility, and the friction or ease of making decisions.

Visibility is not the same as control. A household can have high visibility without moral policing, and it can have low visibility without deception. Visibility is simply information: who can see what, when, and with what emotional tone attached. Discretion is not the same as selfishness. Discretion is capacity: the ability to make small choices without negotiation. Responsibility is not the same as burden. Responsibility is ownership: who ensures bills are paid, renewals are checked, and commitments are not quietly multiplying in the background. These features are the moving parts. They determine whether money becomes a battleground or a tool.

Consider first the fully joint system, often favoured by couples who want simplicity and shared identity. It can be remarkably efficient. Income flows into a single pool. Bills and commitments are paid. The household makes decisions from a shared picture of reality. For certain couples—especially those with children, or those who view the household as a single enterprise—this can feel natural and relieving. There is no mental accounting of "mine" and "yours". There is only "ours".

Show: a couple uses one current account, one credit card, and a shared dashboard. Both can see the numbers. Neither person has to ask permission to buy groceries or book a train. Name: pooled clarity. Explain: pooled clarity is the reduction of ambiguity created by one shared financial picture; it can reduce anxiety and duplication because both people are working from the same information. Implication: pooled clarity can free attention for higher-value decisions—work choices, family priorities, generosity—because the household isn't constantly negotiating micro-transactions.

The problem is that a fully joint system can tip into surveillance if the couple has mismatched spending instincts or unresolved trust wounds. The same visibility that creates clarity can create friction: every purchase becomes visible, and visibility can be interpreted as judgement. If one partner is more anxious, they may check obsessively. If the other is more autonomy-oriented, they may feel watched. The system itself becomes a trigger.

This is where the hybrid system earns its keep. A well-designed hybrid preserves a shared centre while protecting personal lanes. Shared money covers shared priorities: housing, bills, groceries, childcare, planned giving, agreed savings. Personal money covers personal discretion: hobbies, clothing, gifts, spontaneous lunches, the small choices that keep adults feeling like adults rather than like employees in the household enterprise. The crucial point is that personal lanes are not a loophole. They are a deliberate design feature to prevent constant negotiation and to reduce resentment.

A five-word sentence makes it plain. Autonomy prevents petty wars.

Show: a couple contributes to a shared account each month and keeps separate personal accounts. They agree that shared commitments must be funded first. They also agree that personal spending is not interrogated unless it threatens shared priorities. Name: bounded autonomy. Explain: bounded autonomy is the practice of maintaining personal discretion within clear household constraints; it recognises that adults need some financial self-determination to feel respected. Implication: bounded autonomy reduces the frequency of money conflicts by removing the need to litigate every choice, while still protecting core goals.

Notice what the hybrid system demands: explicit agreement. It cannot be run on vibes. The couple has to decide what counts as shared, what counts as personal, and how to handle irregular costs that sit in the grey zone—holidays, support for extended family, large gifts, personal development courses, big hobby purchases. The hybrid system also demands a basic level of fairness, not necessarily mathematical equality. If one partner earns significantly more, the household must decide whether contributions are proportional, equal, or otherwise negotiated. The aim is to avoid the corrosive dynamic where one partner feels like a sponsor and the other feels like a dependent.

Now consider the mostly separate system. This is sometimes chosen by couples with strong independence, second marriages, complex family structures, or simply a deep preference for personal control. It can work extremely well when both partners are organised and when shared obligations are clear and reliably funded. It can also protect against certain kinds of conflict, because each person bears the consequences of their own discretionary spending. Separate systems can be particularly attractive when partners have different spending styles and do not want constant friction.

Show: two partners keep finances mostly separate and split shared costs via fixed transfers each month. They each fund their own discretionary purchases. They review shared bills quarterly. Name: parallel tracks. Explain: parallel tracks are financial arrangements where partners run individual systems alongside a shared agreement for joint obligations. Implication: parallel tracks can preserve autonomy and reduce day-to-day conflict, especially when partners value independence and have stable income.

The weakness of parallel tracks is that they can hide drift and create asymmetry. One partner may quietly accumulate savings while the other carries more lifestyle spending. One partner may shoulder invisible labour—remembering renewals, managing household admin—while the other enjoys the freedom of not thinking about it. Separate systems can also make it harder to plan for shared future goals, because the household lacks a single "truth" about capacity. The cost is not only financial. It is relational. People can start feeling like flatmates rather than collaborators.

This is why "matching structure to life stage" matters. A couple without children, renting, with similar incomes and a strong preference for autonomy may thrive with parallel tracks. The same couple, five years later, with a mortgage, childcare, and one partner taking a career break, may find the same structure suddenly feels unfair or brittle. Structures are not promises. They are tools for a season.

A concrete illustration makes this clearer. Household One is a couple in Edinburgh with two children and a heavy schedule. They run a largely joint system because cognitive load is already high. Income flows into a shared account. Regular transfers fund an irregular-costs pot and a giving fund. Each partner also has a modest monthly personal allowance that goes into individual accounts. The result is that the household can pay for essentials and planned generosity without drama, while each adult retains discretion and dignity.

Household Two is a couple in Bristol in their late thirties, both self-employed, with fluctuating income and prior experiences that make them allergic to financial enmeshment. They keep finances mostly separate. Each month they transfer an agreed amount into a shared account for rent, utilities, and groceries, with an additional buffer for variable bills. They keep separate accounts for taxes and business expenses. They maintain a shared view of the household's commitments and hold a scheduled review to adjust transfers when income swings. The result is a sense of autonomy with a shared safety net.

Both households are "coordinated". Both households are "adult". Both structures work because they match values, personalities, and constraints. They also work because the couples are not pretending the structure will do the emotional work for them. Structure reduces friction. It does not manufacture trust.

Trust, here, must be tethered to behaviours. Trust shows up as consistency: agreed transfers arrive on time, bills are paid, commitments are disclosed, surprises are explained rather than hidden. Trust also shows up as restraint: one partner does not use visibility to criticise, and the other does not use autonomy to evade shared responsibilities. These behaviours can be measured. Does the shared account regularly run low unexpectedly? Do "temporary" upgrades become permanent commitments without discussion? Does one partner repeatedly discover new subscriptions or debts after the fact? Those are not abstract issues. They are signals that the structure and the behaviour are misaligned.

A credible counter-example belongs in any honest discussion: no structure can compensate for bad faith or coercion. If one partner uses money to control the other—restricting access, demanding receipts, preventing employment, accumulating debt in the other's name—then the issue is not "joint versus separate". It is safety and power. Conversely, if one partner repeatedly hides spending or lies about obligations, a separate system may reduce immediate damage but will not resolve the underlying breach. In such cases, structure can become a way of avoiding the real conversation. And yet, in the much more common scenario where both people are trying but keep colliding, structure is often the fastest way to reduce conflict and protect priorities.

The reconciliation is to treat money structure as a design choice with clear criteria. The best structure is not the one that looks most romantic. It is the one that makes the household's values easier to enact. If the household values generosity, does the structure make planned giving effortless or perpetually "extra"? If it values freedom, does the structure create breathing room or lock in commitments?

If it values peace, does the structure reduce day-to-day negotiation or invite constant monitoring? If it values equality, does the structure produce fairness in practice, not merely in theory?

A quiet motif from the chapter opening returns: the bridge. Jointness is the shared bridge deck. Autonomy is the railing that keeps each person upright. Too much deck without railing feels like exposure; too much railing without deck feels like separation. The art is to build a bridge that can carry real life: the messy, expensive, generous, human life that does not arrive in neat monthly increments.

The forward test is simple to state and difficult to answer honestly. When the next money tension arises—a purchase, a bonus, a family request, a sudden bill—does the household's current structure make the conversation easier, or does it turn it into a fight about control and respect? If the structure is not serving the relationship, the question is not who is wrong. The question is what should be redesigned so that shared priorities and personal dignity can coexist without constant strain.

Aligning goals and tradeoffs

In October 2007, in Oslo, the Nobel Peace Prize went to the Intergovernmental Panel on Climate Change and Al Gore. The concrete outcome was a spotlight on a particular kind of argument: that long-term risks deserve present-day decisions, even when the costs are immediate and the benefits diffuse. For many households, the lesson is oddly intimate. Couples do not fall apart because they cannot compute. They fall apart because they cannot agree on what the future is for—and therefore cannot agree on which present-day sacrifices are tolerable.

Goals without trade-offs are fantasies.

A five-word sentence makes it sting usefully. Every yes is also no.

Partners often claim to share goals. They say they want security. They want freedom. They want a good life for their children. They want to be generous. The words are agreeable because they are abstract. The conflict arrives when the abstract has to become a calendar entry, a standing order, a school application, a decision about overtime, a decision about whether to buy time by paying for help, a decision about how much support to give extended family. In other words: when goals collide with reality.

Show: two partners repeatedly promise to "save more", but each month the surplus evaporates into small upgrades, occasional treats, and the subtle creep of recurring commitments. Name: goal fog. Explain: goal fog is the condition where a household holds high-level intentions without translating them into explicit, shared trade-offs; the fog allows drift because nothing concrete is being protected. Implication: money decisions become reactive and interpersonal, with each partner blaming the other for failures that are, in truth, failures of design.

Aligning goals is therefore not about writing a poetic vision statement. It is about choosing which outcomes the household will defend when choices get tight. It is about knowing which tensions are likely to recur and agreeing, in advance, how to navigate them. The discipline is not romantic. It is stabilising. A relationship that has an agreed method for handling trade-offs is less likely to treat every decision as a personal betrayal.

Trade-offs show up first in time, then in money. Work hours are a trade: income, status, and security exchanged for presence, rest, and flexibility. Schooling decisions are a trade: opportunities purchased at the cost of fees, commuting, and sometimes a narrower social world. Housing is a trade: space and convenience exchanged for long-term obligations. Support for extended family is a trade: moral duty and love balanced against the household's capacity, and against fairness between partners' families. These are not minor matters. They shape the texture of daily life.

To align goals, partners must do something many couples avoid because it feels too stark: they must name their "sacred cows" and their "acceptable sacrifices". Sacred cows are the non-negotiables—the few priorities that define the household. Acceptable sacrifices are the things the household is willing to dial down or delay to protect the sacred cows. Without this clarity, couples often end up defending different sacred cows without realising it. One partner may be defending stability; the other may be defending connection. One may be defending generosity; the other may be defending autonomy. Both are legitimate. The conflict is not legitimacy. The conflict is that the household cannot protect everything at once.

Show: one partner insists on private schooling because they believe it protects their child's future; the other resists because they believe it will require work hours that reduce family life. Name: competing goods conflict. Explain: competing goods conflict is disagreement not between good and bad, but between two genuine goods that cannot both be maximised simultaneously. Implication: moralising the disagreement ("you don't care about our child" versus "you care more about status than family") destroys trust; naming it as a trade-off opens room for shared reasoning.

Shared reasoning requires a shared frame. The most useful frame is blunt and freeing: "If we say yes here, what are we saying no to?" That sentence does not end debate; it starts an honest one. It forces the household to talk about opportunity cost—the reality that resources, including time and attention, are finite. It also prevents a common distortion in affluent households: treating every desirable option as if it can be funded by "just trying a bit harder". Trying harder often means working more, delegating more, consuming more convenience, and quietly eroding the very life the household claims it wants.

A five-word sentence names the trap. Effort can become a leak.

The mechanism is simple. When a household avoids trade-offs, it tends to solve every problem with expenditure: pay for speed, pay for relief, pay for image, pay for smoothing. This can work for a while. Then commitments accumulate. Freedom shrinks. The household becomes wealthy on paper and tight in practice. The emotional consequence is that partners start arguing about symptoms—subscriptions, meals out, small purchases—when the real issue is that the household has not chosen its priorities with enough specificity to contain drift.

Specificity does not require spreadsheets. It requires decisions that can be observed. A shared goal should be tied to at least one visible behaviour or metric. "Security" might be tied to maintaining a buffer in a designated account. "Freedom" might be tied to limiting fixed monthly commitments. "Family time" might be tied to a cap on work travel nights or a commitment to certain evenings being protected. "Generosity" might be tied to a giving fund being funded before lifestyle upgrades. These are not prescriptions. They are examples of what it means to make a goal real enough to defend.

Show: a couple claims to value "time with children" yet repeatedly schedules additional work commitments because the household's spending has expanded to require them. Name: values inversion. Explain: values inversion is when spending patterns force behaviour that contradicts stated priorities; the household then experiences ongoing cognitive dissonance and resentment. Implication: partners fight about work stress, exhaustion, and "lack of support" without seeing that the household's commitments are dictating the calendar.

The trade-off conversation must therefore include friction points. Friction points are predictable disputes that recur because they sit at the intersection of values and constraints. Common friction points include: how much to spend on housing, how much to outsource domestic labour, what "reasonable" spending on children looks like, how to handle bonuses, how much to support family members, how often to travel, how much to spend on status-linked categories (cars, wardrobes, gadgets), and how to balance giving with lifestyle. Each friction point contains a moral story. Partners must surface the stories or they will keep colliding.

A quiet motif from this chapter's earlier sections returns here: the bridge. Goals are the far bank. Trade-offs are the river. Couples need crossings that can bear weight. The crossing is not a single conversation. It is a repeatable method: a way to return to shared priorities without re-litigating the relationship every time.

Two named, checkable examples from public life illustrate the difference between stated goals and enacted trade-offs. In the United Kingdom, the introduction of the National Minimum Wage in April 1999 required explicit trade-offs in public policy—balancing worker protections against business costs. Whether one agrees with every detail is beside the point. The point is structural: goals became law because trade-offs were argued, negotiated, and made explicit. By contrast, in personal life, many couples keep goals in the realm of aspiration while making trade-offs implicitly, through drift. Drift is the private version of policy by neglect.

A second example comes from the world of organisations. When Toyota's lean manufacturing ideas became globally influential in the late twentieth century, the principle was not mystical: reduce waste by making choices explicit, building feedback, and aligning daily behaviours with a clear definition of value. Households are not factories, and the analogy should not be stretched into absurdity. Yet the underlying insight holds: if a system does not define what it is optimising for, it will optimise for what is easiest, most immediate, and most rewarded in the moment.

Now consider the "simple exercise" that fosters joint prioritisation. It must be simple because busy households have limited patience for elaborate rituals. It must also be emotionally intelligent because money is rarely just arithmetic. The exercise, at its core, is a paired translation task: translate abstract goals into concrete trade-offs, and translate trade-offs back into the life they are meant to protect.

In practice, partners can begin by each naming three outcomes they care about over the next few years that are concrete enough to picture. Not "wealth", but "the option for one partner to reduce hours without panic", or "the ability to help a parent if health declines", or "a household rhythm with fewer evenings spent exhausted". Then each partner names one fear: not a complaint about the other person, but a fear about what could go wrong—"I'm afraid we'll get locked into costs we can't reverse", "I'm afraid we'll postpone life indefinitely", "I'm afraid we'll become ungenerous", "I'm afraid I'll be judged for spending". The aim is not therapy. The aim is information. With those outcomes and fears on the table, the couple then identifies the two or three friction points most likely to threaten the outcomes. They do not solve everything. They choose the main battlegrounds. Then they ask, for each friction point: if we say yes to one path, what are we saying no to? The question forces the household to name costs explicitly—money, time, stress, autonomy. It also forces the household to notice which trade-offs feel acceptable and which feel corrosive.

Show: a couple realises that a larger house would require higher fixed commitments and therefore more work hours; they also realise that staying smaller would require stricter boundaries with clutter and possibly less entertaining space. Name: honest constraint mapping. Explain: honest constraint mapping is the act of making the real costs of each option explicit, including non-financial costs such as time and stress. Implication: couples can argue about choices rather than about each other's character; the conversation becomes collaborative design.

A credible limitation must be admitted. Some trade-offs are not fully under a household's control. Health can change. Employers can demand more. Family crises can arrive. Children's needs can evolve. Economic conditions can tighten. Aligning goals does not prevent shock. It does, however, give a household a compass in shock. Without alignment, external pressure tends to exploit internal ambiguity. With alignment, partners have a better chance of responding as a unit rather than as rivals.

The reconciliation is that alignment does not demand identical preferences. It demands a shared hierarchy of priorities and a shared method for revisiting it. Partners can disagree on taste, on risk tolerance, and on what counts as "enough" in specific categories, and still coordinate effectively if they agree on the core trade-offs they are willing to make. A household can even treat certain decisions as experiments rather than final commitments: try a different work pattern for a season; trial a schooling route; set a temporary boundary on supporting extended family while building capacity. The key is that experiments have pre-decided review points. Drift does not.

A five-word sentence protects against drift. Decide, test, then decide again.

The forward test appears at the moment of the next tempting "yes": a bigger house, a pricier school, an upgrade, a new commitment, an offer that flatters the ego or promises convenience. The household will feel the pull to treat the decision as isolated. It is not isolated. It is another stone placed in the river. The question that determines whether the bridge holds is whether partners can look at the stone together and say, without accusation and without fantasy, what they are willing to trade away—and what they are no longer willing to sacrifice—so that the life they claim to value can remain not merely desired, but lived.

Handling disagreements constructively

On 26 April 1986, in northern Ukraine, the Chernobyl nuclear power plant suffered a catastrophic accident whose consequences rippled far beyond the immediate blast and fire: whole regions were evacuated, trust in institutions fractured, and the word "risk" acquired a grim new weight. The concrete outcome, measured in displacement and contamination, is a reminder that risk is rarely experienced as a tidy probability. It is experienced as dread, denial, and argument—often after the fact, often when it is too late to rewind the decision. In households, money disagreements are rarely catastrophic in that literal sense, yet they are often catastrophic in the small way that matters day after day: they erode trust through unresolved tension.

Disagreement is not failure.

A five-word sentence puts the task in focus. Repair is the real skill.

Couples who never disagree about money either have a rare symmetry of temperament and circumstance, or they are not talking honestly. Most partners have different risk tolerances, different spending instincts, and different thresholds for what feels safe. These differences are not pathologies. They are variations in how humans cope with uncertainty. The problem is not the clash. The problem is what the clash produces when it is handled badly: contempt, secrecy, scorekeeping, and the slow retreat from shared planning. If money is meant to support a life together, then disagreement is one of the main places where togetherness is tested.

Show: one partner makes an impulsive purchase—a new laptop, a premium pram, a surprise weekend away—believing it will improve life. The other sees the charge and feels blindsided. Name: the surprise tax. Explain: the surprise tax is the relational cost of unanticipated spending, especially when it intersects with shared commitments; the tax is paid in trust, not money. Implication: even when the purchase is affordable, the relationship can feel poorer because predictability has been damaged.

Handling disagreements constructively begins with accepting that money conflicts are often proxy conflicts. The laptop is not the laptop. It is autonomy versus shared control. The donation is not the donation. It is values versus security. The investment risk is not the investment risk. It is optimism versus caution, identity versus fear, the future versus the present. If partners argue only about the surface choice, they keep missing the deeper pattern. Constructive handling requires a way to talk that surfaces the underlying concern without turning it into a moral indictment.

The first guideline is to slow the fight down. That sounds banal until one notices how often couples fight about money in a state of physiological agitation: raised voice, quick speech, narrowed attention, mental certainty. In that state, people do not reason well. They prosecute. They defend. They gather evidence. They remember old grievances. A cooling-off period is not avoidance; it is a commitment to speak when the brain is capable of cooperation.

Show: a partner sees a charge and immediately confronts the other, voice already sharpened. The other responds defensively. Within minutes they are rehashing months of unrelated grievances. Name: escalation spiral. Explain: escalation spiral is the rapid widening of a specific disagreement into a generalised attack on character and history. Implication: the original problem—how to handle a purchase—remains unsolved, while resentment accumulates.

Cooling-off works best when it is pre-agreed. A couple can decide, in calm moments, what "pause" looks like. Is it twenty minutes to walk and breathe? Is it a rule that money conversations do not happen after 10 p.m.? Is it a commitment to sleep on any purchase above a certain amount? The details vary. The principle is consistent:

protect the conversation from the physiology of panic. Couples who do this are not repressing conflict. They are choosing the conditions under which conflict can be metabolised rather than poisoned.

The second guideline is to define spending thresholds that trigger discussion. Thresholds are not about permission. They are about coordination. Without thresholds, partners are forced to improvise what "significant" means, and improvisation invites disagreement precisely when emotions are already running hot. A threshold externalises the decision: it becomes a rule the couple agreed, rather than a judgement one partner is imposing in the moment.

Show: a couple has no threshold; each partner has a different internal definition of "big purchase". One considers £200 trivial; the other considers it significant. Name: threshold mismatch. Explain: threshold mismatch is the gap between partners' implicit spending norms; the mismatch generates repeated conflict because each person experiences the other as unreasonable. Implication: even small purchases become battlegrounds because the dispute is really about norms, not amounts.

Thresholds also clarify autonomy. If partners know what they can decide alone, they feel less infantilised. If they know what must be coordinated, they feel less exposed. The household becomes calmer because decision rights are clear. Decision rights are a form of respect.

A third guideline is to create a method for revisiting decisions without scorekeeping. Scorekeeping is the quiet killer of money peace. It turns the household into a courtroom where each partner accumulates precedent: "You spent on that, so I can spend on this." "You made that mistake, so you owe me." "I gave up this, so you should give up that." The ledger never clears because it is not a financial ledger. It is a moral ledger. Once partners are keeping moral accounts, generosity shrinks and suspicion grows.

A five-word sentence warns against it. Ledgers breed resentment, not fairness.

Constructive revisiting is different. It treats a regretted expense as data, not as a character verdict. The question becomes: what did we miss? What signal did we ignore? What assumption failed? How can we design a guardrail that makes this less likely next time? That approach keeps dignity intact while still demanding learning.

Show: a couple books an expensive holiday during a stressful season, hoping it will provide relief. The trip is underwhelming; the cost lingers. The partners are tempted to blame each other. Name: regret reframing. Explain: regret reframing is the shift from "who caused this?" to "what conditions produced this decision?" Implication: regret becomes a source of system improvement rather than a seed of lasting resentment.

A concrete debrief example makes this vivid. Imagine a couple who buys a high-end exercise bike on impulse after a persuasive sales pitch and a wave of New Year motivation. Six months later it has become an expensive clothes horse. One partner feels embarrassed and defensive; the other feels annoyed and vindicated. An unconstructive debrief sounds like this: "I told you so." "Stop rubbing it in." "You always fall for marketing." "You never support my goals." The bike becomes a symbol of disrespect.

A constructive debrief starts differently. It begins with shared reality: "We spent £X on this and we've used it Y times." That is not cruelty. It is clarity. It then moves to meaning: "What were we hoping it would do for us?" Perhaps the answer is not "fitness" but "a sense of control", "an identity shift", "a way to cope with stress". Then it moves to the process failure: "We bought it on a high-emotion day. We didn't test whether we'd use it. We didn't set a cooling-off period." Finally, it moves to redesign: "Next time we consider a big purchase like this, can we agree to trial first, or to wait a week, or to decide together after checking where it fits in our priorities?" Notice what is absent: humiliation. Notice what remains: accountability.

This debrief method does not eliminate regret. It prevents regret from fossilising into contempt. It also respects a truth adults often resist: people make worse decisions when they are stressed, tired, hungry, time-poor, or emotionally unsettled. Households cannot remove those conditions. They can design around them.

The fourth guideline is to treat disagreements as signals about underlying risk tolerance rather than as proof of irrationality. Risk tolerance is partly personality and partly biography. Someone who watched a parent lose a job may crave buffers. Someone who grew up with chronic scarcity may fear any reduction in cashflow. Someone who spent years working for stability may feel entitled to enjoy it. Someone who has experienced betrayal may need control to feel safe. These are not excuses. They are explanatory maps. A household that acknowledges risk maps can negotiate with far less cruelty.

Show: one partner prefers conservative choices and wants to keep commitments low; the other pushes for upgrades and sees caution as fear. Name: risk narrative collision. Explain: risk narrative collision is the clash between partners' internal stories about what danger looks like and what safety requires. Implication: unless those narratives are made explicit, partners keep attacking each other's motives instead of negotiating trade-offs.

At this point, a credible counter-example must be faced. Some disagreements are not merely differences in temperament. They are symptoms of deeper relational breakdown: repeated dishonesty, hidden debts, compulsive spending, or coercive control. In such contexts, "constructive disagreement" can become a polite veneer over a fundamental breach. A cooling-off rule does not repair chronic deception. A spending threshold does not protect someone whose access is being restricted unfairly. It is important not to romanticise techniques as universal solutions. Techniques work when both partners are acting in good faith and are capable of repair.

The reconciliation is that most couples who fight about money are not enemies. They are two people trying to protect a shared life with different instincts and imperfect tools. In those cases, guidelines act like guardrails. They do not force agreement. They prevent the argument from becoming destructive. They preserve the relationship's capacity to collaborate even when the decision remains contested.

Two additional, named, checkable examples help anchor the plausibility of repair-focused approaches. The psychologist John

Gottman, whose research on marital stability has been widely cited since the 1990s, popularised the importance of repair attempts—small actions or phrases that de-escalate conflict and restore connection. One does not need to treat any researcher as an oracle to recognise the pattern: couples who can repair after tension are more resilient than couples who insist on being right. A second example comes from the legal concept of "without prejudice" discussions in the UK: negotiations can be held in a way that allows exploration without immediate penalty. Again, the household is not a courtroom, but the principle translates: create spaces where partners can explore solutions without turning every suggestion into ammunition.

A quiet motif from earlier in the chapter returns: the bridge. Disagreements are the gusts that test the structure. Cooling-off periods are the moments when the couple stops walking to brace. Spending thresholds are the load limits that prevent collapse. Debriefs without scorekeeping are the maintenance checks that keep small cracks from spreading.

The forward test arrives sooner than anyone prefers. A new opportunity appears. A child needs something. A family member asks for help. A tempting upgrade flashes across a screen. A partner's anxiety spikes. Another partner's desire for relief spikes. The household will feel the pull to settle it quickly, or to win, or to retreat into silence. The question is whether, in that moment, the couple can hold the tension long enough to choose a process that protects both money and meaning—because the argument they are having is never only about the purchase. It is about whether their shared life has a reliable way to absorb disagreement without turning love into a ledger.

Chapter 10
Systems For Busy Earners

At 06:12 on a Tuesday in March 2023, a commuter train slid out of London Bridge and the carriage filled with the soft percussion of modern life: notification pings, thumb-swipes, the tinny leakage of someone else's podcast. A woman in a navy coat opened a banking app, stared for three seconds, then closed it as if it had burned her. She was not broke. She was, by any ordinary measure, successful. Yet the sight of the balance still carried a faint sting—less fear of ruin than irritation at the sheer *management* of it all, the sense that money, like email, had become an always-on system demanding attention at precisely the moments attention was already scarce.

For busy earners, scarcity often hides in plain sight. It is not pounds. It is minutes.

And attention leaks faster than cash.

The paradox is that high incomes do not buy a simpler financial life; they frequently buy a more complex one. A larger home arrives with more direct debits and maintenance decisions. Career momentum arrives with travel, outsourced help, and purchases made at speed. Children arrive with irregular costs that refuse to be neatly monthly. Success arrives with more choice, and choice is a cognitive tax. The household becomes a small organisation with payroll (income), procurement (spending), compliance (tax and bills), risk management (buffers and insurance), and philanthropy (if values are honoured rather than postponed). Yet most households run this organisation with no operating system—only memory, guilt, and last-minute firefighting.

This chapter is about building an operating system.

Not a rigid regime. Not an obsession. A set of systems that quietly carry the load when life is full. The aspiration is not to become a miniature accountant. The aspiration is to make money behave like plumbing: mostly invisible, reliably functional, and noticed only when something genuinely needs attention. The difference between a household that feels financially "tight" and one that feels free is often not income. It is whether the household has designed its flows so that important priorities happen by default and distractions have to fight for oxygen.

A system is a bet about human nature. It assumes tired people exist. It assumes busy seasons arrive. It assumes willpower fluctuates and that decisions made under pressure are often worse than decisions made with a little structure around them. The mainstream imagination of "being good with money" still leans towards discipline, self-control, and constant vigilance. Those virtues can matter, but they do not scale. They break under stress. They also waste a resource that affluent, time-poor people rarely have in surplus: sustained attention. A system is how a household protects attention for what only humans can do—relationships, meaningful work, rest, generosity—by delegating routine consistency to structure.

To see why this matters, consider the difference between two kinds of stress. There is the stress of genuine insufficiency: the hard limits of not having enough. And there is the stress of constant monitoring: the sense that things are probably fine, but could turn not-fine if one stops watching. Many comfortable households live in the second. They are not in immediate danger, yet they feel perpetually on call. This is where money starts to resemble a demanding colleague rather than a tool. Each month becomes a small negotiation with uncertainty: which bills are due when, whether the card balance is "higher than it should be", whether something has slipped through unnoticed, whether generosity will be possible once everything else is handled. The household pays a steady tax in micro-anxiety.

Systems reduce that tax by shifting the household from reactive to designed. That shift is not merely practical. It is philosophical. A reactive household lives at the mercy of whatever is loudest: the urgent bill, the tempting purchase, the emotionally charged request. A designed household lives according to what has been intentionally placed on autopilot: essentials funded first, irregular costs smoothed, giving set aside as a normal commitment rather than an occasional impulse, and discretionary spending contained without being suffocating.

The first strand of this chapter is automation—because predictable actions should not require repeated decisions. It is strangely modern that people who automate the heating, the lighting, and the grocery delivery still manage their money as if it requires constant manual intervention. Predictable inflows and outflows exist: salaries, mortgages or rent, utilities, childcare, subscriptions, loan payments. Many households allow these to happen in a chaotic order, and then wonder why the middle of the month feels like a squeeze. Automation, properly understood, is not the elimination of choice; it is the elimination of repetitive choice in areas where repetition adds no value. When bills are scheduled, transfers to key accounts occur automatically, and sinking funds are fed regularly, money begins to "move itself". The monthly experience changes. Stress decreases not because spending has become saintly, but because timing and predictability have been engineered.

The second strand is purpose-built accounts or "pots" that give money visible roles. A single large balance is deceptively comforting. It invites a form of optimism that is often expensive: if the number looks big, everything seems affordable, even when a portion of that number is already spoken for by upcoming bills, annual renewals, and irregular costs. Visual separation counters this illusion by making commitments legible. When essentials sit in one account, irregular expenses in another, discretionary spending in another, and giving in its own lane, the household gains clarity without needing constant calculation. The mind stops performing a silent subtraction exercise all day. It sees, at a glance, what is available for what.

This is not about hiding money from oneself like a Victorian aunt hiding biscuits. It is about reducing cognitive load. Humans are not naturally good at tracking multiple future obligations inside a single number, especially when fatigued. A pot for irregular expenses—birthdays, car maintenance, school trips, annual subscriptions, repairs—smooths the psychological shock of "surprise" bills. The bill may still be annoying, but it is no longer destabilising. The household is no longer forced into a sudden choice between raiding savings, adding debt, or cancelling plans. That is freedom in its most unglamorous form: fewer emergency decisions.

The third strand is the lightweight dashboard: a way to stay aware without becoming consumed. The budgeting industry has often treated awareness as a kind of virtue—track everything, categorise everything, review everything. Busy earners often reject this not because they lack intelligence, but because they have a life to live. The antidote is not ignorance. It is a smaller, sharper set of indicators. Households do not need to watch every transaction to remain in control; they need to watch the variables that predict drift. Total fixed commitments. The health of the irregular-expenses pot. The buffer. The amount of truly free cash. These indicators can be reviewed quickly, tied to a recurring ritual, and used to prompt timely adjustments rather than late regret.

Awareness does not have to be heavy to be real. It has to be honest.

This introduces a useful distinction between information and noise. Many households consume enormous amounts of financial noise: price comparisons for minor purchases, endless scrolling through deals, constant app notifications, the dopamine flicker of "saving" money by buying something discounted. This noise steals time and attention while pretending to be responsible. A good system reduces noise by deciding, in advance, where precision matters and where it does not. It makes some categories boring and automatic so that the household can reserve thought for decisions that truly shape the future—work choices, housing decisions, family priorities, generosity, and the handful of purchases where quality and longevity matter.

The fourth strand, therefore, is protecting time and attention from the modern machinery designed to extract them. Marketing is no longer occasional; it is ambient. Shopping apps are engineered to turn boredom into purchasing. Comparison research is endless because there is always another review, another "best of" list, another marginal improvement. For high earners, the temptation is not merely to buy more; it is to spend more life managing buying. The cost is invisible until one notices that the household's evenings are punctuated by little decisions that do not improve happiness but do exhaust attention. This chapter takes that cost seriously. A household that spends less time thinking about spending has more capacity to enjoy what it already funds, and more capacity to notice what it truly wants.

A quiet motif threads through this chapter: the household as a cockpit. The aim is not to stare at every gauge. The aim is to ensure the essential instruments are readable, the autopilot is properly set for routine flight, and alarms are reserved for genuine issues rather than for every flicker of turbulence. Busy earners do not need more data. They need better defaults. They need fewer decisions of low importance, and clearer moments for decisions of high importance.

There is also a moral dimension here, though it rarely gets named. When a household's money system is chaotic, generosity becomes fragile. Giving is treated as something that can happen only when the month goes unusually well, or when guilt spikes, or when a moving story crosses a screen. That is not wicked. It is merely unplanned. Yet it leaves the household's values at the mercy of circumstance. A well-designed system changes that. When giving is funded as a normal outflow, it no longer competes with last-minute obligations. It becomes part of the household's identity, enacted quietly, even in busy seasons. In that sense, systems do not merely reduce stress. They protect character.

Still, systems have limits. A system can automate bills, but it cannot decide whether the household has chosen too many commitments. A system can create pots, but it cannot resolve deeper disagreements about priorities. A system can present a dashboard, but it cannot force honesty about what the numbers imply. The point is not to replace judgement. The point is to create the conditions in which judgement can function without being drowned by noise.

The deeper promise of this chapter is a kind of calm competence. When core cashflow is automated, when accounts have purpose, when reviews are light but real, and when attention is guarded as fiercely as money, the household begins to feel different from the inside. The month stops being a sequence of small surprises. Conversations become less emotionally charged because fewer issues arrive as emergencies. Decisions become more deliberate because the system has bought the household time.

The closing question, the one that gives this chapter its forward tension, is not whether a household can build a perfect system. Perfection is a mirage that keeps people trapped in perpetual tweaking. The question is whether the household can build a system that holds under pressure: when work intensifies, when children are demanding, when family needs arise, when a tempting upgrade appears, when fatigue makes everything feel harder. In that moment, does money continue to "move itself" in service of what matters—or does the household fall back into firefighting, with freedom and generosity postponed yet again?

Automating core cashflow

On 27 June 1967, in Enfield, North London, Barclays unveiled the first cash machine in the United Kingdom, and the local press treated it as a curiosity: a box that could dispense money outside banking hours. The concrete outcome was simple and quietly radical. People no longer had to organise their day around a counter and a queue; a routine transaction could happen while the branch was shut and the world carried on. The air that evening would have held the familiar London mix—warm pavement after rain, petrol, cigarette smoke—yet the novelty was not sensory. It was temporal. A portion of financial life had slipped free of the diary.

That is the promise of automation.

Autopilot is mercy on Mondays.

Busy households tend to treat financial control as an activity: log in, check, shuffle, remember, correct. The result is a weary form of vigilance. Things usually work, until they do not, and the household pays for the failure twice—once in money, and again in attention. The irony is that the most predictable parts of cashflow are often managed in the least predictable way, through memory and mood. Predictable bills are paid when someone remembers. Transfers happen when guilt spikes. Irregular costs arrive like ambushes because no lane exists for them in the month. The household then confuses turbulence with danger: the numbers wobble, and anxiety interprets the wobble as a warning siren.

A predictable bill is a known object. It has a due date, a payee, and a typical amount. When such a bill is repeatedly handled manually, the household is choosing to spend attention on something that is, by nature, stable. Show: a partner opens an app on a Friday night to make a manual transfer for a bill due Monday, gets distracted by messages, and forgets. The bill goes out late. A fee appears. Name: the attention penalty. Explain: the attention penalty is the cost of requiring human focus for tasks that do not reward focus; it appears as late fees, bounced payments, time spent repairing mistakes, and the low-grade stress of being "not quite sure" whether everything is covered. Implication: the household's energy is consumed the way a slow leak consumes water—quietly, persistently, until the tank feels inexplicably low.

Automation is the antidote precisely because it is boring. It takes the repetitiveness of modern household finance—mortgage or rent, utilities, insurance, childcare, subscriptions, debt repayments where relevant—and turns it into a sequence of pre-committed movements. The household is not "more disciplined". It is less dependent on discipline. The system carries the load when people are tired, distracted, travelling, or simply living.

The phrase "money moving itself" can sound like surrender, as if agency has been outsourced. The reality is the opposite. Automation is agency expressed in advance. It is a decision made in a calm moment that continues to execute in hectic ones. It moves choice upstream, away from the point of temptation or exhaustion. That shift is not merely practical; it alters the emotional texture of money. When core outflows are reliably handled, the household stops rehearsing worst-case scenarios every time the balance dips. The mind can interpret fluctuation as rhythm rather than threat.

A useful way to see automated cashflow is as a conveyor belt. The belt does not eliminate choice about what is placed on it; it ensures that once something is placed, it moves consistently through the system. A household chooses which items belong on the belt: fixed bills, planned transfers, regular allocations to known categories of future expense. The belt then does the unglamorous work of carrying.

Show: a household receives income on a predictable cadence, yet the account balance swings wildly during the month, and the household responds by checking constantly. Name: cashflow whiplash. Explain: cashflow whiplash is the destabilising pattern created when the timing of income and the timing of bills are misaligned or unmanaged; the household experiences artificial scarcity mid-month even when annual capacity is healthy. Implication: anxiety increases, and spending decisions become reactive—either overly restrictive in the trough or overly indulgent in the peak.

Automating inflows is usually straightforward when income is salaried, yet automation is not limited to salary. Any predictable inflow—a regular dividend, a rental payment, a stipend, a fixed draw from a business—can be integrated. The deeper point is that timing matters as much as amount. A household that earns well can still feel constrained if commitments are clustered, if transfers happen late, or if the month is treated as one undifferentiated pool rather than a sequence of predictable obligations. Aligning bill dates, where possible, to income rhythm is less about optimisation and more about reducing avoidable friction. A bill paid two days after payday feels different from the same bill paid two days before, even when the annual numbers match. Psychology is not impressed by arithmetic.

Automation becomes more powerful when it includes deliberate transfers to "key accounts" or "pots" that serve specific roles. This is where automation stops being mere bill-payment and becomes cashflow design. A household can treat certain categories of spending as if they are bills owed to the future: irregular expenses, annual renewals, planned generosity, maintenance, travel, gifts. When these categories are funded through regular, automated contributions, the household converts surprise into schedule. The month becomes less dramatic.

Consider a simple illustrative flow, not as a prescription but as a demonstration of how a conveyor belt can be built. Imagine a household where income lands twice a month. On each payday, the first movements are fixed and unromantic: the mortgage or rent allocation, utilities, council tax, childcare. Next, a transfer feeds an irregular-expenses pot—so that car servicing, school trips, and annual subscriptions are not treated as emergencies. Another transfer feeds a giving fund, not because giving is always easy, but because values do not deserve to exist only in leftover space. A final transfer feeds a discretionary spending lane that is explicitly allowed to be spent without constant negotiation. What remains in the main account is then genuinely available for day-to-day variable essentials. In such a system, the balance in the primary account becomes meaningful rather than misleading: it is not pretending to include money already promised elsewhere.

The stress reduction here is not mystical. It is mechanical. Show: an unexpected annual insurance renewal hits a household that has no dedicated pot, and the partners scramble—moving money, cancelling plans, or feeling the sting of having to "fix" something that was entirely foreseeable. Name: foreseeable shock. Explain: foreseeable shock is the experience of surprise triggered by an expense that was predictable in existence but not prepared for in structure. Implication: partners blame each other for carelessness, and the household's sense of competence erodes, even though the event was not truly unpredictable.

Automation also creates a subtle but important fairness within relationships. When the system moves money according to agreed priorities, the household is less reliant on one partner's vigilance. Many couples fall into an unspoken pattern where one person becomes the de facto financial manager—tracking, remembering, nudging—while the other remains pleasantly detached until something goes wrong. Detachment is comfortable until it becomes a source of resentment. A well-automated system reduces the need for one person to act as the household's human reminder app. It can therefore be a relational tool as much as a financial one.

This is also where the limits appear. Automation is powerful, but it is not morally intelligent. It will execute what it is told to execute, whether or not the underlying commitments are wise. A household can automate itself into a corner by setting up transfers that reflect an unrealistic picture of its own capacity, or by allowing recurring luxuries to harden into structural costs. Automation can conceal drift because the month runs smoothly until the buffer is quietly eaten. It can also create complacency: the household stops paying attention entirely, and only notices problems when they are large.

Show: a household automates everything and stops looking, then gradually accumulates subscriptions, upgrades, and creeping renewals; the system continues to pay them faithfully. Name: automated drift. Explain: automated drift is the tendency for recurring commitments to multiply and intensify when payments are frictionless and oversight is absent. Implication: the household feels blindsided by a slow tightening that, in truth, occurred incrementally and invisibly.

The credible counter-example is therefore a household with irregular income. For freelancers, business owners, and commission-based earners, aggressive automation can be risky if it assumes a steady inflow that does not exist. In such cases, the principle still holds—reduce repetitive decisions—but the execution must respect variability. Automation may focus on minimums rather than full amounts, on building buffers during high months, and on scheduling reviews around known volatility points. The system becomes a set of adaptable defaults rather than fixed commands. Flexibility is not the absence of structure; it is structure designed to bend without breaking.

A useful measure for whether automation is helping is not how "sophisticated" the set-up looks, but what it does to behaviour. Does the household check balances less compulsively? Do late fees disappear? Do surprise bills become merely inconvenient rather than destabilising? Does generosity occur without drama? Does the household spend fewer evenings doing financial admin? These are visible outcomes. They are the difference between money as a background tool and money as a constant mental task.

Efficiency, here, should be paired with a human metric: time. If a household can reduce money oversight from daily checking to a brief, scheduled review, it has not merely saved minutes. It has changed the quality of its attention. It has made space for deeper choices. It has reduced the emotional noise that makes partners short-tempered and impulsive. In that sense, automation is not about becoming more mechanical. It is about protecting what is most human.

The conveyor belt motif returns because it explains a final, crucial idea: what is not placed on the belt remains a choice. A household does not automate everything. It automates the boring essentials so that the remaining decisions can be made with care. Travel plans, meaningful purchases, support for family, changes in work patterns, decisions that reflect identity and values—those deserve deliberation. The belt is not a tyrant. It is a servant.

The unresolved tension that remains, and that makes this chapter more than a hymn to convenience, is this: when the household automates core cashflow, does it also become honest about what the automation reveals? A system that "moves money itself" can expose a sharp truth. If the conveyor belt cannot carry the household's stated priorities—buffers, freedom, generosity—then the issue is not the belt. It is what the household has chosen to load onto it, and what it has refused to unload.

Using accounts with purpose

On 16 May 1861, the Post Office Savings Bank opened in London with a plain, almost audacious promise: ordinary people could place small sums somewhere safer than a biscuit tin or a landlord's drawer, and retrieve them without humiliation. The concrete outcome was not merely financial; it was architectural. A new kind of boundary entered daily life, one built of ledgers and procedures rather than locks. One can imagine the scene in a Victorian post office—ink, damp wool coats, the scratch of pens—yet the real innovation was invisible: money could be *named* and kept in its own place.

Labels change what we notice.

That sentence sounds modest. It carries a sharp truth. A single account balance, however large, is a blunt instrument. It collapses different kinds of money—money already committed to essentials, money intended for giving, money waiting to cover irregular costs, money genuinely available for discretionary pleasures—into one undifferentiated number. The mind then performs an exhausting mental act of translation: it tries to remember what the number really means. Under pressure, it often fails. The household's experience becomes paradoxical: the bank balance looks healthy, yet the month still feels tight, because the "health" is partly an illusion created by mixing categories that behave differently.

Show: a household glances at a main account and sees a comfortable sum. Within ten days, council tax, utilities, school costs, and an annual renewal leave the number noticeably smaller. The household feels whiplashed, as if money has disappeared. Name: balance ambiguity. Explain: balance ambiguity occurs when a single figure is forced to represent multiple obligations at once; the figure becomes psychologically unreliable because it cannot communicate which portion is actually free. Implication: people either spend too freely at the start of the month or clamp down too hard mid-month, not because they are irrational, but because the instrument they are reading is imprecise.

Accounts with purpose—separate accounts or digital "pots"—solve this problem by turning money into a set of labelled containers. The value of the container is not aesthetic. It is cognitive. A labelled pot reduces the need for constant subtraction in the head, which is where many households quietly burn their attention. This is not a theory about virtue. It is a theory about how human minds handle complexity. When categories are visible, decision-making becomes calmer because the question changes from "Can we afford this?" to "Which pot does this come from?" That is a smaller question. Smaller questions are easier to answer well, especially when life is busy.

The intellectual underpinning of this approach has an unglamorous name: *mental accounting*. Richard Thaler, writing at Cornell University in Ithaca, New York, gave the concept its enduring shape in the 1980s, notably in work such as his 1985 paper "Mental Accounting and Consumer Choice". The idea is simple and unflattering: people do not treat all pounds as identical. They place money into mental categories and behave differently depending on the label. "Holiday money" feels spendable. "Rent money" feels untouchable. "Bonus money" feels like a windfall, even when it is part of overall capacity. Economists can complain that this violates pure rationality. Households, meanwhile, discover that the labels are not merely quirks; they are tools.

Show: someone receives a tax refund and spends it quickly on a treat, while simultaneously feeling anxious about a future bill. Name: label-driven behaviour. Explain: label-driven behaviour is the tendency to follow the story attached to a pot of money rather than the overall arithmetic of wealth. Implication: labels can cause waste when they encourage thoughtless spending, but they can also prevent waste when they protect priorities from being casually raided.

The trick, then, is to make labels serve the household's real values rather than the market's temptations. A single main account is a blank canvas upon which impulses can paint whatever justification they like. Purpose-built pots reduce that narrative flexibility. They create gentle friction against self-deception. The household does not need to be morally puritanical; it needs to be structurally honest. If irregular costs exist every year, they deserve a visible lane. If giving matters, it deserves a visible lane. If enjoyment matters, it deserves a lane that does not constantly steal from safety or generosity. Structure is not austerity. Structure is clarity.

A useful historical mirror sits far from Victorian London. In 1904, in Tokyo, the Japanese journalist Hani Motoko popularised a household budgeting method that became known as *kakeibo*. It was not a financial product. It was a practice: money was allocated intentionally, and spending was recorded with a reflective spirit rather than a punitive one. The cultural specifics are distinct, yet the underlying insight travels well. When money is assigned a purpose, the household's choices become legible to itself. The household can see its own story unfolding in numbers, and the story can be revised with less drama because it is visible.

Show: a household carries all spending through one account and later struggles to explain where the month went. Name: narrative fog. Explain: narrative fog is the sense of disorientation created when spending leaves no meaningful trace of intention; the household cannot connect outcomes to choices. Implication: fog encourages either resignation ("That's just how it is") or guilt ("We're terrible with money"), neither of which leads to better alignment.

Purpose-built accounts turn fog into contours. The most common, and often most transformative, contour is an "irregular expenses" pot. Irregular expenses are not rare; they are merely non-monthly. Car maintenance, annual subscriptions, birthdays, school trips, seasonal costs, minor repairs, professional fees that arrive once or twice a year—these are regular features of life disguised as surprises. When they are treated as surprises, they steal both money and mood. They force last-minute reallocations. They spark arguments. They create the sensation that progress is always being undone by something unexpected.

A case example makes the mechanism concrete without turning it into a morality play. Consider a household in Bristol where two working adults juggle intense jobs and school-age children. Their income is strong; their calendar is stronger. In October 2022, a car service and MOT land in the same week as a school residential payment. The household can afford both, yet the timing creates stress because the main account is also carrying the month's normal outflows. One partner pays the service and feels responsible; the other sees the balance drop and feels alarmed. A small disagreement follows—not about the MOT, which is unavoidable, but about the feeling of being caught off guard. The household's problem is not income. It is structure.

Show: the same household later routes a regular amount into an irregular-expenses pot. The MOT arrives, is paid from that pot, and the main account barely flinches. Name: shock absorption. Explain: shock absorption is the household's capacity to meet predictable irregularities without destabilising the rest of cashflow. Implication: fewer emergencies are created by timing, and fewer conflicts are created by the psychological meaning of timing.

Notice what changed. The household did not become more frugal in the moralistic sense. It became less surprised. Surprise is expensive. Surprise steals time, creates friction, and invites poor decisions under pressure. A pot is, in effect, a buffer for the mind. It is a way of acknowledging the truth that humans do not experience money as a smooth annual spreadsheet. They experience money as a sequence of weeks in which certain costs land with emotional force.

The same logic applies to giving. If giving is left to whatever remains after a month's spending, it becomes a fragile act—dependent on whether the month happened to go smoothly and whether the household happens to feel virtuous. That fragility is not merely practical; it subtly changes what generosity means. It turns giving into a mood rather than a commitment. A giving pot, by contrast, makes generosity a visible and recurring part of the household's system. It also protects generosity from the silent raid of convenience spending, because the money is not sitting in an ambiguous pool where anything can claim it.

Show: a household wants to be generous, but repeatedly postpones giving because "this month is busy". Name: deferred generosity. Explain: deferred generosity is the pattern of treating giving as an optional extra that can always be delayed; the delay becomes permanent because life remains busy. Implication: the household's identity drifts away from its values, not through malice but through structural neglect.

A "fun" pot can seem frivolous beside essentials and giving, yet it often plays a crucial stabilising role. When discretionary spending has no defined home, it tends to either sprawl or become a source of constant negotiation. Partners start interpreting each purchase as a referendum on character: "Do you really need that?" "Why are you spending again?" "You're always treating yourself." A fun pot does not solve deeper value disagreements, but it does reduce ambient conflict by setting an agreed lane for enjoyment. It can also protect against the toxic pattern where one partner spends secretly out of resentment because every discretionary purchase feels like it will be judged.

Show: one partner buys small treats quietly to avoid conflict, then feels guilty; the other senses secrecy and feels mistrust. Name: hidden spending. Explain: hidden spending is not always the sign of catastrophe; it often emerges when the household's structure makes normal enjoyment feel illegitimate. Implication: trust erodes, and the household becomes less able to coordinate on larger priorities.

Here, the motif of labels becomes more than a metaphor. Labels are a form of social contract between present and future selves, and between partners. A labelled pot says: "This portion is for this purpose." It reduces the need for constant renegotiation. It also makes trade-offs visible. If the fun pot is low, the household sees scarcity in the only place where scarcity matters in that moment—discretionary spending—rather than feeling a vague, global panic about the whole financial picture.

The counter-example deserves honesty. Some people find multiple accounts oppressive. They experience it as fragmentation, as if life is being turned into compartments that resist spontaneity. Others discover that too many pots create their own form of confusion: money becomes hard to track, transfers proliferate, and the household starts to feel like it is managing a miniature bureaucracy. There is also a subtle psychological risk: pots can become moralised. Someone begins to treat the "fun" pot as guilty money, the "essentials" pot as worthy money, and the whole system becomes a theatre of self-judgement. Structure, in that case, does not create freedom. It creates new opportunities for shame.

This limitation is real. It is also reconcilable. The usefulness of purpose accounts is not proportional to how many exist. The usefulness comes from choosing a small number of categories that reflect actual household realities—essentials that must be protected, irregular costs that must be smoothed, giving that must be honoured, enjoyment that must be permitted—and making those categories visible. The system should reduce cognitive load, not increase it. When the system starts producing more admin than clarity, it has ceased to be a tool and has become a hobby.

Risk, too, becomes clearer when pots exist. A household can measure risk not by a general feeling, but by a visible metric: the buffer pot, the irregular-expenses pot, the commitments lane. Risk becomes less theatrical because it is less mysterious. The household can see whether it is living off a single account that is doing too many jobs, or whether it has built some redundancy into its structure. Redundancy is often mocked as inefficiency. In household finance, redundancy is resilience.

A final layer is philosophical. Using accounts with purpose is, in a quiet way, a refusal of the market's favourite story: that all money is for maximising consumption. A labelled giving pot refuses that. A labelled irregular-expenses pot refuses the illusion that life is smooth. A labelled fun pot refuses the puritan fantasy that enjoyment must be earned through suffering. A labelled essentials pot refuses the casual risk of letting basics be jeopardised by impulses. In each case, the household is choosing to live by a more honest narrative.

The image to keep is simple: a kitchen with clearly marked jars. Flour is not stored with salt. Tea is not stored with screws. One could, in theory, tip everything into a single drawer and rummage each time dinner is made. Dinner would still happen. It would simply cost more time, more frustration, and more small mistakes. A household's money is similar. One big number can work, until the day it does not, and the day it does not is often the day everyone is tired.

The forward test is not whether a household can create pots. The test is whether the labels will be honoured when desire spikes and uncertainty rises—when an "irregular" bill arrives, when a tempting upgrade appears, when generosity is asked for at an inconvenient moment, when the fun pot feels tight and the main balance looks deceptively spacious. In that moment, does the household respect the meaning it assigned to its money, or does it dissolve the labels and return to ambiguity, trading a brief hit of freedom for the slow, familiar cost of confusion?

Light dashboards and reviews

On 14 January 1986, the Space Shuttle *Challenger* launched from Kennedy Space Center in Florida. Seventy-three seconds later, it broke apart. In the investigations that followed, one theme returned with chilling clarity: complex systems can fail while the people operating them feel, in the moment, that everything is normal. The sensory details from that morning—the sharp brightness of the Florida sky, the distant roar, the public spectacle—are famous, yet the deeper lesson is quieter. A system can look stable right up until the point it is not, because the operators are watching the wrong signals, or because the signals are drowned in noise.

Household finance is not spaceflight. The stakes are different. The principle is the same.

What you monitor shapes what you notice.

High-income households often oscillate between two unhelpful modes of "awareness". One is obsessive tracking: the meticulous logging of every transaction, the categorisation of every coffee and cab fare, the daily checking of balances as if vigilance itself prevents drift. The other is deliberate avoidance: the vague hope that as long as income remains strong, everything will be fine, coupled with a dread of looking closely because looking might invite guilt. Both modes are understandable. Both are inefficient. The first wastes attention on trivia; the second postpones reality until reality becomes louder.

A light dashboard is a third way: a small set of indicators that tells the truth quickly.

Show: a professional couple in Manchester checks their banking app multiple times a day, yet still feels uncertain about whether they are "on track". Name: anxious monitoring. Explain: anxious monitoring is the habit of frequent checking without a clear question in mind; it creates the sensation of control while providing little actionable insight. Implication: the household spends time and emotional energy without improving decisions, and money becomes a daily irritant rather than a supportive tool.

The antidote is not more data. It is better questions. In complex work, dashboards exist precisely because the human mind cannot hold every detail. A hospital does not run on a line-by-line log of every supply used that hour; it runs on key measures that flag meaningful changes. A pilot does not watch the fuel molecules; the pilot watches the gauges that matter for safe flight. The household, likewise, should monitor what predicts drift and what protects priorities. That is the function of a lightweight review: not to perfect the past, but to keep the system aligned with what it is supposed to do.

The intellectual basis for this approach is well established outside personal finance. Herbert A. Simon, working in the mid-twentieth century and later publishing *Administrative Behavior* (first published 1947), argued that human rationality is bounded: people cannot process everything, so they satisfice—choose options that are good enough given limited attention. The mistake many households make is to pretend attention is unlimited and then feel ashamed when it is not. A light dashboard respects bounded rationality. It assumes busy people exist. It builds a system that fits the human organism rather than fighting it.

Show: a household creates a spreadsheet with dozens of categories, uses it for three weeks, then abandons it. Name: precision collapse. Explain: precision collapse is the pattern where a highly detailed system fails because it demands more attention than the household can sustainably give. Implication: the household concludes, wrongly, that "we can't stick to anything," when the true issue is that the system was poorly matched to real life.

A light dashboard begins with deciding what "truth" is needed. For most affluent, time-poor households, truth is not found in the third decimal place of spending categories. It is found in a few structural indicators: the total weight of fixed commitments; the health of buffers and purpose accounts; the availability of genuinely free cash; and the presence of any creeping recurring costs that are quietly hardening. These indicators turn vague feelings into visible metrics. They also reduce the moral theatre that often surrounds money. Instead of arguing about whether someone is "careless," the household can look at whether commitments have drifted from an agreed range.

Show: partners feel friction about spending, yet cannot locate the cause. Name: attribution error. Explain: attribution error is the tendency to blame character when the problem is structural; if the system gives unclear signals, people argue about personalities rather than adjusting design. Implication: relationships absorb stress that should have been absorbed by structure, and money becomes a proxy battlefield.

A single number can be surprisingly clarifying: total fixed commitments. This includes the recurring obligations that happen regardless of mood—housing, utilities, childcare, subscriptions that remain, loan repayments where relevant, insurance, and other predictable outflows. When this number grows quietly, the household's freedom shrinks, even if income also grows. Tracking total commitments is a way of measuring how much of future life has already been sold to obligations. It pairs an abstraction—freedom—with a visible metric.

Another useful indicator is free cash: what remains after essentials and planned allocations are accounted for. "Free cash" is not a moral licence; it is a diagnostic measure. When it is healthy, the household can experiment, enjoy, and give with less fear. When it is thin, the household can admit that something must change—either commitments must drop, or priorities must be renegotiated. Free cash is the household's room to breathe. Breathing room matters.

A third indicator is the stability of the irregular-expenses pot, the quiet workhorse that turns predictable surprises into planned costs. When that pot is regularly drained to zero, it signals that the household is either under-allocating to irregular costs or facing a genuinely unusual season. Either way, the system needs attention. When that pot steadily grows and is used as intended, it reduces the emotional spike of "how did this happen again?" It produces calm. Calm is a measurable outcome.

Now consider how a light review might actually appear in the life of a busy household. The image to hold is not a conference room and a PowerPoint deck. It is a kitchen table with a notebook. It is fifteen minutes with a cup of tea. It is a brief pause with a few numbers written down, not to worship them, but to interpret them. The purpose is to locate the household's current position in relation to its own design.

A case example can make the point without turning it into a template. Imagine a household in Edinburgh with two earners and one child. Their money moves through purpose accounts: essentials, irregular costs, giving, and discretionary spending. Each month, on the first Sunday evening, they open a one-page "dashboard"—not a spreadsheet of transactions, but a short record of four numbers. The first is total fixed commitments. The second is the balance of the irregular-expenses pot. The third is the buffer amount. The fourth is the available free cash for the month. They do not track every purchase. They do not debate every coffee. They simply note whether fixed commitments have crept up, whether the irregular pot is being refilled at a reasonable pace, whether the buffer is intact, and whether free cash feels proportionate to the life they want. The review takes less time than a scroll through shopping apps.

Show: in one month, the dashboard reveals fixed commitments have risen because of a new subscription bundle and a "small" upgrade to a service contract, and free cash has shrunk. Name: creeping commitments. Explain: creeping commitments are recurring costs that increase incrementally, often justified in isolation, but collectively narrowing freedom. Implication: the household can see the trade-off plainly; the issue becomes choice rather than confusion.

The power here is not the numbers themselves. It is the change in conversation. Instead of the household feeling vaguely irresponsible, it can see that it has made a structural shift. It can then decide whether that shift is worth it, using the book's central lens: does the spending contribute to the household's version of a good life, or does it merely add weight? A dashboard does not enforce an answer. It clarifies the question.

There is a subtle moral hazard in dashboards, too. People can become seduced by the illusion of control that dashboards offer. A household can stare at the indicators and still avoid the deeper decisions: the right-sizing of lifestyle, the alignment between partners, the courage to say no to certain upgrades. Another hazard is metric fetishism: choosing indicators that are easy to measure rather than those that matter. A household might track net worth obsessively while ignoring the monthly experience of stress and conflict. Numbers can become a distraction from meaning if they are not chosen thoughtfully.

Show: a household celebrates a rising investment account balance while increasing monthly commitments until it feels trapped. Name: metric misdirection. Explain: metric misdirection occurs when a household optimises a headline number while neglecting the lived experience of cashflow and freedom. Implication: wealth increases on paper while wellbeing decreases in practice, and the household feels strangely ungrateful for a life that looks impressive.

The credible counter-example is the household in genuine instability—income volatility, sudden expenses, or a life transition such as a new baby or a move. In such seasons, a monthly review might be too infrequent, and indicators might need to be checked more often. The principle still holds, though: do not drown in detail. In volatile seasons, the dashboard should become even simpler, not more complex. The household should watch the few indicators most sensitive to risk—buffer health, commitments, and the rate at which discretionary spending is being consumed—without turning the season into an endless audit. The dashboard is meant to support life, not replace it.

A useful way to evaluate any review ritual is to ask whether it changes behaviour without requiring constant willpower. If a dashboard produces a few clean decisions—pausing a subscription, adjusting a transfer to the irregular pot, noticing that commitments have grown, deciding that a season requires tighter boundaries—then it has done its job. The goal is not to feel virtuous. The goal is to stay oriented. Orientation is what prevents drift.

The motif from earlier in the chapter—the cockpit—returns here with precision. A pilot does not need to understand every component of the aircraft in flight; the pilot needs reliable instruments and a regular scan. The scan is brief. The scan is disciplined. It is not obsessive. It exists to catch problems early enough that the corrections remain small. Household finance can be run the same way. A light dashboard is a scan. It lets a household correct course before resentment accumulates, before generosity is squeezed out, before "just this once" upgrades harden into permanent commitments.

The closing tension is the one that separates a dashboard from a mere document. A household can create a one-page overview and still avoid the moment of honesty it invites. The forward test is this: when the indicators reveal drift—commitments rising, free cash shrinking, buffers thinning—does the household treat the dashboard as a mirror and respond with real trade-offs, or does it treat the dashboard as a talisman, glance at it, and carry on, hoping that numbers will be kind on their own?

Protecting time and attention

In 1971, in Baltimore, Johns Hopkins University Press published a volume titled *Computers, Communications, and the Public Interest.* Buried in Herbert A. Simon's contribution, "Designing Organizations for an Information-Rich World", is a line that has aged with unnerving grace: "a wealth of information creates a poverty of attention" (Simon, 1971). It reads like a memo from the future. Paper on a desk, the faint smell of ink, the soft rasp of a page turned—an old scene, yet a modern consequence. Attention, Simon argued, becomes the scarce resource. Scarcity, once named, changes the calculus.

Time does not stretch.

Affluent households often assume they have purchased relief from scarcity. Money should buy time. Money should buy ease. And yet many busy earners discover a stranger equation: the more options available, the more attention is demanded. Subscription menus multiply. Delivery services promise frictionless living. Shopping apps compress a department store into a pocket and then keep nudging, suggesting, whispering. The household, meanwhile, remains finite. The day still has twenty-four hours. The mind still tires. The problem is not simply that things cost money; it is that they cost *thinking.* The quiet waste is not just pounds leaving the account, but minutes and focus leaving the life.

Show: a professional checks an app "for a minute" and emerges twenty minutes later with a basket of items, half of which were never planned. Name: attention leakage. Explain: attention leakage is the unplanned loss of focus caused by environments designed to convert curiosity into consumption; it often leaves the person feeling oddly dissatisfied, because the time was not spent on something they would have chosen deliberately. Implication: the household pays twice—once for the purchase, and again for the reclaimed time that never returns.

Modern commerce is not neutral. It is competitive. Platforms compete not only on price and convenience but on how effectively they can hold attention long enough to trigger action. That is not conspiracy; it is business logic. When a retailer can measure conversion rates, scroll depth, and abandonment, it naturally tests designs that reduce hesitation. The psychological term "choice architecture", popularised by Richard Thaler and Cass Sunstein in *Nudge* (2008), describes this reality without melodrama: the way choices are presented shapes what people choose. A household can be entirely intelligent and still be steered by a well-designed interface, in the same way a skilled driver can still be guided by road layout.

Show: an online checkout pre-selects add-ons, insurance, or a subscription, and the purchaser accepts without noticing. Name: default capture. Explain: default capture is the process by which pre-set options quietly become commitments, not because the household endorses them, but because attention is elsewhere. Implication: recurring costs harden, and later reviews feel like unpleasant archaeology—digging for forgotten decisions.

The scarcity of attention is not merely about advertising. It is also about research. Affluent, conscientious households often fall into a peculiar trap: they spend hours comparing options for mid-level purchases while remaining oddly casual about large, structural commitments. The household will read thirty reviews for a coffee machine and then renew a service contract on inertia. It will agonise over the "best" luggage and then accept the default school expense structure without ever calculating what it does to flexibility. There is a mismatch between the *felt* stakes and the *real* stakes. Attention goes where it is tugged, not where it is most valuable.

Show: someone watches an hour of videos comparing vacuum cleaners, then forgets an annual renewal until it quietly charges at a higher rate. Name: misallocated scrutiny. Explain: misallocated scrutiny is the tendency to concentrate research on decisions that are emotionally engaging or heavily marketed while neglecting the less glamorous decisions that have larger cumulative impact. Implication: the household feels "careful" without becoming strategically careful, and time is spent without proportional gain.

A simple way to understand this is to picture attention as a small torch in a large, cluttered room. Wherever the torch points feels urgent and vivid. Everything outside the beam fades. Shopping apps and marketing are skilled at pulling the torch towards what they want illuminated. A household that wants wealth without waste must learn to control the beam—not by becoming humourless, but by becoming deliberate about when attention is spent and when it is conserved.

This is where boundaries matter. Boundaries are often framed as moral self-control. In reality, boundaries are environmental design. The household does not need heroic willpower; it needs fewer points of frictionless failure. A marketing email arriving at 7 a.m. with a "today only" discount is not merely information. It is a timed cognitive interruption. When such interruptions become constant, attention is fragmented into a thousand tiny shifts. That fragmentation has a cost: decisions become impulsive or avoidant, because the mind is already tired.

Decision fatigue is the useful name here. Roy F. Baumeister and colleagues popularised the concept in the late 1990s and 2000s, arguing that self-control draws on a finite resource that can be depleted by repeated choices (Baumeister et al., 1998). The specific mechanisms remain debated in later research, but the lived phenomenon is recognisable: when people make too many small decisions, later decisions become worse. They either choose the easiest option, or they refuse to choose at all. Households feel this every week. It is not a character flaw. It is physiology meeting modern commerce.

Show: after a long workday, someone orders expensive takeaway not because it is cherished, but because choosing anything else feels like climbing a hill. Name: end-of-day surrender. Explain: end-of-day surrender is the pattern of defaulting to the easiest purchase when cognitive resources are low; it is often rational in the moment and regretted later. Implication: convenience becomes a tax on exhaustion, and the household's spending drifts in the direction of whatever requires the least attention.

Protecting time and attention therefore requires distinguishing between decisions that deserve deep research and decisions that deserve swift resolution. Not every purchase should be a project. A useful heuristic is to treat certain decisions as "one-way doors" and others as "two-way doors", a distinction popularised in business circles by Jeff Bezos at Amazon. The idea is plain: some choices are hard to reverse and carry long-term consequences; others are reversible experiments. When a decision is reversible, perfectionism is waste. When a decision is hard to reverse, careless speed is waste.

Show: a household spends weeks deliberating over a small, reversible purchase, while making a structural commitment quickly because it feels familiar. Name: reversal blindness. Explain: reversal blindness is the failure to match decision effort to reversibility; it leads to overthinking the trivial and underthinking the structural. Implication: time is squandered, and the household's future becomes more rigid than it needed to be.

A named, checkable example shows how the environment is engineered to exploit reversal blindness. Amazon's "1-Click" purchasing system was patented in the United States in 1999, and it became emblematic of an era in which hesitation itself was treated as a defect to be designed out. The purpose was not sinister; it was conversion. Yet the behavioural impact is obvious. When the friction between desire and purchase is reduced to nearly nothing, the household must supply the missing friction from its own attention. If attention is depleted, the purchase happens. The system is doing exactly what it was built to do.

A second example makes the marketing logic more vivid. In February 2012, *The New York Times* published Charles Duhigg's report on Target's use of customer data to predict life events, including pregnancy, drawing on internal analytics described in the piece. The story included a case in Minnesota where a father complained about maternity-related coupons sent to his teenage daughter, only to later learn she was pregnant. Whatever one thinks of Target's practices, the broader point stands: marketing has become probabilistic. It does not wait for explicit intent. It infers vulnerability and times the nudge. The household is not being advertised to in a generic way; it is being profiled into a likely moment of purchase.

Show: a person receives a perfectly timed promotion when tired, stressed, or newly interested in a hobby, and the purchase feels oddly "self-initiated". Name: predictive persuasion. Explain: predictive persuasion is the use of data to time marketing prompts for maximum responsiveness; it makes impulses feel like choices. Implication: the household's sense of agency weakens, because decisions are increasingly initiated by external triggers rather than internal priorities.

None of this means households should live in a bunker. The counter-example matters. Some research is genuinely worth doing. When a purchase affects safety, health, or long-term satisfaction—think car safety features, home maintenance decisions, accessibility needs, or tools that underpin daily work—careful comparison can prevent waste and regret. There is a difference between attentive discernment and anxious scrolling. The aim is not to reject information. The aim is to refuse the *endless* loop of information that produces no decision and no peace.

Show: a household spends time comparing replacement options for a boiler after repeated failures, and that time prevents repeated call-out fees and winter discomfort. Name: high-stakes diligence. Explain: high-stakes diligence is the deliberate investment of attention where consequences are meaningful and reversibility is low. Implication: time spent researching becomes a form of protection rather than a form of procrastination.

The reconciliation is simple: attention should be budgeted like money, with the same question in mind—what earns its keep? A household that wants to spend less life managing spending must be willing to declare that some decisions will be made quickly, on "good enough" criteria, and some decisions will be given a defined research window and then closed. The research window matters. Without it, research becomes entertainment dressed as responsibility. It becomes another open tab.

Open tabs multiply.

That motif is more than metaphor. A browser with thirty tabs feels like productivity, yet it is often deferred discomfort. The same is true of a mind with thirty half-made purchasing decisions. Each unresolved choice creates a small cognitive burden: remember to compare, remember to decide, remember to revisit. In aggregate, these burdens become a background hum. They steal the very time that convenience purchases claim to buy back.

Show: a person keeps a running list of "things to buy soon", revisits it weekly, adds items, removes few, and feels perpetually behind. Name: deferred decision load. Explain: deferred decision load is the accumulation of postponed choices that continue to demand attention even when no purchase occurs. Implication: the household experiences chronic mental clutter, which can lead to impulsive "clear the list" spending sprees.

A practical boundary with marketing is not primarily about virtue; it is about input control. When inputs are constant, outputs will be messy. Marketing inputs arrive through email, push notifications, social feeds, and even search results shaped by past browsing. Each input is a request for attention. A household that treats attention as scarce will decide where requests are allowed to enter. The behavioural metric is visible: how often does the household encounter shopping prompts when it did not seek them? If the answer is "often", the environment is doing the steering.

A boundary with shopping apps is similar. The phone is the most efficient impulse-delivery device ever invented. The question, therefore, is not whether the household is disciplined enough to resist; it is whether the household wants a casino in its pocket. That is not moralising; it is descriptive. Casinos are designed for frictionless continuation. Many retail interfaces are, too. When the path from curiosity to purchase is smooth, attention must supply the brakes. When attention is tired, the brakes fail.

Show: someone intends to buy one item and ends up buying three because "recommended for you" feels like helpfulness. Name: basket drift. Explain: basket drift is the expansion of a purchase beyond its original scope due to interface prompts and low-friction add-ons. Implication: spending becomes less aligned with values, and the household accumulates items that do not meaningfully improve life.

The final layer is relational and philosophical. Time and attention are not private possessions; they shape relationships. A parent distracted by shopping decisions is less present at dinner. A partner absorbed in researching an upgrade is less available for conversation. The household may have money, yet feel oddly impoverished in the currency that matters most: undivided presence. Protecting attention is therefore a form of generosity towards one's own life and towards other people. It supports the book's deeper claim that freedom and generosity reinforce each other. Attention is where freedom begins.

The motif returns again because it offers a forward test. When a household faces a purchase decision, does it open more tabs—literal or mental—until the decision becomes exhausting, or does it decide where the decision belongs: quick lane or deep lane? Does it let marketing choose the moment, or does it choose the moment itself? And when it notices that money management is consuming too much life, does it treat that as an acceptable cost of "being responsible", or as a form of waste that must be designed out, with the same seriousness given to any other leak?

Chapter 11
Handling Bonuses And Bumps

On 15 September 2008, Lehman Brothers filed for bankruptcy in New York. In London, the news travelled faster than the commuters. Screens flickered in Canary Wharf; headlines refreshed; the air in glass-walled offices seemed to tighten. The sensory memory of that month is not merely visual—there was the dry hum of printers, the metallic taste of bad coffee, the odd quiet between phone calls when people tried to work out what, exactly, was now true. For many households, the shock was not only about markets. It was about the fragility of assumptions. Money that had felt like a steady climate revealed itself as weather.

Windfalls feel like weather too. A bonus arrives like a gust: sudden, energising, slightly unreal. It can lift plans, shift moods, and make yesterday's restraint feel unnecessary. And because it is not part of the ordinary monthly rhythm, it carries a peculiar psychological power. It does not land in the mind as "income"; it lands as permission.

That is why the handling of extra money is rarely a technical question. It is an interpretive one. The same sum, arriving under two different narratives, will be treated differently. A refund is framed as a correction, so it is spent with a shrug. A bonus is framed as reward, so it is spent with theatre. An unexpected cheque from an old account is framed as found money, so it is spent as if it were not truly part of the household at all. In each case, the pounds are identical; the story attached to them is not. The household is not simply allocating cash. It is allocating meaning.

Behavioural economists have a name for the mental filing system that makes this happen. Richard Thaler described "mental accounting" in work spanning decades, including *The Winner's Curse* (1992): people separate money into imagined categories and treat those categories as if they were separate pools with separate rules. It is a profoundly human habit. It is also a source of gentle self-deception. A household can be disciplined with monthly spending and reckless with a windfall, then describe itself as "generally responsible". The windfall is treated as an exception. Exceptions, repeated, become a lifestyle.

Show: a household receives a year-end bonus, books a more expensive holiday than planned, upgrades a car finance package because the monthly difference seems small, and adds a new subscription bundle to "make life easier". Name: the windfall cascade. Explain: a one-off sum often triggers not only one-off purchases but a cluster of small recurring upgrades; each feels harmless in isolation, and each is justified by the temporary feeling of abundance. Implication: the bonus is spent twice—once as cash outflow, and again as a permanent lift in commitments that narrows future breathing room.

The cascade is not greed. It is normal cognition meeting a consumer environment that is extremely good at turning moments of joy into ongoing obligations. A single celebratory decision—fine, deserved, human—can easily be bundled with other decisions that ride along unnoticed. The household thinks it is spending the bonus; in reality, it is rewriting the monthly baseline. That baseline is where freedom lives or dies. Monthly commitments are the architecture of future days. They determine how easily a household can absorb a surprise expense, reduce working hours, give with consistency, or simply feel calm.

A striking paradox sits at the centre of this chapter's theme: why do households that manage monthly cashflow well often mishandle the money that should be easiest to handle? A bonus has no rent attached to it. It is, by definition, extra. And yet it is precisely because it is extra that it becomes psychologically slippery. Ordinary income is already spoken for by ordinary life. Extra income arrives with less structure and therefore more vulnerability to impulse, performance, and narrative.

That vulnerability is intensified by social comparison. A bonus is rarely private. It is discussed at work, hinted at among friends, implied in lifestyle cues. It becomes part of the ambient competition of adulthood: who is "doing well", who is "moving up", who is still in the game. Even when nobody speaks openly, people notice. The human mind then does what it always does: it tries to translate status into purchases that can be seen. The gust of money becomes a gust of signalling.

Show: a team of colleagues talks loosely about bonus season, one person mentions a new watch, another mentions business class, and a third quietly feels behind without knowing why. Name: bonus benchmarking. Explain: bonus benchmarking is the subtle comparison process that turns a personal windfall into a social yardstick; it nudges households towards visible upgrades rather than invisible freedom. Implication: the windfall is used to buy belonging, which is an expensive commodity because its price rises with the crowd.

Modern relevance sharpens the stakes. Many earners now receive income in lumpy forms: annual bonuses, quarterly profit shares, stock awards, freelance invoices, consulting retainers, seasonal business surges. Even within salaried employment, certainty has thinned in many sectors. The household that expects smoothness can be wrong-footed by reality. That is why bumps—bonuses, refunds, commissions, tax reconciliations, unexpected costs—deserve a deliberate way of thinking. Without a way of thinking, the household reacts. Reaction is where waste breeds.

The emotional texture of windfalls matters as much as the arithmetic. Some windfalls arrive with relief, some with pride, some with grief, some with exhaustion. A performance bonus after a brutal year can feel like compensation for time that cannot be bought back. A redundancy package can feel like both a cushion and a verdict. A tax refund can feel like a small vindication. When money carries emotion, it becomes tempting to use it to manage emotion. Sometimes that is benign. Sometimes it is costly. The question is not whether feelings should be involved; they always are. The question is whether the household can see them clearly enough not to be driven by them blindly.

Show: someone receives a bonus after months of overwork and spends it quickly, not from joy, but from a need to prove that the sacrifice was worth it. Name: compensatory spending. Explain: compensatory spending is the use of money to soothe the discomfort of effort, resentment, or fatigue; it is often less about the object purchased and more about the story it tells. Implication: the bonus is consumed as emotional anaesthetic, and the underlying problem—an unsustainable work-life bargain—remains untouched.

Still, it would be dishonest to pretend windfalls are only dangerous. They can be beautiful. A windfall can fund generosity that feels alive rather than dutiful. It can create a buffer that turns the household from brittle to resilient. It can buy time in ways that genuinely matter, such as reducing stress in a demanding season. It can also be used for joy without apology. The point is not to moralise the windfall. The point is to handle it with the same precision that this book advocates everywhere else: spending that earns its keep, aligned with what matters.

That is why simple allocation rules—gentle, flexible, not doctrinal—become useful. When a windfall arrives, the household can treat it as a gust that must be shaped before it becomes a storm of small decisions. The shaping is not about a perfect percentage. It is about preventing the two classic failures: spending it all as if tomorrow were guaranteed, or hoarding it all as if joy were irresponsible. Both extremes are forms of misalignment. One sacrifices the future. The other sacrifices the present. Wealth without waste requires a third posture: deliberate division that honours freedom, generosity, and lived satisfaction in the same breath.

An example clarifies the difference between deliberate division and reactive spending without turning the moment into a sermon. A household receives a mid-year bonus and experiences the familiar buzz: new possibilities appear. They notice, perhaps, an urge to upgrade a recurring service—faster broadband, a pricier gym, a more expensive school add-on, a monthly delivery subscription. The monthly price looks small. The bonus makes it feel free. But then the household asks a different question, a question that changes the entire mood: is this a reversible experiment, or is it a structural commitment? If it is structural, the decision deserves more gravity than its monthly number suggests, because it will echo long after the windfall is gone. If it is reversible, the household can trial it for a defined period without letting it silently become the new normal. A subtle shift. A major outcome.

This distinction—reversible experiments versus structural commitments—runs through the chapter like a seam of ore. Structural commitments are the lifestyle ratchet: once clicked into place, they resist moving back. Housing is the obvious ratchet, but it is rarely the only one. Vehicles, schooling choices, recurring luxuries, even certain social obligations can behave like ratchets. A household can afford them and still be constrained by them. This is not a contradiction; it is the difference between capacity and flexibility. Capacity is about whether the money exists. Flexibility is about whether the money is free.

Show: successive "small" upgrades accumulate—slightly higher rent, slightly higher car payment, slightly higher monthly services—until the household's free cash becomes thin and generosity feels risky. Name: the ratchet effect. Explain: the ratchet effect is the gradual conversion of variable surplus into fixed obligation; it feels like progress while it is happening and feels like a trap once established. Implication: the household experiences a quiet narrowing of choices, even while earning well, and begins to confuse comfort with freedom.

This is where the earlier themes of the book converge. The value hierarchy matters because it determines what upgrades are worth becoming structural. Guardrails matter because they prevent the windfall from being absorbed by low-value drift. The giving practice matters because generosity, when planned, is less vulnerable to the emotional swings of "feast" and "famine". The system matters because systems, not moods, are what keep households aligned across changing seasons.

The chapter also widens its lens beyond bonuses. Many intelligent professionals live with irregular income. Freelancers, business owners, consultants, commission-based earners, creatives, and people with multiple income streams know the psychological whiplash of feast-and-famine cycles. In feast months, optimism rises and spending loosens. In lean months, anxiety rises and spending tightens. The household becomes reactive. Reaction is exhausting. It also creates waste, because decisions made in feast are regretted in famine and decisions made in famine can become unnecessarily restrictive. Stability, here, is not a product; it is a design. It comes from how the household interprets income variability and how it chooses to smooth its lived experience.

Show: an irregular earner has a strong quarter, upgrades recurring costs, then faces a quiet month and feels pressured, even while annual income remains healthy. Name: seasonal illusion. Explain: seasonal illusion is the tendency to treat a high-income month as representative and a low-income month as anomalous, rather than seeing both as part of a predictable rhythm. Implication: the household's commitments become mismatched to its true baseline, and stress becomes cyclical.

The motif of weather returns because it is faithful to the subject. Windfalls and bumps are not simply "extra money"; they are changes in pressure. They can bring relief or turbulence, and they can reveal the integrity of the household's design. A well-designed system does not depend on perfect predictability. It accommodates gusts. It uses them. It does not let them dictate.

The page-turning payoff of this chapter is not a magic rule. It is something more durable: a clearer relationship with surplus. Surplus is often treated as an invitation to consume, or a mandate to optimise, or a reason to compare. It can be none of those. It can be an instrument of freedom. It can be fuel for generosity that is calm rather than performative. It can be a way to make the household less fragile—financially, relationally, psychologically—without making it austere.

And so the forward tension, the one that lingers after the last paragraph, is a test disguised as a moment. When the next gust arrives—bonus, refund, unexpected invoice, a month that is unusually strong—what will be made permanent? What will be treated as a one-off joy? What will be used to widen breathing room rather than decorate the cage? The household does not need to control the weather. It needs to decide what the weather is allowed to change.

Psychology of extra income

On 12 June 2012, in Stockholm, the Sveriges Riksbank Prize in Economic Sciences in Memory of Alfred Nobel was awarded to Alvin E. Roth and Lloyd S. Shapley for work on stable allocations and the practice of market design. The phrase sounds bloodless, but the core idea is intimate: rules shape outcomes, often more than intentions do. Outside a lecture hall, in households, the same principle plays out in miniature whenever an unexpected sum lands. A bonus, a refund, a belated rebate—money arrives like a gust through an open window. It changes the room. It changes the decisions. The interesting part is not that people spend it. The interesting part is *how* they decide what it is.

A windfall feels different from wages. It carries a different flavour in the mind: lighter, freer, less entangled with duty. A salary is earned in hours, meetings, performance reviews, and fatigue. A refund arrives as a correction, almost an administrative apology. A bonus arrives as reward. Each narrative nudges behaviour. The pounds are identical; the meaning attached to them is not. That meaning determines whether the money becomes a fleeting pleasure, a quiet strengthening of the household's foundations, or—most commonly—a mixture so muddled it is only understood months later.

The mind files money.

That short sentence hides a great deal of human psychology. People do not experience money as a single neutral pool that can be allocated with perfect rationality. They experience it in categories—rent money, holiday money, "treat" money, "emergency" money—each with its own unwritten rules. Richard Thaler, a foundational figure in behavioural economics, described this tendency as *mental accounting* in work spanning decades, including *The Winner's Curse* (1992). The point is not that people are foolish. The point is that the brain uses categories to reduce complexity. Categories feel like control. Categories also create loopholes.

Show: a household receives a tax refund and immediately books an upgraded hotel for an upcoming trip, while simultaneously worrying about rising monthly commitments. Name: mental accounting. Explain: the refund is placed in a "found money" category, mentally separated from "real money" earned through routine effort. Implication: decisions that would feel reckless in the salary category feel harmless in the windfall category, even though the bank balance makes no such distinction.

The windfall category is especially prone to what might be called permission spending. It is not necessarily extravagant. It can be modest: a few dinners out, a new gadget, an impulse weekend away. But the permission is the key. The windfall arrives as justification to relax constraints that have been held, often with quiet tension, during the year. It can feel like a moral release: *we have been good; now we can be good to ourselves*. For many high earners, this is not a childish impulse. It is a response to a real pressure. A demanding professional life can make ordinary pleasures feel scheduled, negotiated, and rationed. The windfall punctures the rationing.

And yet windfalls have a second, subtler effect. They do not only invite one-off treats. They invite upgrades that stick.

The upgrade is the stealth move. It often disguises itself as a small decision. The household sees a one-off sum and decides to improve something ongoing: a slightly larger mortgage payment, a higher-tier phone plan, a new car on a slightly higher monthly finance package, a subscription bundle that promises convenience, a cleaner twice a week instead of once, a private club membership that feels like a sensible network investment. The numbers, presented monthly, appear tame. The windfall makes the first few months feel "covered". The household tells itself it can always dial back later. Later rarely arrives, because once a feature becomes part of the lived baseline, removing it feels like loss rather than choice.

Show: an annual bonus funds a new monthly commitment—a premium childcare add-on, a pricier gym, a "full package" insurance plan—because the first year feels affordable. Name: baseline drift. Explain: baseline drift is the gradual elevation of fixed outgoings following a temporary increase in cash; the mind treats the new baseline as normal, then defends it. Implication: future months feel tighter, not because income fell, but because optionality was converted into obligation.

The paradox is easy to miss because the household can remain comfortable. Bills get paid. Holidays happen. Life looks fine. The cost shows up elsewhere: less breathing room, more anxiety about "unexpected" expenses, reduced ability to change course, and a vague feeling of working hard without getting freer. The windfall was meant to be a gift. It becomes a tiny architect of constraint.

Why does the mind choose upgrades over freedom? Partly because upgrades are legible and freedom is abstract. A nicer car is visible. A thicker buffer is not. A new service that saves time is tangible. A reduced sense of fragility is felt only when something goes wrong—and people prefer not to imagine what could go wrong. There is also a cultural script at play: success should look like something. Windfalls become moments when households feel obliged to produce evidence of progress.

Here the psychology of comparison does its quiet work. The windfall is rarely a solitary event. It is social in its implications, especially in professional environments where "bonus season" becomes a whisper network. People do not always discuss numbers, but they discuss outcomes: the holiday, the renovation, the watch, the school decision, the car. A windfall can become a social marker, and markers invite performance. That performance is not always boastful; it can be defensive. The household spends to avoid feeling left behind.

Show: colleagues exchange hints about their bonuses; one mentions a ski trip, another a kitchen renovation, a third a new electric car. Name: status anchoring. Explain: status anchoring is the process by which visible spending in a peer group sets an implicit reference point for what is "normal" for people like us. Implication: windfalls become fuel for conformity, not because people are shallow, but because belonging is a basic human need and money is one

Simple windfall allocation rules

On 9 October 2017, in Stockholm, the Royal Swedish Academy of Sciences announced that Richard H. Thaler would receive the Sveriges Riksbank Prize in Economic Sciences in Memory of Alfred Nobel. The press release did not mention bonuses, tax refunds, or unexpected inheritances; it spoke of bounded rationality, nudges, and the quiet oddness of human choice. But the moment matters here because it formalised, in public daylight, what most households already know in private: money is not only arithmetic. It is story. It is permission. It is fear. It is identity. A windfall arrives as a story with a sum attached, and the story often spends faster than the sum.

Rules make freedom feel real.

The difficulty is not that windfalls invite spending. The difficulty is that they invite *unplanned meaning*. A single payment can become four different things in the same week: a celebration, a repair, a promise, an escape. Without a prior logic, the household tends to improvise. Improvisation has a glamour when it happens on stage; in cashflow, it becomes a habit of reacting. The result is not always wasteful in the vulgar sense. It is, more often, misaligned: money moves in a way that is hard to defend later, even to oneself.

A rule of thumb is not a moral instruction; it is a constraint that makes behaviour more predictable. In engineering, constraints prevent collapse. In music, constraints create style. In domestic finances, constraints prevent a windfall from quietly turning into a permanent monthly commitment that nobody explicitly chose. The prior discussion of mental accounting matters because rules can harness that tendency rather than fight it. If the mind insists on categories, then categories can be designed: not to punish, but to prevent drift.

The most useful windfall rules are gentle. They avoid the fantasy of perfect optimisation. They also resist the opposite fantasy: that money is merely for enjoyment because it is "extra". A windfall is extra only in timing. It still belongs to the same life, the same obligations, the same values. The trick is to allocate it in a way that does not overfit the emotion of the moment. A workable rule performs two jobs at once: it honours the pleasure that a windfall naturally suggests, and it protects the freedom that a windfall can create.

Show: a bonus lands and the household wants to book a holiday immediately, because exhaustion has been building for months. Name: emotional liquidity. Explain: emotional liquidity is the sense that cash can dissolve fatigue, friction, and deferred desires; windfalls intensify that sensation because they arrive as a surprise. Implication: without a pre-commitment to allocate some portion elsewhere, the household risks turning a temporary relief into a permanent pattern of spending to cope.

The simplest allocation logics usually share four destinations: giving, enjoyment, security, and future goals. Those words are abstract until they are connected to visible behaviours. "Enjoyment" becomes a booked meal with friends rather than a month of vague upgrades. "Security" becomes a buffer that prevents a credit card balance from creeping. "Future goals" becomes an intentional reduction of an obligation, a planned expense, or a time horizon extended—something that increases room to manoeuvre. "Giving" becomes a deliberate act that expresses values without waiting for guilt or a dramatic moment. These are not moral categories; they are functional ones. They map onto the ways windfalls can either dissipate or compound.

To see why the four-way split works, consider what happens when one destination dominates. If everything goes to enjoyment, the household may feel briefly lighter, then oddly unchanged. If everything goes to security, the household may feel prudent but resentful, as though the windfall was confiscated by the spreadsheet. If everything goes to future goals, the household may feel responsible but emotionally undernourished; deprivation has a way of returning later, dressed as "deserved" spending. If everything goes to giving, the household may feel noble and frightened at the same time, because generosity without a plan can trigger an aftertaste of vulnerability. A mixed allocation is not compromise for its own sake. It is stabilisation across competing human needs.

Economists have studied how households actually treat windfalls, and the findings are a useful corrective to self-mythology. When the United States issued tax rebates in 2001, subsequent analysis by Nicholas S. Souleles, Jonathan A. Parker, and David S. Johnson used household expenditure data to observe a measurable increase in spending following the rebates (Johnson, Parker & Souleles, 2006). The point is not the exact magnitude; it is the pattern: even when households know a payment is temporary, a portion tends to be spent quickly. A rule of thumb acts like a pre-built channel, directing some of that quick spending towards destinations that do not create future regret.

Show: a temporary payment produces a short-term rise in consumption. Name: immediacy bias. Explain: immediacy bias is the tendency to privilege near-term relief over distant benefit, especially when the money feels unearned or exceptional. Implication: a windfall rule that earmarks a portion for security or future goals counterbalances the brain's default tilt without requiring heroic willpower.

A second checkable example comes from the 2008 US stimulus payments, analysed using household transaction and survey data by Parker and colleagues in work such as Parker et al. (2013). Again, the exact percentages are less important here than the robust observation: spending rises in the weeks following receipt, particularly on certain categories. Windfalls behave like a pulse. Without a plan, the pulse diffuses through whatever habits are already present. With a plan, the pulse can be converted into something more durable than a few unusually expensive weeks.

The design question, then, is not whether to enjoy a windfall. It is whether enjoyment will be treated as an event or as a leak. The difference is behavioural and visible. Event enjoyment is time-bound, chosen, and memorable. Leak enjoyment is frictionless, forgettable, and oddly hard to explain later. A rule of thumb can be built to privilege event enjoyment: a set-aside portion for a specific experience rather than a general licence to upgrade.

A quiet motif helps here: the envelope. Not the literal brown envelope of old budgeting folklore, but the envelope as a boundary that turns a feeling into a finite decision. The windfall arrives as a gust; the envelope turns the gust into a directed current. It also prevents the common sleight of hand where "just this once" becomes "from now on".

Consider a plausible scenario. A household receives a one-off bonus. The sum is large enough to feel significant, small enough to disappear if scattered. The household is tired. There are a few outstanding niggles: an overdue service on the car, a creeping sense that the emergency buffer is thinner than it should be, an itch for a holiday, and a desire to support a cause that matters to them without making it performative. The windfall, unallocated, becomes a competition between these claims, and the loudest claim often wins.

A sample rule—one among many—might allocate the windfall into four envelopes with deliberately imperfect proportions: a meaningful portion for enjoyment, a meaningful portion for security, a meaningful portion for future goals, and a meaningful portion for giving. The proportions are not sacred. The proportions are a mirror. If the household claims to value generosity, the giving envelope should exist in visible form. If the household claims to value freedom, security and future-goal envelopes should exist in visible form. If the household claims to value a rich life, enjoyment should not be treated as contraband.

What counts as "security" in such a scenario is not an abstract virtue; it is a metric. It might be the number of months of essential outgoings that could be covered without stress. It might be the absence of revolving consumer debt. It might be the reduction of a specific fragility, such as a known annual bill that tends to cause a scramble. "Future goals" is equally concrete: it might be a planned expense on a defined timeline, a reduction in a recurring obligation, or a contribution to a longer-term aim that has been named and agreed. The aim here is not to prescribe what those goals ought to be. The aim is to make them legible enough that an envelope can hold them.

This is where rules of thumb earn their keep. They take a windfall out of the realm of mood and into the realm of structure. A household that decides, in advance, that some share always goes to security prevents the most common windfall tragedy: converting an irregular gift into a regular cost. A household that decides, in advance, that some share always goes to giving prevents generosity from becoming an afterthought reserved for years when everything feels easy. A household that decides, in advance, that some share always goes to enjoyment prevents the grim pattern where people become financially "responsible" while emotionally starving, only to splurge later in an act of rebellion against their own rules.

Still, no rule can dissolve reality. Some windfalls arrive in households with immediate, serious pressures. A boiler fails. A relative needs support. A job loss is looming. In such cases, the elegant four-envelope split can feel naïve. This is the credible limitation worth stating plainly: allocation frameworks assume some degree of choice. When urgent needs dominate, the windfall is not an opportunity for balance; it is triage. That does not invalidate the framework. It clarifies its role. The framework is most useful when the household has enough stability to choose, and least useful when stability is absent.

Reconciling that limitation requires honesty about what the rule is for. It is not a way to force every windfall into the same pattern regardless of circumstances. It is a way to prevent default behaviour from pretending to be a decision. In a triage season, the "security" envelope may swallow most of the sum because security is the dominant value at that moment. The discipline is not the ratio; it is the naming. When the household can say, without self-deception, "This windfall is being used to reduce fragility," it prevents the later confusion of wondering where the money went and why the month still feels tight.

The other reason ratios should stay flexible is psychological. A windfall rule must be easy enough to apply when people are tired. Complexity invites procrastination, and procrastination invites accidental spending. The household that feels obligated to calculate an optimal split may delay the decision; the money sits unassigned, and the mind treats unassigned money as available for anything. The envelope motif matters again. An envelope is simple. An envelope is finite. An envelope is psychologically satisfying because it converts ambiguity into a boundary.

Show: a household delays deciding what to do with a bonus, and the money slowly disappears into "normal" spending over several months. Name: ambiguity leakage. Explain: when funds lack a named destination, everyday spending expands to meet the available balance, often through small upgrades and conveniences that do not feel like decisions. Implication: an imperfect, quickly applied split can preserve more intentionality than a perfect plan applied too late.

There is also a deeper philosophical reason to include giving explicitly, even in small proportion. Giving is not merely altruism; it is an anchor for "enough". Households that treat windfalls as pure personal reward risk reinforcing the narrative that satisfaction is always purchased and always private. A giving envelope, even modest, disrupts that narrative. It reminds the household that money is also relational: it can express gratitude, solidarity, and responsibility without requiring grand gestures. The giving envelope is not there to drain the household. It is there to prevent the household from becoming sealed.

The enjoyment envelope deserves equal respect. Enjoyment is not frivolous when it is aligned. It becomes waste when it is mindless. A windfall rule that allows enjoyment to be deliberate protects against two common failures: the grimness of always postponing pleasure, and the chaos of pleasure appearing only as impulsive spending. Deliberate enjoyment can be surprisingly economical, not because it is cheap, but because it is memorable. A single chosen experience can outvalue months of casual upgrades.

The security envelope is where the rule feels least glamorous and most powerful. Security is rarely posted on social media. It is felt in moments when the household's life throws an unplanned demand: a family emergency, a sudden bill, a change at work. Security reduces the sense of being cornered. It also makes generosity safer, because giving from a position of fragility tends to trigger backlash later. The security envelope is the quiet partner of the giving envelope; together they prevent the oscillation between guilt-driven generosity and fear-driven hoarding.

Future goals are where windfalls become directional rather than reactive. A windfall allocated to a future goal does something subtle to the household psyche: it turns "someday" into a calendar. It turns hope into a sequence. Not every future goal is financial in the narrow sense. Some goals are about time—reducing the need for overtime, creating space to change roles, enabling a sabbatical, supporting a family transition. A windfall can serve those aims only if it is allocated with that story in mind. Otherwise, it becomes another pleasant week that leaves the long horizon unchanged.

The windfall, then, is a diagnostic instrument. Its allocation reveals the household's true hierarchy more honestly than any stated values. When the money arrives, what gets protected first? What gets indulged first? What gets deferred yet again? The question is not meant to accuse. It is meant to illuminate. A rule of thumb is an attempt to ensure that the answer is chosen, not stumbled into.

The envelope appears one last time as a test of character disguised as a test of process. After the windfall is divided, the household faces a deceptively simple decision: will any portion of the money be converted into a new recurring cost? That is the moment when a windfall becomes a ratchet. A gentle rule of thumb can include an implicit restraint here—not as punishment, but as protection. The household can treat recurring upgrades as a separate, slower decision that requires more evidence than a single flush month. That separation is not asceticism. It is realism about how hard it is to reverse a new normal once it has been lived.

A windfall feels like speed. A rule introduces braking distance. The unresolved tension that remains is practical and uncomfortable: when the next unexpected sum arrives—whether it is large or small—will it be treated as a gust that rearranges the room, or as a current channelled through envelopes that reflect what the household claims to value?

Avoiding lifestyle ratchets

On 15 September 2008, in New York, Lehman Brothers filed for bankruptcy protection, and a particular kind of confidence evaporated overnight. The headlines were about markets and contagion, but the private shock landed in kitchens and lift lobbies:

households whose income had recently stepped up discovered that their outgoings had stepped up too, and the second step was the one that refused to move. The scent of burnt coffee in office reception areas that morning was ordinary; the feeling in many stomachs was not. A windfall, a promotion, a string of strong years—none of these are mistakes. The mistake is letting a temporary crest harden into a permanent baseline. The ratchet makes a sound. Then it holds.

It rarely feels dramatic.

The lifestyle ratchet is not a vice; it is a mechanism. A ratchet is useful precisely because it resists reversal. In tools, that is the point. In household finances, it quietly turns flexibility into obligation. The household does not decide, in one theatrical moment, to sacrifice freedom and generosity for comfort. It makes a sequence of small, plausible upgrades that each feel deserved, each feel manageable, and each adds teeth to the gear. The tragedy is not that people enjoy their lives. The tragedy is that they begin to require a more expensive version of their lives to feel normal.

Show: a bonus arrives and a family upgrades their car, not extravagantly, just to something "reliable", and with it comes a slightly higher insurance premium, slightly higher servicing costs, and the expectation that the next car will be in the same class. Name: the ratchet effect. Explain: the ratchet effect is the tendency for living standards to rise with income in a way that is psychologically sticky; once the new standard is experienced, it becomes the reference point rather than the treat. Implication: one-off gains start to finance recurring costs, and recurring costs are the most stubborn form of spending.

Economists have a long memory for this pattern. James Duesenberry's relative income hypothesis (1949) framed consumption as social as well as personal, shaped by comparison and habit rather than need alone. Later work on hedonic adaptation—often associated with the "hedonic treadmill" described by Brickman and Campbell (1971)—gave the phenomenon its psychological spine: people adjust to improved circumstances faster than they expect. The practical consequence is simple enough to sting. A higher income can raise the floor of expectations without raising the ceiling of satisfaction. The ratchet clicks again.

Comparison supplies the lubricant. A household does not only respond to its own history; it responds to the visible world. An upgraded postcode, a school gate, an office culture with a certain uniform of competence—these environments bring genuine advantages, but they also normalise higher costs. Abstractions like "status" and "belonging" become visible behaviours: the default restaurant for meetings, the type of holiday that counts as a proper break, the way children's activities are scheduled and paid for. None of this requires vanity. It requires only immersion.

Show: a couple moves house after a promotion, choosing an area with better commute options and good schools, and quickly discovers that the new neighbourhood has a different baseline for everything from tradespeople to birthday parties. Name: baseline inflation. Explain: baseline inflation is when the everyday price of "normal" rises because the household has moved into a higher-cost ecosystem of goods and expectations. Implication: the move that was meant to reduce stress can increase monthly commitments, making future flexibility harder, not easier.

The ratchet is most dangerous when it hides inside decisions that feel like character. Housing is the clearest example because it is both a shelter and a statement. A larger mortgage is not merely a number; it is a promise to keep earning at a certain level for a long time. Vehicles play a similar role, especially when they are financed in ways that convert a purchase into a monthly contract. Schooling can do this too, not only through fees but through the web of associated costs and the social world that often comes with them. Then come the recurring luxuries that are not quite luxuries because they arrive labelled as efficiency: the premium memberships, the "small" monthly charges for convenience, the upgrades that save time. Each one has a plausible justification. The ratchet does not argue. It accumulates.

The psychology is amplified by mental accounting, the tendency to treat money differently depending on its source or label, explored in Richard Thaler's work and widely discussed in behavioural economics. A pay rise can be mentally earmarked as "room" rather than as "capacity". Room is spent. Capacity can be designed. The difference is not mathematical. It is interpretative. A household that experiences additional income as permission is far more likely to convert it into ongoing lifestyle costs than a household that experiences it as optionality.

Show: a household receives a pay bump and immediately adds new subscriptions, upgrades flights to premium economy, and increases regular takeaway, each change "small" relative to income. Name: commitment creep. Explain: commitment creep is the gradual increase of fixed or semi-fixed outgoings that is hard to notice because each step is minor and the household still feels solvent. Implication: the household becomes more vulnerable to shocks despite earning more, because the margin—the part of income that can flex—shrinks.

This is why "avoid lifestyle creep" is a weak phrase. It sounds like scolding, and it misses the technical point. The real issue is not spending more; it is spending in ways that become hard to reverse. There is a moral difference between an expense that can be turned off next month and an expense that requires a move, a contract break, or a change in identity to undo. The ratchet's teeth are structural. A one-off celebratory holiday is not the same kind of risk as a larger mortgage. A special purchase is not the same kind of risk as a higher monthly run-rate. Freedom lives in reversibility.

That distinction—reversible experiments versus structural commitments—deserves to be treated as a serious intellectual tool rather than a vague intuition. A reversible experiment is time-bound, with a clear endpoint and low exit friction. A structural commitment is open-ended, with high exit friction and social or psychological consequences. This is not a binary; it is a spectrum. But naming the spectrum changes what can be seen. It makes the household's risk profile legible: not the risk of being poor, necessarily, but the risk of being trapped in a lifestyle that requires constant performance to maintain.

A useful historical illustration of "upgrade shock" comes from Denis Diderot, the French philosopher. In 1769, after receiving money associated with the sale of his library to Catherine the Great, he wrote the essay commonly translated as "Regrets for My Old Dressing Gown", describing how one new, finer item made his older possessions feel shabby, prompting a cascade of replacements. The details are domestic, almost comic, and that is why they endure. Show: a single upgrade alters perception of the entire environment. Name: the Diderot effect. Explain: the Diderot effect describes how acquiring a new item can trigger a series of additional purchases to restore a sense of coherence. Implication: the first upgrade is rarely the full cost; the second and third purchases arrive as "matching", not spending.

Modern households enact this essay without reading it. A new kitchen makes the rest of the house feel dated. A higher-end car makes the old coat feel wrong. A job change into a more senior bracket changes what "appropriate" looks like, and appropriateness is expensive. The ratchet clicks because the mind seeks coherence. It is not trying to be wasteful. It is trying to feel at home in its own choices.

Still, the counter-example matters. Some upgrades are not ratchets; they are repairs to a system that was under strain. A move to safer housing, a more reliable vehicle for a family with complex care needs, higher childcare costs that make work sustainable, changes that reduce chronic stress—these can be rational and humane. The danger is not the existence of structural commitments. The danger is mistaking every structural commitment for a harmless treat, or treating every treat as if it were harmless because the household can "afford it". Affordability is not only about income; it is about how much of that income remains uncommitted.

Show: a household increases housing costs significantly to reduce commute time and gain stability for children, and the quality-of-life improvement is real. Name: value-aligned commitment. Explain: a value-aligned commitment is a structural cost chosen because it directly serves core priorities rather than social comparison or default escalation. Implication: the same category of spending—housing, for example—can be either a freedom-eroding ratchet or a freedom-supporting foundation, depending on what it displaces and what it enables.

This is where the book's through-line returns without being reintroduced: wealth without waste is about contribution, not cheapness. The ratchet is wasteful when it consumes margin that would otherwise support freedom, relationships, and generosity. It is not wasteful merely because it is expensive. A high-cost choice can be aligned; a low-cost choice can be misaligned if it generates constant friction, poor health of the household system, or time loss. The question is not "Is this upgrade indulgent?" The question is "Does this upgrade reduce or increase dependence on continued high earnings?"

The visible metric here is the household's fixed-cost ratio: the share of regular income consumed by obligations that cannot easily be paused. Even without quoting numbers, the logic is clear. A household with high fixed costs must protect income more aggressively. That protection takes time and attention. It can also shape career decisions, forcing people to keep roles they have outgrown, to avoid sabbaticals, to say no to opportunities that would temporarily reduce income but improve life. These are not small effects. They are philosophical consequences expressed through bank transfers.

Generosity is often the first casualty because it is the easiest to postpone. A household can always promise to give later, when things are calmer. The ratchet thrives on that promise. A new structural commitment arrives and the giving becomes "for next year". Next year arrives with a new commitment. The point is not that generosity must be large. The point is that generosity reveals whether the household has preserved margin. When giving disappears entirely, it is often a sign that the lifestyle has become brittle.

The ratchet also creates a peculiar kind of anxiety. People assume that earning more should feel like relief. Sometimes it does, briefly. Then the household's commitments catch up, and the feeling returns: tight month, vague unease about the future, a sense of running to stay still. That discomfort is frequently interpreted as personal failure—surely competent people should be able to manage this. But the discomfort is often a design signal. The system has too many teeth engaged. The household has built a life that requires constant forward motion.

A final subtlety: ratchets often enter through time-saving purchases. Convenience is not an enemy, but it can be a Trojan horse for permanence. The premium version of everything promises to buy time back. Sometimes it does. Sometimes it simply raises the baseline of spending while leaving the calendar unchanged. The risk is not that convenience is chosen; it is that convenience is chosen as a default and then defended as necessary because life has been built to be too full. A household can end up paying to cope with its own busyness, which is a strangely circular transaction.

The sound returns here. The click.

If the ratchet's teeth are structural, then the most useful mental model is not moral restraint but optionality. Optionality is a technical word that becomes human the moment it is applied to a life: the ability to choose, to pause, to change direction without panic. Structural commitments consume optionality. Reversible experiments preserve it. This is why distinguishing them matters. It is also why windfalls and bumps are such pivotal moments. They arrive as apparent surplus and tempt the household to purchase permanence.

The unresolved tension at the end of this section is not whether a household will ever upgrade. It is whether the next upgrade will be an experiment or a lock. When the next bump arrives—promotion, bonus, unexpected project fee—will it be converted into a monthly obligation that requires another bump to feel safe, or will it preserve enough margin to make the household less dependent on the next bump? The diagnostic question is simple and unpleasant: if income fell for six months, which recent upgrades would still be chosen, and which would reveal themselves as ratchets that clicked too easily?

Planning for irregular incomes

On 26 March 2020 in London, at the daily Downing Street briefing, Chancellor Rishi Sunak announced the Self-Employment Income Support Scheme for the UK's self-employed. The cameras caught the formal language, but the real audience was quieter: kitchens where invoices had stalled, spare rooms where laptops glowed late, and small offices that smelled faintly of printer ink and reheated tea. For people whose earnings arrived in waves, the pandemic did not merely reduce income; it exposed how thin the shoreline could be between a high tide month and a low tide month. The announcement mattered not only as public policy, but as a stark reminder of what variable earnings always imply: cashflow is not a line, it is weather.

Volatility is not your fault.

That sentence is not consolation. It is diagnosis. When income is lumpy, the household experiences a peculiar psychological whiplash: abundance and constraint can sit a fortnight apart, each feeling equally "true". A strong quarter can invite confidence, while a slow month can trigger premature austerity, even when the annual picture is fine. The mind tends to treat the most recent data point as the whole story. Behavioural economists have named this tendency "recency bias", and in money it becomes visible as decisions made at the peak or trough of the tide: signing up to ongoing costs after a good month, or cancelling valued spending after a lean one. The implication is not that variable earners are irrational; it is that they live closer to the emotional edge of timing.

A simple scene makes it concrete. A consultant finishes a demanding project, sends an invoice, and waits. The work is complete, but payment sits behind procurement processes and polite delays. The household's calendar moves faster than the client's accounts department. Rent, childcare, insurance, and tax do not wait for the invoice to clear. This gap between effort and cash is not a moral failing; it is the structural reality of many forms of independent work. Once that gap is named—timing risk—it becomes easier to see why some "high earners" still feel fragile: the average may be high, but the troughs still exist, and obligations are timed to the calendar, not to earnings.

The central design move for irregular income is to separate "how much is earned" from "how life is funded". In salaried work, those are typically the same stream. In variable work, they are better treated as two related systems: the income stream, and the household draw. The household draw is the amount that leaves the business or income pool to fund the household's core life, regardless of whether this month is exuberant or thin. In business language it resembles a salary paid to oneself, but the useful point is not the label; it is the stabilising function. When the household draw becomes consistent, the household stops making decisions in a fog of temporary scarcity or temporary euphoria. The implication is psychological as much as practical: steadier funding supports steadier judgement.

This is where the buffer enters, not as a product, but as a principle. A buffer is simply stored slack: money that sits between income variability and life's fixed rhythm. In households with salaried income, the buffer can be implicit, hidden inside predictable pay cycles and employer risk-bearing. In variable households, the buffer must be explicit because nobody else is holding it. The act of making it visible changes behaviour. When a buffer exists, a low tide month is no longer interpreted as emergency by default; it becomes data. When no buffer exists, a low tide month turns every decision into an existential referendum on the person's competence.

The tide motif matters because it captures the real hazard. A coastline erodes not because there is always a storm, but because the water returns, again and again, until the land's margin is gone. The lifestyle ratchet discussed earlier is one form of erosion: commitments rise when the tide is high, and then remain when it drops. For variable earners, the ratchet is especially dangerous because the tide is not merely seasonal; it can be project-based, market-based, or health-based. A household that builds its monthly baseline around peak months is building on high tide sand.

A second checkable example sharpens the modern context. On 27 March 2020 in Washington, D.C., the United States enacted the CARES Act, which included the Paycheck Protection Program for small businesses facing pandemic disruption. Whatever one thinks of the policy design, the episode highlighted something that independent earners already know: "stable income" is often an institutional achievement, not a natural state. Employment, credit terms, government supports, and corporate payment norms all distribute timing risk. When a freelancer waits sixty days for payment, the client has effectively borrowed the freelancer's resilience at zero interest. That is not a complaint; it is an accurate description of where risk sits. The implication is that building a buffer is not merely prudent; it is a way of reclaiming agency in a system that routinely pushes timing risk downhill.

A useful scenario brings the abstraction down to the level of decisions. Consider a small business owner in Manchester running a two-person design studio. In April, two clients pay promptly and one delays. The month looks good on paper because the delayed invoice is large, but the bank balance does not reflect it. In May, the delayed invoice arrives alongside new work, and the month looks spectacular. In June, work slows. If the household responds directly to each month's surface—tightening in April, splurging in May, worrying in June—it will live inside the tide. If, instead, the household draw remains steady and the surplus in May replenishes the buffer depleted in April, June becomes less dramatic. The key movement is not the perfection of forecasting; it is the refusal to treat each month's emotion as truth.

This is also where language matters. "Feast and famine" is a familiar phrase, but it can be misleading because it implies drama and scarcity, when the reality for many professionals is subtler: it is not famine, it is timing. A high-income freelancer may never be "poor" in annual terms, and yet still experience months where cash feels tight because obligations are smooth while income is jagged. Naming the jaggedness protects the person from an unhelpful identity story. The problem is not that the household lacks discipline; the problem is that the household is trying to run a smooth system on a spiky input.

Tax timing is one of the most common spikes because it converts annual liability into concentrated payment moments. The detail varies by country and circumstance, and no single description fits everyone, but the underlying design issue is consistent: when a liability is real but postponed, it can masquerade as disposable cash. The behaviour is visible: a strong month leads to higher spending because the bank balance looks healthy, while the future tax bill is treated as an abstract. When the bill arrives, the household feels ambushed by its own past self. The name for this pattern is deferred obligation blindness. The implication is that a household can feel both affluent and startled, repeatedly, without any change in underlying earning capacity.

The antidote is not constant vigilance; it is clearer partitioning of what is already committed. Partitioning can be psychological—mental accounts that match reality rather than wish—or it can be structural—separating pools so that future liabilities do not impersonate surplus. The important point is that irregular earners benefit disproportionately from visibility. A salaried household can often coast with a single balance because timing is predictable. A variable household can misread a single balance because it mixes money meant for life, money meant for future obligations, and money meant for business costs. When everything sits in one pot, every purchase becomes an argument with the future.

This is where the notion of a baseline becomes intellectually useful. A baseline pay-yourself amount is not a claim about what someone deserves; it is an attempt to measure what the household can sustain through low tide months without eating into the shoreline. The baseline is best thought of as a hypothesis, not a badge. It can be tested against real patterns over time. If the hypothesis is too high, the buffer erodes. If it is too low, the household may become unnecessarily restrictive and miss the point of earning well. The implication is that stability is not achieved by optimism; it is achieved by setting a baseline that respects the troughs.

A credible limitation deserves to be faced squarely. Some forms of irregular income are not merely variable; they are discontinuous. A key client leaves. A regulation changes. Health interrupts earning capacity. A market collapses. In such cases, a buffer can soften the landing but cannot cancel reality. The pandemic itself was an extreme demonstration: many businesses experienced not lumpy months but sudden shutdowns. The honest reconciliation is that cashflow design is not an amulet. It cannot prevent every shock. What it can do is reduce the number of shocks that are self-inflicted—shocks caused by over-committing in high tide months, or by failing to notice obligations accumulating in the background.

The counter-example on the positive side is also real. Some freelancers and business owners create revenue structures that are less tidal: retainers, subscriptions, long-term service agreements, or diversified client bases that smooth demand. There is no need to romanticise irregularity as the "price of freedom" when parts of it can be redesigned. Yet even relatively stable independent income tends to carry more timing risk than salaried income because payment can still be delayed and costs can still cluster. The implication is that smoothing revenue helps, but does not eliminate the need for a household draw and a buffer; it simply makes them easier to maintain.

Time and attention return here as scarce resources. The temptation for variable earners is to over-monitor: checking balances daily, obsessing over forecasting, and reacting to each incoming payment as if it were a verdict. That attention has an opportunity cost. It can also degrade decision quality by keeping the household's nervous system permanently activated. A better design is one that reduces the number of moments requiring judgement. When the household draw is steady and obligations are anticipated, the household makes fewer decisions under stress. The work shifts from constant monitoring to occasional calibration. The implication is not only calmer finances, but calmer cognition.

The tide image makes one last appearance because it offers a practical question that is less about money and more about freedom. High tide months feel like proof of competence. Low tide months feel like threat. The question that separates brittle systems from resilient ones is whether the household's core life is built to survive the low tide without drama. If the answer is yes, the high tide can be used for choice—future projects, generosity, time—rather than for patching holes. If the answer is no, the high tide will be spent shoring up commitments made in optimism.

The forward test is therefore uncomfortable but precise: when the next unusually good month arrives, will it be treated as permission to raise the household's baseline, or as an opportunity to deepen the buffer and buy optionality? That decision is rarely announced. It is embedded in small agreements, quiet upgrades, and the stories people tell themselves about what the good month "means". The shoreline holds, or it erodes, one tide at a time.

Chapter 12
Keeping The System Alive

On 9 November 2018 in London, a set of documents quietly landed on the public record: the UK National Audit Office published its report on Carillion's collapse. The headlines tended to gravitate towards the drama of failure, but the most unsettling detail was mundane. Contracts, cash pressures, optimistic assumptions, weak oversight, warning signs noticed late. Nothing in the story suggests that intelligent people sat down intending catastrophe. The tragedy is that systems rarely die in a single blow. They die by drift. A little delay becomes a habit. A temporary workaround becomes normal. Then, when the crunch arrives, everyone discovers that the "system" was mostly belief.

Money systems fail like that too, only with less paperwork and more plausible deniability. A household can be doing objectively well and still find itself, six months later, wondering why the savings rate has thinned, why generosity has become sporadic, why the sense of breath has tightened. It is rarely because anything dramatic happened. It is because attention moved elsewhere, the calendar filled, the friction softened, and spending quietly re-attached itself to default. The graph is almost never a cliff. It is a slope.

A good system is a living thing.

That sentence is not sentimental. It is a practical observation about time. The earlier chapters have built tools for precision: lenses for judging purchases, structures for cashflow, ways to coordinate between people, and methods for catching leaks before they become identity. But a design that works on paper can still fail in the wild, because life is an excellent saboteur. New jobs do not arrive with a pause button. Children do not ask whether a month is financially convenient. Parents age on their own schedule. Even good news—an unexpected bonus, a brilliant opportunity, a new relationship—can knock a system off balance simply by changing the rhythm of decisions. The question here is not whether the system is "right". The question is whether it can stay right when the weather changes.

The first villain is not spending; it is invisibility. When money is flowing smoothly, the mind stops looking. When the mind stops looking, small deviations become the new normal. This is the paradox of comfort: stability can breed neglect, and neglect can erode stability. A household that once measured its commitments can, over time, forget to measure them, and then be surprised when commitments begin to feel heavy again. The implication is quietly radical: the purpose of reviews is not control. It is sight.

Reviews are often misunderstood because the cultural image of review is punitive—an audit, a scolding, a grim spreadsheet. That image is not merely unappealing; it is counterproductive. When review feels like judgement, people avoid it, and the system dies by drift. When review feels like a brief conversation with reality—what is still earning its keep, what is not, what has crept in—people can stay engaged without turning their finances into a second job. The difference is visible in behaviour. In one mode, the household hides from its own data. In the other, it makes a small appointment with it, the way one checks a calendar rather than litigates it.

There is also a deeper, almost philosophical reason reviews matter. The project of wealth without waste is not merely economic. It is moral in the broad sense: it is about deciding what kind of life the household is building, and then noticing whether daily choices are cooperating. Values are not static declarations; they are patterns of attention. If attention never returns to the pattern, the declared value slowly becomes theatre. The implication is not that people are hypocrites; it is that life is loud, and values require occasional quiet.

A short narrative moment makes the point without sermon. Imagine a couple with two children whose system worked beautifully last year. Essentials were smooth. Irregular costs were anticipated. Giving was steady. Then one child starts a new school. The commute changes. After-school clubs appear. Meals tilt towards takeaway for a month. A new subscription arrives for learning support. None of this is outrageous. None of it is a moral lapse. It is life. But if the household never revisits its money design, those changes harden into a new baseline and quietly squeeze the freedom that the system was supposed to protect. The "leak" is not the club fee; it is the failure to notice the cumulative shape.

The maintenance layer therefore begins with rhythm. A monthly glance is not an obsession; it is a pulse check. It catches drift while it is still gentle. It also keeps the emotional temperature low. People fight about money more when it is discussed only in crisis, because the conversation arrives already loaded with fear. When money is discussed as routine maintenance, it becomes less like a courtroom and more like steering. The implication is relational as well as financial: small, regular noticing reduces the need for big, tense reckoning.

Annual reflection plays a different role. Monthly checks notice movement; annual checks notice meaning. A year contains enough life to reveal whether the household's spending story is coherent: whether the things that were supposedly precious actually received time, money, and attention. It also reveals whether generosity has become a lived practice or an occasional aspiration. This is not about perfection. It is about alignment. A person can spend handsomely and still be deeply misaligned; another can spend less and be richly aligned. The annual review is where that truth can be seen without panic, because it is seen in hindsight rather than in the heat of a single month.

If reviews are the heartbeat, adaptation is the immune system. Systems that cannot change become brittle, and brittle systems break in predictable ways: they either collapse under new demands or force the household into a guilt-fuelled performance of discipline that nobody can sustain. Life changes are not exceptions; they are the operating environment. A career shift can alter income rhythm, commuting costs, social spending, even identity. Health fluctuations can change time, energy, and the value of convenience overnight. Relatives needing support can re-order priorities without warning. The crucial move is not to pretend these changes are temporary. The crucial move is to recognise "trigger moments" that deserve a deliberate revisit to the design.

The idea of triggers matters because it respects time and attention. People do not need endless tinkering; they need a small set of moments that are worth pausing for. A move. A new baby. A redundancy. A new business. A major caregiving responsibility. A significant change in working hours. Each of these events tends to rearrange obligations and desires. If the system is treated as fixed, it will fail. If the system is treated as living, it will be adjusted before resentment and confusion accumulate. The implication is soothing in a strange way: change is not proof that the system was wrong; it is proof that the household is alive.

Safeguards are the next layer, and they are often misunderstood as restriction. In reality, safeguards are how freedom is protected in an attention economy designed to steal it. Marketing is not neutral. Shopping apps do not exist to help households make wise decisions quickly; they exist to keep people browsing, comparing, and buying. The modern household is not merely managing money; it is managing an environment engineered to provoke impulse. A system that relies on willpower alone is like a house built without doors in a windy city. It may look elegant in theory. It will be cold in practice.

The gentlest safeguards are behavioural, not technological. A pause before a big purchase is not a deprivation; it is a way to let the future self vote. A practice of decluttering is not a minimalist aesthetic; it is an economic signal that storage has a cost and regret has a shape. Even written "money principles"—brief statements of what the household will not do, and what it will prioritise—can act as a stabilising spine, especially when the calendar is full and decisions are made on the run. These are not grand gestures. They are small structures that stop drift becoming destiny.

Accountability deserves its own nuance. The word can sound heavy, yet the reality can be light: a trusted friend, a partner, even a periodic conversation that makes choices less private and therefore less slippery. The reason it works is simple. People are storytelling creatures. When nobody else hears the story, it is easier to narrate a purchase as "necessary", a subscription as "hardly anything", an upgrade as "sensible". When another person is present, even kindly, the story becomes clearer. The implication is not surveillance. It is honesty with warmth.

All of this maintenance work—reviews, triggers, safeguards—serves a purpose that can be forgotten if the household is too focused on technique. The purpose is not to become a financially managed person. It is to live a life that feels rich, not merely expensive. That richness has two recurring signals in this book: *enough* and generosity. Enough is not a number that can be solved once and filed away. It is a felt sense that must be refreshed, because comparison and ambition are renewable resources. Generosity is not what happens after everything is settled; it is one of the forces that settles the heart.

Celebration, in this context, is not self-congratulation. It is noticing. Noticing that a month passed without money anxiety spiking. Noticing that a purchase earned its keep. Noticing that giving was steady, not heroic, and that it connected the household to something beyond itself. Noticing that the system did not merely prevent waste; it made room for relationships, for time, for the kind of comfort that does not demand constant earning to sustain it. Without noticing, the household risks becoming efficient but joyless, disciplined but restless—technically correct, existentially poor.

The ending of a book like this cannot be a neat finish, because the point is not completion. The point is ongoing authorship. The system is alive, which means it will always be tempted to drift, always be asked to adapt, always be invited to grow. The forward tension is therefore not "can the system work?" but "can the household keep choosing it when life is busy and the world is persuasive?" The most honest diagnostic question is also the simplest: when the next season of change arrives—good or bad—will the household tighten into fear and improvisation, or will it return to its rituals, adjust the design, and keep its version of enough intact?

Monthly and annual reviews

On 2 May 2008 in Omaha, Nebraska, Warren Buffett stood in front of thousands of shareholders at Berkshire Hathaway's annual meeting and did something that looks almost quaint from the outside: he answered questions for hours about decisions already made. The room, by all accounts, had its own sensory texture—the low churn of conversation, the paper rustle of note-taking, the slightly stale warmth of an arena full of people. The purpose was not spectacle. It was review. A disciplined return to what was done, why it was done, what worked, what did not, and what should be watched next. Few households will ever hold a shareholder meeting. And yet the underlying act is universally available: a scheduled, non-dramatic appointment with reality.

The paradox is that people who are busiest often need this most. When the calendar is full and income is strong, the money story can feel "handled" by default. Bills get paid. The balance is not terrifying. The card works. But comfort can breed invisibility, and invisibility breeds drift. A review ritual, done well, is not an audit. It is steering.

Steering beats scolding.

The first claim is simple: without a rhythm of review, households outsource their financial narrative to their bank app and their mood. The show is familiar. A person glances at a single large balance, feels briefly reassured, then spends with speed because speed is the currency of the week. Later, an insurance renewal arrives at a higher price, a subscription quietly ticks over, a social season produces more dinners than expected, and the month ends with a faint pinch that seems inexplicable. Name the concept and it becomes less mysterious: *status-blind spending*. The mind responds to a headline number rather than the underlying commitments that make that number fragile. Explain it and the mechanism is obvious. A household can have a healthy income and still be structurally tight if obligations are large, lumpy, or poorly timed. The implication is not that spending must shrink; it is that spending must become visible in the way that matters.

A monthly review is visibility with restraint. It is a small loop, short enough to survive busy seasons, frequent enough to catch drift early, and gentle enough to avoid the guilt spiral that makes people abandon systems altogether. The right emotional tone matters because shame is not a financial tool; it is a sabotaging solvent. When review becomes punishment, the household avoids it, and drift wins by default. When review becomes a brief conversation, the household returns.

Consider a concrete scene. A professional couple in Manchester, March 2024. Two salaries. One child. A kitchen table with a laptop, a mug cooling beside it, and an email subject line that begins "Your subscription has renewed". The month's spending was not reckless;

it was merely unexamined. Two streaming services. A meditation app. A cloud storage plan. A premium delivery membership. A gym membership used sporadically since winter. None of these is absurd. Each looks small in isolation. Together they form a pattern of commitments that do not match actual use. Show: the couple scrolls through a banking feed, surprised by how many lines end in "monthly". Name: *recurring inertia.* Explain: humans discount small repeating costs because each instance feels trivial; the pain is diluted over time, and attention moves on. Behaviourally, the mind treats recurring charges as part of the environment, like background noise. Implication: without monthly review, a household pays for a past identity—who it meant to be—rather than its current life.

A monthly ritual works best when it focuses on a handful of metrics rather than a catalogue of transactions. This is not because details are unimportant, but because attention is finite. A household does not need to become its own forensic accountant. It needs a few decisive signals that reveal whether money is supporting the chosen life. The most revealing signal is not "how much did we spend?" but "how much of our future is already promised?" That promise is visible in commitments: mortgages or rent, childcare, insurance, school costs, car finance, subscriptions, minimum debt payments, and recurring giving. Put simply, commitments are the gravity of a household. When they rise quietly, everything else becomes harder, and the household often misdiagnoses the problem as a willpower issue.

This is where the metaphor of steering becomes practical. A driver does not constantly stare at every bolt in the engine. A driver checks the speed, the fuel, and the road. In money terms, a monthly review can check the household's "speed" (commitments as a share of income), its "fuel" (free cash after commitments and planned allocations), and its "road conditions" (any lumpy bills due soon). These are not moral measures. They are navigational measures. The implication is relief: the household can spend generously and enjoyably when it knows what it has actually made available for that purpose.

A second checkable example shows how small rituals prevent large regrets. In January 2019, the Financial Conduct Authority in the UK published a market study on general insurance pricing practices, including the so-called "loyalty penalty" in home and motor insurance. The details vary by product and provider, but the phenomenon is well-established: many households pay more over time because renewals happen on autopilot. Show: an annual renewal arrives, a price rises, and it is paid because nobody has time to compare. Name: *renewal drift*. Explain: the renewal system relies on inertia; it trades on the fact that busy people treat non-events as safe defaults. Implication: the value of a monthly review is not that it forces constant comparison, but that it makes room to notice what is coming and decide intentionally at a few key moments.

Still, it is important to be honest about a limitation. Review rituals can become a new form of procrastination—an illusion of control that replaces action. A person can spend an hour perfecting categories and still avoid the real decision: to cancel the unused membership, to ring-fence giving, to admit that the "aspirational" subscription is no longer serving them. The reconciliation is straightforward. A good review ends with one or two decisions that change reality, not a longer list of insights that merely decorate it. The point is not to admire the dashboard. The point is to steer.

Annual reviews operate at a different altitude. Monthly reviews answer, "Are we drifting?" Annual reviews answer, "Are we becoming who we said we wanted to be?" The show is more reflective. A year contains enough evidence to see whether spending aligns with declared values, whether generosity is steady, whether comfort has quietly expanded into entitlement, whether convenience is buying back time or merely buying off discomfort. Name the concept: *narrative alignment*. Explain: humans live inside stories about what matters, but money is one of the most honest editors of those stories because it reveals what actually received resources. Implication: an annual review is a chance to reconcile the story with the ledger—not to scold, but to clarify.

A useful annual review looks at "leaks, joys, and generosity" because these three categories map onto the book's central concerns without collapsing into moralism. Leaks are spending that undermines freedom and attention. Joys are spending that earns its keep and makes life feel rich. Generosity is the outward flow that tests whether "enough" has become real. Each category can be paired with a visible behaviour or metric. Leaks show up as recurring charges with low use, as convenience spending that does not actually save meaningful time, as upgrades that created more maintenance than pleasure. Joys show up as high-use, high-value purchases, as experiences remembered months later, as decisions that reduced friction in daily life. Generosity shows up not as a heroic one-off gesture but as consistency: what did the household support, how often, and did it feel precarious or normal?

The phrase "checklist" can sound clinical, yet the human version is more like a conversation with a clear agenda. Start with what changed: job, school, housing, health, caregiving, social life. Change is not an inconvenience; it is data. Then look at commitments: did they rise, fall, or shift shape? Then look at free cash: did it become more abundant or more volatile? Then look at leaks: what quietly persisted despite low value? Then look at joys: what earned gratitude, not merely consumption? Then look at generosity: what was given, and did giving feel anchored or squeezed? Each question is concrete. Each has a visible trace in bank feeds, calendars, or memory. None requires self-flagellation. The implication is that reflection becomes actionable without becoming exhausting.

A subtle motif can help unify the practice: steering. Monthly reviews are small steering corrections. Annual reviews are route checks. A household that never checks its route may still move quickly, but speed without direction is only an impressive way to get lost. The act of review slows things down just enough to recover agency. It is not financial virtue-signalling. It is behavioural design.

There is also a social dimension that deserves respect. Many people avoid reviews because they fear what they will find, or because they associate money talk with conflict. A private, gentle review ritual can lower the temperature before any shared conversation occurs. It allows each person to meet the facts alone first, without defensiveness. Then, if the household reviews together, the conversation begins from observation rather than accusation. Trust is not built by pretending everything is fine; it is built by returning to reality together without cruelty.

Evidence from behavioural economics helps explain why ritual works even when willpower fails. Mental accounting—popularised by Richard Thaler—describes how people treat money differently depending on its label or source, even when the pounds are identical. The practical implication is that a review is partly a re-labelling exercise. It takes money out of the fog of "general funds" and returns it to meaning: commitments, freedom, giving, joys. This is not about tricking oneself; it is about respecting how the mind actually functions. Ignoring the mind's quirks does not produce rationality. It produces expensive surprises.

The danger, again, is turning review into a performance of diligence. A household can create elaborate systems and still feel anxious because the system became another task that competes for time and attention. The better standard is minimal sufficiency. Does the ritual reliably surface the handful of facts that change decisions? Does it happen even in hectic months? Does it reduce stress rather than add it? If not, the ritual is too heavy. A review that is skipped is not a ritual; it is an aspiration.

The closing tension is therefore practical and philosophical at once. Money drift rarely announces itself with a siren. It announces itself with a slightly tighter month, a slightly more frequent "we'll make it up later", a slightly delayed gift, a slightly resentful conversation about another small upgrade that somehow became permanent. The forward test is simple to state and hard to dodge: when the month turns, will the household look at the road and steer, or will it keep driving by feel and hope the route stays true?

Adjusting as life changes

On 23 March 2020 in London, Boris Johnson looked into a television camera and told the United Kingdom to stay at home. The announcement was not delivered in a household register, yet it landed at household scale: kitchens became offices, spare rooms became classrooms, and the familiar hum of commuting was replaced by the faint whirr of a laptop fan. In thousands of homes, the same private realisation arrived almost at once. A financial arrangement that worked in February no longer fit in April. The old pattern was not "wrong"; it was simply built for a different week.

Life changes; money must follow.

That sentence is not a slogan. It is an observation about design. A household's money system is a living arrangement between income, obligations, relationships, time, and the unavoidable fact that bodies and families are not static. When the arrangement is treated as fixed, it tends to fail at the worst moments—precisely when attention is scarce and decisions are emotionally loaded. When it is treated as living, it can absorb shock and keep faith with what matters.

The first claim is that life changes do not merely add costs; they change *shape*. The show is subtle: a new baby does not only introduce childcare, nappies, and equipment, it reorganises time, sleep, work capacity, and the household's tolerance for friction. A career shift does not only adjust salary, it changes the rhythm of cashflow, the predictability of expenses, and sometimes the social expectations that cling to a role. Name the concept and it becomes easier to handle: *structural change*. Explain why it matters. Most money systems are built for steady-state living, with assumptions about monthly pay, stable energy, and enough spare time to notice small problems early. Structural change breaks those assumptions. The implication is bracing but freeing: the problem is not personal weakness. The design simply needs to match the new conditions.

A useful system anticipates that conditions will change again. That does not require constant tinkering. It requires knowing what should prompt a revisit. In engineering, maintenance is planned around stress points, not around perfect schedules. Households have stress points too: the moments when commitments shift, when risk changes, when care responsibilities expand, when income becomes more variable, when travel increases, when health demands more attention. The point is not to predict every turn. The point is to decide which turns deserve a deliberate pause.

A second claim follows: households often delay redesign because they confuse "reviewing" with "admitting failure". The show is familiar. A family senses that the old plan is no longer working, so they try harder to execute it: tighter tracking, more self-denial, more anxious checking of balances. It feels responsible. It is also often futile. Name the concept: *plan loyalty*. Explain the mechanism.

Human beings become attached to systems they have invested in, particularly if those systems once worked. That attachment can become a quiet form of sunk-cost thinking: abandoning a plan feels like wasting effort, so the household doubles down even as the plan becomes misaligned. The implication is counterintuitive. Flexibility can be a form of integrity, because it protects the underlying commitments—freedom, relationships, generosity—when the surface conditions shift.

A checkable example from outside the home makes the point clearer. On 19 February 2021 in London, the UK Supreme Court ruled that Uber drivers are "workers" under UK law in *Uber BV v Aslam*. Whatever one thinks of gig work, the decision illustrates something practical: when the legal definition of work changes, income patterns can change too, and with them the assumptions a household makes about predictability, benefits, and bargaining power. Show: a person whose earnings arrive irregularly, who faces periods of feast and famine, and whose schedule changes week to week. Name: *income texture*. Explain: money is not only an amount, it is a rhythm—when it arrives, how predictable it is, how tightly it is tied to time and energy. Implication: a household can feel "fine" on annual income and still be stressed by monthly volatility, because commitments are often rigid while income is not.

Seasonal change is not always dramatic. Many households experience what might be called slow drift: the gradual increase of responsibilities, the creeping expansion of convenience spending, the subtle rise of standards, the quiet accumulation of subscriptions and upgrades that once felt like treats but now feel like baseline. This is where pre-deciding revisits matters most. Sudden shocks force attention. Slow drift does not. And yet drift can be more dangerous precisely because it feels normal.

The notion of a "trigger" can sound mechanistic, but the most useful triggers are human. They are the moments when the household's emotional bandwidth changes. A new child, an elder-care responsibility, a change in health, a move, a shift in work demands, the start or end of schooling, a change in household composition, the arrival of a dependent relative—these events alter the household's risk profile and its capacity to manage complexity. The show is measurable in behaviour: more late fees, more rushed purchases, more reliance on last-minute solutions, more arguments that begin with small spending and end with bigger fears. Name the concept: *bandwidth compression.* Explain: when time and energy are squeezed, systems that require frequent attention collapse, and spending decisions become reactive. The implication is not to romanticise simplicity, but to respect it. A living plan is one that can simplify when life becomes crowded.

A case example makes this concrete without pretending to be universal. In September 2022, a family in Bristol welcomed a second child while one partner changed roles from a stable salaried post to contract work. Nothing about their values changed. Everything about their constraints did. The old system assumed two predictable pay cheques and a household rhythm in which admin could be done on a quiet evening. The new reality included unpredictable income timing, disrupted sleep, and a weekday schedule that behaved like a puzzle missing several edge pieces. The show: they began paying for convenience in scattered ways—extra deliveries, duplicate subscriptions, and a handful of "small" upgrades that felt like coping. Name: *friction purchasing.* Explain: under pressure, people buy the removal of friction more than they buy objects; they pay to avoid thinking, planning, or waiting. Sometimes that is exactly right. Sometimes it becomes an unnoticed drain. Implication: the question is not whether convenience is good or bad, but whether the pattern of convenience matches the household's changed life, rather than merely soothing it.

This is where treating the plan as living becomes more than a pleasant metaphor. Living things have joints. They bend where they are designed to bend. A household plan needs joints too: places where it can flex without breaking. The quiet hinge in a money system is often the boundary between fixed commitments and adjustable spending. When fixed commitments rise—through housing changes, schooling choices, vehicles, or long contracts—the hinge stiffens. The household has less room to respond to the unexpected. When the hinge is kept supple, the household can absorb change without panic.

The third claim is that people often underestimate how much identity drives resistance to adjustment. The show is not just practical; it is psychological. A person who has always seen themselves as prudent may feel ashamed to admit that the system no longer works. A person who has always seen themselves as generous may feel frightened when generosity feels risky. A person who has climbed into a higher-income bracket may feel an unspoken obligation to maintain a certain lifestyle even when life conditions change. Name the concept: *identity drag*. Explain: spending patterns and money systems become part of "who we are", and changing them can feel like changing the self. The implication is delicate. If the household can separate values from habits—what it honours from what it repeats—it becomes easier to adjust without feeling unmoored.

At this point, a credible limitation deserves daylight. Not every change arrives as a neat event. Some shifts are gradual, ambiguous, or private: a slow decline in health, a long season of caring for a relative, a relationship becoming strained, a child's needs changing over time, a creeping loss of joy in work. These do not always produce a crisp moment that says "redesign now". A trigger-based approach can miss them. It can also become exhausting if the household treats every wobble as a reason to rebuild the entire system. The reconciliation is to recognise two modes of adjustment: small steering corrections that keep the system aligned, and occasional redesigns when the underlying assumptions truly change. The hinge matters again. A household does not rebuild the door each time it is opened; it checks whether the hinge is loose, whether it needs oil, whether the frame has shifted.

A well-timed redesign is often less about money and more about clarity. When conditions change, the household can become hazy about what is non-negotiable. Under stress, spending decisions can be driven by immediate relief rather than long-run coherence. This is why pre-deciding revisits is emotionally protective: it moves the moment of reassessment away from crisis. It allows the household to ask, with a cooler mind, which parts of the system must remain stable and which can flex. "Stability" is not a virtue in itself; it is a tool to support what matters. When stability becomes rigid, it turns into a trap.

Another public example shows how quickly normal assumptions can become obsolete. On 15 September 2008 in New York, Lehman Brothers filed for bankruptcy, triggering a severe phase of the global financial crisis. Most households did not hold complex securities. Many still felt the consequences through employment uncertainty, tightened credit, and a change in collective confidence. Show: a household that assumed steady income and rising opportunity suddenly facing job insecurity and delayed plans. Name: *assumption shock*. Explain: households build systems around what they believe is stable—work, markets, health, family availability. When those beliefs are disrupted, the system's weak points appear fast. Implication: the value of a living plan is not that it predicts crises, but that it creates a habit of revisiting assumptions before they calcify.

The most humane way to think about adjustment is to treat the money system as a tool for protecting relationships under pressure. Many conflicts that look like spending arguments are really arguments about safety, autonomy, fairness, or care. When life changes, those underlying concerns become sharper. A redesigned system can reduce conflict not by forcing agreement, but by making trade-offs visible and shared. When the plan is treated as fixed, every change becomes a fight against the system. When it is treated as living, change becomes a shared design problem. The difference is moral as well as practical: it reduces blame.

Notice how this framing keeps returning to the same image. The hinge is small, unglamorous, and decisive. It is what allows movement without collapse. A household's living plan should have hinges: points of flexibility that allow the household to open into new seasons without breaking what it values. If those hinges are absent, life changes turn into expensive improvisation.

The closing tension is unavoidable. Life offers trade-offs that are not neat. Supporting a relative can compress freedom. A career shift can increase fulfilment while reducing predictability. A new child can intensify joy while shrinking time. A health change can clarify priorities while tightening resources. In those moments, the question is not whether the household is "good with money". The question is whether the household is willing to revisit its assumptions before reality forces a harsher revision. The forward test is simple to state and difficult to ignore: when the next major season arrives—expected or not—will the household treat its plan as a fixed rulebook, or as a living design with a hinge ready to move?

Building habits and safeguards

In April 2013 in Amsterdam, the behavioural economist Dan Ariely wrote a public apology after a colleague spotted that a dataset underpinning one of his papers had been manipulated. The paper was subsequently retracted, and a career built on studying human irrationality was forced to confront a different kind of fragility: the ease with which a system drifts when the safeguards are weak. The drama was academic, but the lesson is domestic. Most financial trouble among busy earners does not arrive as a single catastrophe. It arrives as drift: a sequence of small, defensible decisions that accumulate into a life that feels tighter than it should.

Drift is quiet. It is also predictable.

Five words, no theatrics, no moralising. Just a fact about humans in systems. We adapt. We normalise. We stop noticing. A money design that works in January can be quietly undermined by July, not because anyone became reckless, but because the environment changed and attention followed it. The safeguard is not heroic discipline. The safeguard is a set of small habits—boringly repeatable behaviours—and a few structural backstops that catch you when you are tired, stressed, busy, or simply human.

The first claim is that willpower is the wrong tool for long-run alignment. Show it. Consider the Friday afternoon scroll: an exhausted professional, brain glazed from meetings, opens a shopping app "just to look", sees a limited-time offer, and buys a £180 item that seemed unnecessary at 9 a.m. but now feels like relief. The behaviour is ordinary. Name the mechanism: *ego depletion* is debated as a precise scientific effect, but the underlying reality is hard to deny—self-control feels harder when cognitive load is high. Explain why this matters for money. Many financial systems implicitly assume that people will make careful decisions repeatedly, even when busy. That is an unrealistic design brief. The implication is sharp: if a money system relies on constant restraint, it is not a system; it is a recurring test.

A better approach is to reduce the number of high-stakes decisions. Habits do that by turning choices into defaults. Safeguards do that by adding friction where drift is likely. Both shift the burden away from moment-by-moment judgement and towards earlier, calmer design.

The second claim is that small habits work because they are *cheap to execute*. Show it with a metric. A monthly review that takes sixty minutes is frequently skipped by busy people; a ten-minute check-in can survive almost any calendar. A declutter ritual that requires a weekend is postponed; a five-minute "one surface" reset can occur even on a Tuesday. Name the design principle: *minimum effective dose*. Explain it plainly. The point is not to do everything; it is to do the smallest action that reliably prevents the worst drift. The implication is both practical and philosophical: your money habits should respect your life, not demand that you become a different person to keep them.

The third claim is that drift is not random; it clusters around predictable categories. Busy earners tend to drift where purchases are frequent, automated, or emotionally soothing: subscriptions, convenience spending, upgrades, and "improvements" that become permanent. A safeguard is most effective when it is aimed at a predictable leak, not sprayed everywhere like a disinfectant fog.

Take the "pause rule" before big purchases. Show it in behaviour: a household sets a threshold—say, any non-essential spend above a certain amount requires a 48-hour pause and a second look. The crucial detail is that the pause is not a punishment; it is a time buffer that interrupts impulse and invites comparison with values. Name it: *cooling-off*. Explain why it works. The pause creates a gap between desire and action, letting immediate emotion decay and allowing the brain to test the purchase against longer-term priorities. The implication is that you are not trying to eliminate desire. You are trying to stop desire from impersonating necessity.

This is not merely folk wisdom. Public policy has long used cooling-off periods in contexts where regret is common. In the European Union, consumers buying online typically have a right to withdraw within 14 days under the Consumer Rights Directive (2011/83/EU), a structural acknowledgement that distance purchases can be impulsive or poorly informed. You do not need law to mimic the logic at home. You need a habit that treats regret as a design problem, not a personality flaw.

A second habit is regular decluttering—not as a lifestyle trend, but as a financial safeguard. Show it. A household notices that when cupboards fill, they re-buy things they already own, because the cost of finding them exceeds the cost of replacing them. They also overvalue bargains because they have space to store them. Name the mechanism: *search cost*. Explain: clutter raises the time cost of using what you have, which nudges you towards new spending that feels like solving a problem. The implication is deliciously paradoxical: decluttering is not about being tidy. It is about lowering future spending by increasing the usability of your existing possessions.

A third habit is the "two-question purchase prompt". Not a spreadsheet. Not a sermon. Just two questions asked consistently, especially when you are tempted: "What problem does this solve?" and "What will I stop paying for if I buy it?" Show the behaviour: someone is about to buy a premium kitchen gadget; the questions reveal the real desire is for weekday ease, which might be better met by simplifying meals rather than adding equipment. Name: *replacement thinking*. Explain: money systems drift when additions are not paired with removals. The implication is that every new commitment should have a visible trade-off, otherwise your life becomes an ever-expanding set of obligations.

Habits alone, however, have limits. A credible counter-example is obvious: a household can have excellent habits and still be derailed by a high-stress season—bereavement, a sudden move, a demanding project, a health crisis. In those moments, even small habits can collapse. The reconciliation is not to guilt-trip the household into "staying consistent". It is to build safeguards that do not require you to be at your best.

Safeguards are structural. They sit in the environment like guardrails on a mountain road. You do not install guardrails because you expect to drive badly every day. You install them because everyone, sooner or later, will meet fog, fatigue, or distraction. The metaphor matters because it keeps you out of moral language. A guardrail is not an insult. It is respect for reality.

One safeguard is the written set of "money principles". Not slogans. Not vague aspirations. Written, specific, and short enough to be remembered. Show it. A couple writes four principles on a single page and stores it somewhere visible: for example, "We avoid permanent commitments based on temporary income"; "We buy time back only when it protects sleep or relationships"; "We keep giving predictable"; "We research deeply only for high-impact choices". Name: *pre-commitment.* Explain: writing a principle in calm conditions creates a reference point that can overrule the emotional weather of a hard week. The implication is that you are not negotiating from scratch each time. You are consulting a prior version of yourselves—the ones who had time to think.

Pre-commitment is not a self-help gimmick; it is a recognised strategy in behavioural economics. Thomas Schelling wrote about self-command and the ways people bind their future choices, and later work in behavioural science popularised "commitment devices"—structures that make desired behaviours easier and undesired behaviours harder. Households can use the same idea without turning life into an experiment. The trick is to pre-commit only where drift is most expensive.

Another safeguard is an accountability partner. Show it in a way that avoids melodrama. Two friends, or two colleagues, agree to a simple practice: once a month they each answer one question aloud—"What is the one spending pattern you are proud of this month, and the one you want to change?" The act of saying it to another person changes behaviour because it makes it real. Name: *social proof* and *accountability*. Explain: humans are exquisitely sensitive to what is witnessed. An unshared intention dissolves easily; a witnessed intention has weight. The implication is not surveillance. It is companionship for a task that can otherwise feel solitary and shame-prone.

A third safeguard is setting spending thresholds that require a second person's consent or, at minimum, disclosure. The behaviour is clear: anything above a threshold requires a conversation; smaller spends do not. The threshold is not about control; it is about preventing resentments built from surprises. Name: *shared veto.* Explain: couples and households fight less about the money itself than about the feeling that decisions are unilateral. The implication is that a threshold is a relationship tool masquerading as a finance tool.

Now, an example that shows how a few habits can anchor the whole system. In January 2024, a household in Manchester—two professionals, one child at primary school—noticed a familiar pattern: spending was not "out of control", yet money felt oddly absent. They did not have debt spirals or obvious extravagance. They had drift. The behaviour was a series of small upgrades: the nicer grocery delivery slot, the premium app subscriptions, the occasional taxi instead of the bus, the "better" version of routine products, and one recurring service they kept meaning to cancel. None of these decisions, individually, was irrational. Together, they created a new baseline of costs that squeezed freedom.

They installed three habits and two safeguards. The habits were: a 48-hour pause on non-essential purchases over a chosen threshold; a Sunday evening five-minute "commitments glance" where they looked only at upcoming automatic charges and bills; and a fortnightly declutter of one small area to keep the house usable. The safeguards were: a one-page set of money principles pinned inside a cupboard door, and a simple rule that any new recurring subscription had to replace an old one within the same month.

Watch what happened. The pause rule did not eliminate spending; it changed *timing.* Several purchases still occurred, but fewer occurred when one partner was depleted and seeking relief. The commitments glance did not require categorising every transaction; it made the "invisible" visible, catching creeping renewals before they became normal. The subscription replacement rule attacked drift at its most dangerous point: recurring commitments that feel small but accumulate relentlessly. The declutter habit reduced duplicate buying and made the household less vulnerable to "we need this because we can't find the old one".

Name what this bundle created: *system integrity*. Explain: integrity here is not virtue; it is coherence between intention and reality. The implication is that the household regained a sense of agency without adding a heavy administrative burden. The system became lighter, not heavier.

The motif worth threading through this is the guardrail. A pause rule is a guardrail for impulse. A declutter habit is a guardrail for hidden duplication. Written principles are guardrails for identity under stress. An accountability partner is a guardrail for avoidance. These are not ornate. They are simple. Their power lies in being present when you are not at your best.

There is, however, a second limitation to acknowledge. Habits and safeguards can become rigid. A household can turn the pause rule into a moral court. They can treat decluttering as punishment. They can use principles as weapons in an argument. The reconciliation is to remember the purpose: these tools exist to protect freedom and generosity, not to create a new tyranny. A safeguard that produces constant guilt is a poorly designed safeguard. It needs redesign, not greater compliance.

The deeper philosophy here is that drift is not a sign of failure; it is a feature of life in a consumer economy. The environment is engineered to pull attention towards spending. Marketing is relentless, friction is removed deliberately, and comparison is always one swipe away. The question becomes: will you rely on inner strength against an outer machine, or will you build a few quiet structures that make your best choices easier?

The forward test is a decision disguised as a question: the next time you feel busy and tempted—when the week is thin and the purchase promises relief—what guardrail will meet you first: a pause that gives you back your own judgement, or the frictionless "buy now" button that treats your attention as a resource to be harvested?

Celebrating generosity and enough

On 7 June 2020 in Bristol, the bronze statue of Edward Colston was pulled from its plinth and rolled into the harbour. Within days the empty space became a kind of civic argument: what deserves honour, what deserves forgetting, and what we owe each other when history is uncomfortable. The air that afternoon, captured in photographs and reports, looked bright and salt-tinged; people's voices carried across the water. It was not a money story. And yet it was. It was a story about value made visible, about a community deciding that the symbols it lives with shape the life it lives. The same is true, in miniature, of every household.

The strange truth is that many people feel poor while being well-funded. They live in warm houses, replace devices when they slow, and pay for convenience when time is tight. They are not pretending. They are experiencing a particular kind of scarcity: not a lack of money, but a lack of *enough*. The question worth holding is blunt: if comfort can expand indefinitely, how does a person know when the expansion has stopped serving life and has started consuming it?

This is not a riddle. It is a design problem.

A life that feels rich is not automatically the life with the highest income. Show it. In 2010, researchers Daniel Kahneman and Angus Deaton published findings using US data suggesting that emotional wellbeing rose with income but levelled off beyond a certain point, while life evaluation continued to climb (Kahneman & Deaton, 2010). Later work complicated the shape of that curve, including analyses suggesting wellbeing continues to rise for many people (for example, Killingsworth, 2021). Name the concept: *hedonic adaptation*. Explain without mystique. Humans get used to improvements; yesterday's luxury becomes today's normal, and the nervous system stops treating it as special. The implication is sharp: if "better" is always normalised, then "better" cannot be the only strategy for feeling secure.

The next claim is that "enough" is not merely a number; it is a practiced perception. Show it in behaviour. A household adds a second streaming service, upgrades the car, and starts ordering takeaway more often because work is relentless. These moves may be reasonable. They also create a new baseline of expectation. Soon, a month without them feels like deprivation, even though the household previously lived happily without them. Name the mechanism: *baseline creep*. Explain: when the baseline rises, the gap between "what we have" and "what we now consider normal" can create anxiety that looks like financial pressure. The implication is that prosperity can paradoxically intensify restlessness unless "enough" is actively maintained.

This is where generosity re-enters the room—not as a virtue display, but as an anchor. Show it with a checkable example. In March 2020, as COVID-19 disruptions spread, mutual aid groups formed across the UK, including in London, to support neighbours with food deliveries, prescriptions, and small cash help. These networks were not only philanthropic; they were relational. People who gave also received something measurable but difficult to price: a sense of belonging and agency in a frightening time. Name the concept: *prosocial spending*. Explain: research has repeatedly found associations between spending money on others and increased subjective wellbeing across different contexts, including early work by Elizabeth Dunn, Lara Aknin, and Michael Norton (Dunn, Aknin & Norton, 2008). The implication is not that giving "buys happiness" like a product. The implication is subtler: giving can counteract the isolating logic of consumption, which often promises connection but delivers private convenience.

Still, generosity is not magic. A credible limitation matters here. Giving can be used as a performance, a way to avoid harder questions, or even a form of control. It can also become destabilising if done impulsively or in ways that create resentment. Reconcile it honestly. The point is not to give in a way that harms the giver or the household. The point is to treat generosity as part of a coherent life, not as a sporadic emotional discharge. When generosity is integrated—planned, reviewed, talked about with care—it can become one of the few forces that reliably says, "This is enough for us," even while the world insists it is not.

"Enough" is also social. That is uncomfortable, but true. Show it. A professional can feel perfectly content with a sensible holiday until a peer posts photographs from a more exotic one. A family can feel settled in a modestly sized home until school-gate comparisons make their choices seem inadequate. Name: *social comparison*. Explain: the mind uses other people as reference points, often without permission. The implication is not to blame social media or pretend comparison can be switched off. The implication is to recognise that "enough" must be defended against reference points that are endlessly curated and rarely contextualised.

One way to defend it is to measure different things. Not obsessively. Just deliberately. A household can measure "free cash" and commitments, yes, but it can also measure moments of enough: evenings not spent shopping, weekends not spent researching upgrades, meals shared without scrolling, giving done without panic. These are behavioural metrics. They are visible. They can be counted. Their presence is evidence that wealth is serving life rather than demanding to be served.

The temptation, particularly for high-functioning people, is to treat "enough" as a finish line: a target to reach so that life can begin. The difficulty is that life does not pause for targets. Children arrive, work expands, parents age, health fluctuates, and the cultural weather changes. The pursuit of enough cannot be postponed until everything is settled, because nothing stays settled for long. Name: *the moving horizon*. Explain: when enough is framed as a future state, it retreats as soon as circumstances shift, and the household remains in permanent preparation. The implication is that enough needs to be practiced in the present tense, not merely planned in the future tense.

Consider a second named, checkable example that keeps the argument grounded. In 2019, the Office for National Statistics in the UK began publishing personal wellbeing measures that include questions on life satisfaction, worthwhileness, happiness, and anxiety. These measures are imperfect, but they do something important: they legitimise the idea that what matters is not only economic output but lived experience. Name the concept: *multi-dimensional prosperity*. Explain: money is instrumental, not ultimate; it supports a life that is evaluated by more than financial indicators. The implication is a quiet rebuke to the culture of endless optimisation. If national statistics can include worthwhileness as a measure, a household can take seriously the question of whether its spending increases worthwhileness or merely increases throughput.

This is where celebration belongs—not as fireworks, but as recognition. Celebration is a form of attention. It tells the nervous system, "This mattered." Without it, the household becomes a machine that processes income into obligations. Show it in scene. A couple notices, at the end of a month, that they hosted friends twice instead of ordering separate meals in front of separate screens. The cost might even be higher in ingredients and wine. And yet the life might be richer. A family notices that they supported a local food bank regularly rather than making one grand donation when guilt peaked. The sums may be modest. The impact—relational, moral, internal—can be steady. Name: *signal amplification*. Explain: noticing strengthens patterns; unobserved patterns fade. The implication is that celebration is not sentimental; it is maintenance for the values that money is meant to serve.

The phrase "wealth without waste" becomes most vivid here. Waste is not always the expensive thing. Waste is the thing that corrodes attention, crowds out generosity, and inflates the baseline without improving life. Conversely, some spending that looks "expensive" can be a defence of enough: paying for childcare to protect a marriage, investing in tools that remove constant friction, travelling to see ageing relatives while time still permits. These choices are not justified by status; they are justified by contribution. The lens is not austerity. The lens is alignment.

A final tension needs to be named, because it is where sophisticated readers often stumble. When people start noticing enough, they can become frightened that contentment will dull ambition. They worry that if they stop chasing, they will stagnate. The reconciliation is straightforward: ambition and enough are not enemies. Enough is the boundary that makes ambition humane. Without enough, ambition becomes appetite—restless, easily manipulated, and never satisfied. With enough, ambition can become craft: precise, chosen, and oriented towards work and relationships that actually matter.

The motif that threads through this ending is the empty plinth. An empty plinth is not nothing; it is an invitation to choose what stands there next. Every household has plinths: the calendar, the bank statement, the space in the garage, the attention given to offers and upgrades. Something will stand there. If it is not chosen deliberately, it will be chosen by default—by advertising, comparison, habit, and the convenient inertia of recurring payments.

The forward test is simple and unsparing. When the next raise, refund, or bonus arrives, when the next stressful season makes convenience feel like salvation, when the next comparison twinge makes an upgrade feel urgent, what will the household be protecting: the feeling of being endlessly "ahead", or the quieter reality of being enough—enough to breathe, enough to give, enough to be present in the life you have already paid for?

About the Author

Ravi Khatekar writes about money as something more human than spreadsheets and status symbols. He is drawn to the everyday tension between comfort and conscience, between wanting a pleasant life and wanting to be useful. ASSUMPTION: Ravi has personal experience navigating money decisions in affluent-but-busy households.

Over the years he has watched friends, colleagues, and families earn more, upgrade everything, and somehow feel less free. Those conversations, often over late-night tea rather than formal meetings, shaped his conviction that the real leverage lies in how we design our cashflow and define 'enough', not in heroic self-denial or secret tricks.

Ravi's thinking is quietly influenced by traditions that prize both thrift and generosity, such as the practice of daan in parts of South Asia: the idea that giving is a normal, integral part of a life well-lived, not a dramatic event. His writing aims to be calm, practical, and kind, helping readers bring their spending back into conversation with their deepest values. He believes that when households become both more intentional and more open-handed, they not only feel lighter themselves, they also strengthen the communities around them.

www.ingramcontent.com/pod-product-compliance
Lightning Source LLC
Chambersburg PA
CBHW031336230926
51848CB00002B/255
* 9 7 8 9 3 7 6 5 5 8 4 5 2 *